The Virtue
of
Giving Up

Growing Up Blind and Autistic

Judith Anne Dent, Ph.D.

BALBOA.
PRESS

A DIVISION OF HAY HOUSE

Balboa Press books may be ordered through booksellers or by contacting:

Balboa Press
A Division of Hay House
1663 Liberty Drive
Bloomington, IN 47403
www.balboapress.com
1 (877) 407-4847

Because of the dynamic nature of the Internet, any web addresses or links contained in this book may have changed since publication and may no longer be valid. The views expressed in this work are solely those of the author and do not necessarily reflect the views of the publisher, and the publisher hereby disclaims any responsibility for them.

The author of this book does not dispense medical advice or prescribe the use of any technique as a form of treatment for physical, emotional, or medical problems without the advice of a physician, either directly or indirectly. The intent of the author is only to offer information of a general nature to help you in your quest for emotional and spiritual well-being. In the event you use any of the information in this book for yourself, which is your constitutional right, the author and the publisher assume no responsibility for your actions.

Any people depicted in stock imagery provided by Thinkstock are models,
and such images are being used for illustrative purposes only.
Certain stock imagery © Thinkstock.

Print information available on the last page.

ISBN: 978-1-5043-7680-8 (sc)
ISBN: 978-1-5043-7679-2 (e)

Balboa Press rev. date: 08/28/2017

Author's Introduction

The greatest triumph of my life is that I'm here, stretched out in my recliner, braille note-taker on my stomach, writing this book. That's saying a lot after six suicide attempts. They failed, as did most endeavors in my life, until I stopped trying, stopped believing in the myth of the American dream, stopped telling myself I had to love my blindness in order to embrace life. Success came when I redefined it, let go of all the nonsense I learned from early childhood, got up the courage, after more than half a century, to do just what I'm doing now. During one of my many trips to the psychiatric hospital, a kind nurse said to me, "Honey, you've been a long time getting here, and you'll be a long time getting back."

No way, I thought. I have to get back to school, back to my over-achieving life in two minutes or less, or the world will end in a major cataclysm. I didn't get back in two minutes, or two years, or ten, but I did get back. It is a tribute to the many who helped me, an admonition to the few who abused me, and an act of reconciliation toward those who thought they were doing the first while actually doing the second. It is about being misunderstood and driving my teachers and caregivers nuts. It's about living every day with blindness, autism, mental illness, and some other vaguely defined developmental delays.

This is the story of what it was like for me growing up as a child with multiple disabilities (most of which nobody understood, least of all myself) and a mother with paranoid schizophrenia, as well as a child who could lie on the floor and scream until she turned blue from the sheer desperation of realizing she was different, not only from sighted children, but from other blind children. The people with power—who didn't crash into the furniture, who could find words in the little pictures on the blank pages, who could color between the lines—did not approve of this behavior.

As for autism, I might as well have said I was a little green person from Alpha Centauri. For people who had ever heard of autism, it meant someone who screamed but never spoke, who sat in the corner and rocked, who bumped his or her head against walls and furniture, who ignored toys and other children, but fell in love with the stove or vacuum cleaner. Asperger's was not even a diagnosis in those days. People just called me "goofball" or "the old prof." So what if I insisted on absolute order in my toy box and desk drawers? So what if I could calculate calendars in my head? So what if I could balance the checkbook in my head before I had a clear idea what a checkbook was?

I was the kind of child who inspired well-intentioned members of the helping professions to quit their jobs and become plumbers. I was the kind of child that only a mother, or in my case, grandmother, could love.

Yet there was sometimes joy in our home, often dark humor, and always an expectancy of good so profound that when it didn't materialize immediately as planned, each of us, in his or her own way, collapsed under the crushing weight of the struggle to be perfect, like Atlas trying to hold up the world.

There was much yelling at our house, not the yelling of raised voices, but of recrimination and blame. My dad, who nevertheless loved me to distraction, called me "Such an idiot!" so many times that I almost thought my name was Idiot. My mother called me "Stupid individual!" with such conviction that I began to believe it. From the time I was diagnosed with blindness at four months, my parents freaked out, and they stayed freaked out until the day they died. While I sucked my bottle, they feared for my future. While I sat in my playpen, they worried about their own mortality and what would happen to me after they were gone. With that in mind, they dedicated themselves to my education with a ferocious tenacity that would have done justice to a pit bull. Every meal, every conversation, every walk in the yard or up the street was a learning experience, some enlightening, others amusing, many horrifying.

This is the background from which I walked into freshman English class on my first day of college. The assignment was to read a short story by Katherine Anne Porter called "The Downward Path to Wisdom," about a four-year-old boy who finds out that his parents don't love him; then we had to write a short essay on "The Day My Childhood Ended." What did we know about the end of childhood? We were still children. I don't remember what anyone else wrote except that when read in class, they were all unremarkable. I wrote some glib, maudlin nonsense about childhood never ending because magic and wonder never stop—this from a child who had experienced precious little magic or wonder. The teacher, who herself had a rather starry-eyed view of the world, gave me an A instead of the C-minus I so richly deserved for being mentally lazy, for circumventing the assignment instead of completing it. In retrospect, the assignment was impossibly romantic for eighteen-year-olds, most of whom lacked the perspective to know when childhood ended, if it had. It took me years to find out. That instructor might have been astonished to learn that my childhood ended on the first day of kindergarten.

Judy Dent
Kirkwood, Missouri
March 2, 2005

Chapter 1

First Day Of Kindergarten (January 1952)

"No, ma'am, you cannot see!"

Dad held my hand with one hand and opened the big door with the other. A burst of sensory experiences washed over me like the vinegar rinse Mother poured over my head after a shampoo. Hot, wet air mixed with hot, wet sound. The clatter and screech of children running through halls. The voices of teachers yelling, "No running!" The smell of mothballs and disinfectant and urine and sweaty socks. Everything about the place said age and decay.

I wanted to turn right around and go home. This stinky, noisy, damp vastness was nothing like the way I imagined school would be. This was not the one-room schoolhouse Grandma had told me about. This was not eight grades in a single space, where everyone studied in a small, cozy group, and the only chaos was the sound of everyone repeating their lessons out loud. There was no pot-bellied stove or cozy coal fire to keep us warm. Instead of books and pencils, there were blocks, dolls, and plastic trucks. The place even had a funny name, "kindergarten." It didn't have grades at all, and it certainly didn't feel like any garden I had ever been in. There wasn't a plant to be touched or smelled anywhere. Where I lived there were no gardens in early January, which is when I started school because my fifth birthday came in October, not September, and my dad thought four was too young to start school. Gardens were outside; we were in this dank dungeon without a whiff of fresh air.

When Dad brought me to Miss Brookshire's kindergarten class at the Wilson School for the Blind, the children were just coming in from recess and the bedlam was like nothing I had experienced in my friendly nursery school. Clang! Clang! Pffft! Heat came into the cold room with a serpentine hiss, as if the sun had turned into a giant reptile cooking us all for breakfast. The steam radiator warmed up quickly, and if you ventured too near and accidentally touched it, you got burned, as I soon learned. The place smelled of wet wool, mothballs, armpits, sweaty socks, and a hint of urine. The ten students gathered to sit cross-legged on a hard floor in a big room in a huge building.

1

"Thank you, Mr. Dent," a cracked, elderly voice said, dismissing Dad like a piece of old luggage being consigned to a garage sale. "The coat rack is over here, Judy. You can hang your coat there." A thin, wrinkled hand that reminded me of the witch in "Hansel and Gretel" grabbed my arm and placed my hand on an object that felt like a metal skeleton with wire cages hanging from it.

"What's this?" I asked. Things were getting more and more mysterious by the minute and I did not like it.

"Coat rack, Stupid," a boy's voice taunted loudly from the back of the room.

That didn't help. Miss Brookshire had already called it a "coat rack." I knew what a coat was; the question was, what was a rack?

"Take your coat off, Judy." Miss Brookshire's syllables made a hard, popping noise as they came out, like icicles falling off a tree. "Take the hanger off the rack, put the hanger in the sleeve, and hang up your coat. Don't take all day. The class has better things to do than wait for you. You were already late this morning. Your father should have left home earlier."

What Miss Brookshire didn't know was that we had left home at 6:30 a.m. in a driving snowstorm. We had spent hours in a huge traffic jam. Dad had spun the wheels and had to get out of the car and put salt on the road. Snow and ice were everywhere. When we finally arrived at school we were more than an hour late. It wasn't fair to be chewed out after trying so hard to get to school on time, but somehow it didn't seem wise to point this out.

Getting back to the momentous challenge of hanging up my coat, I almost asked, "What's a hanger?" but quickly decided against it. This did not seem like a place where question asking would be encouraged. I felt around on the coat rack. The wire things were hanging from it so maybe they were the hangers. I was just about to pat myself on the back for figuring that out when Miss Brookshire's voice interrupted my reverie.

"Hurry up, Judy. Nobody's going to help you."

I took off my coat and pulled one of the hangers off the rack.

"Take note, class," said Miss Brookshire. "When she found out nobody was going to help her, she got to work."

I tried to put the hanger in the sleeve while several of the other students, who I later learned were partially sighted, giggled as if this were the most uproariously funny thing since the last time somebody tipped over a chair. Coat and hanger fell to the floor with a clatter like the sound effects for a sword fight on my "Robin Hood" record.

"Oh, for goodness sake!" Miss Brookshire was really disgusted now. "These children come to school and they can't do a thing for themselves! Didn't your parents teach you anything in the past five years?"

"I thought school was the place to learn things." I was trying to be helpful but Miss Brookshire took it the wrong way as people so often did.

"Not only helpless but a smart aleck. What a big mouth you have for such a small child!"

Big tears began to roll down my face. Nobody had told me that school was a place where you had to put up with continuous shame and humiliation.

Miss Brookshire grabbed my hands and yanked them through the motions of hanging up the coat. It took her about a second. "Let that be a lesson to you, class," she admonished when the task was finished. "Her mommy was too good to her."

If only Miss Brookshire had known how "good" my mommy was, about the angels and devils and Indian chiefs Mother spoke to almost every day, about the screaming and the hitting, about the sudden trips to the doctor, about how she was too groggy and quiet afterward to cook meals or take care of the house because of the pills Dad gave her, how both grandmas tried to fill in the gaps.

"All right, class, let's get started!" said a cracking voice. "Those who can see, raise your hands."

My hand went up in a flash. I could see. My parents always said I saw with my fingers. I could see the warm, throbbing life of my collie puppy Tuffy. I could see the roundness of a tulip, the bunch-of-grapes shape of a hyacinth, the velvet of a pussy willow. I could see my dad's friend's model tanks and battleships. I could see my Uncle Martin's casting rod with a big, wet, scaly trout on the end of it, but I wasn't allowed to touch the hook, so I couldn't see that.

The cracked voice interrupted my thoughts. "Judy, can you see?"

"Yes, ma'am," I answered with the absolute certainty of someone who knew what she was talking about.

Silence. Then, "No, ma'am, you cannot see!"

Kerplunk. Something hit hard inside me. I sensed that I had just received momentous news, something so bad it couldn't be discussed. My parents had never told me I couldn't see. In fact, they never talked about what was wrong with me, about the strange defect in me that made them sad, but in that room, on that day, with all those other kids laughing at me, I knew that this was it.

It made me run into trees when I tried to play tag with my cousins. It was why I could not yet dress myself. It was why I so often bumped my head on the corner of the coffee table in the living room. It was, above all, what made my parents sad.

The finality of that sentence, "No, ma'am, you cannot see!" put everything into sharp perspective. Now I knew why I heard my mother crying in the night, why my dad often said, "For crying out loud! Can't you understand anything? You're the dumbest kid I know." I wondered how many kids he knew, why he thought they were all so much smarter and better than I. It made my mother put holy water in my eyes with a dropper several times a day and make me pray, "Dear God, if it be thy will, please give me sight." Apparently seeing with my fingers wasn't enough. That tone of voice Miss Brookshire, the kindergarten teacher, used to reprimand me for not knowing I couldn't see explained it all, yet raised more questions than my five-year-old mind could grasp. My parents didn't have the solution, and it soon became clear that no one at school did. I didn't realize it then, but I would have to find those answers myself.

"All right, class," Miss Brookshire heaved a resigned sigh with which I was to become all too familiar. "This day is already far too exhausting for work. Let's have game time. Everybody get in a circle."

As usual, I wondered what that meant, and also as usual, I stood around trying to figure out what to do next. Everyone stood together in a cluster, nudging and shoving one another like puppies in a litter.

"Son of a bitch," said one boy, apropos of nothing in particular.

"Richard, we don't use that kind of language in refined society—not that this is refined society, but one can only hope."

Thank you, God, the old battleship was training her weapons on somebody else. I didn't know what a son of a bitch was, but I hoped someone would say it, or something like it again to keep Miss Brookshire's attention off me. I wished I could be as invisible to the people in this awful place as they were to me. That was another of those unfairnesses of which I was becoming so keenly aware. I couldn't see other people, but they sure could see me. It was obvious I wasn't going to get away with a thing here. If I thought home was tough, what was school going to be like?

I waited for Miss Brookshire to get out cards, dominoes, Monopoly, or something else indicative of games. Thank goodness I had a grandma who was interested in those things. She had taught me well, and I was pretty good at games; playing games sure beat hanging up my coat, but this was not my lucky day.

"Class, didn't you just hear me say get in a circle? That doesn't mean stand around pushing and shoving one another. Get in a circle and take hands. We're going to play 'Jim Crow.'"

That wasn't a game I knew; in fact, I had never played a game where you stood in a circle. On one side of me was Richard, the boy who had said "son of a bitch." He kept twisting his hand trying to get away from me. The harder he twisted the tighter I clutched his hand. I clung to him with a fierce death grip, as though he were the only thing standing between me and some nameless catastrophe. He seemed to know what to do, which was more than I did. On the other side was a person—I did not know whether boy or girl—whose hand was clammy with sweat or spit. This hand clung to mine with the same desperation with which I held onto Richard's.

"Your head's crooked," announced this person, apparently a girl. There seemed to be nothing to say to this. I didn't think my head was crooked on the outside, but in this strange world one never knew. How did this girl know how crooked my head felt inside? This whole universe was skewed in a way I found completely baffling. It reminded me of a story my cousin Janice had told me about a visit to a fun house where they had mirrors that made you look fat, thin, tall or short. I had only a vague idea what a mirror was, except that Mother used one to put on her makeup "to hide my wrinkles," and that my parakeet Joey had one in his cage to make him believe there was another bird in there with him when really there wasn't. So apparently a mirror was something that distorted things. Why people wanted things distorted was beyond me. Grandma had read me a book called "Alice Through the Looking Glass." She said a looking glass was a mirror and that the book was about a chess game played backwards. She had tried to teach me to play chess and I thought it was hard enough to play forward. This school must be a kind of distorting mirror. Maybe we were like Alice, playing a game backwards.

"Your head's crooked," Wet Hands declaimed again.

"My name's Judy," I said, searching through my arsenal of adult conversation for only children. I wished Grandma were here to explain what kind of place this was.

"I'm Ellen Anderson," said Wet Hands. "Everybody's head's crooked."

"Right," I agreed, seeing the beginning of a cosmic metaphor just beyond my grasp. When you have an editor for a dad you learn to think in those terms, but keep it to yourself.

"Judy! Ellen! All of you! If you don't get in a circle right now and play this game, I'm going to grab each and every one of you, body and soul, and make you wish you had!"

Miss Brookshire was, as Dad often said about Mother, "getting hostile." Only for emphasis he pronounced it hoss-style, as in "Don't get hoss style."

I had only a vague idea what a circle was. Nickels, dimes, and quarters were circles, but I didn't understand how you could "get in" one. We were still holding hands in what felt to me like a straight line.

"At last you are all doing what you're supposed to do. I'd better enjoy it while it lasts. Hold hands."

That remark seemed unnecessary because we were already holding hands. It never occurred to me that maybe not all of us were holding hands. I was so concerned about pleasing the teachers, and my parents by proxy, that I never thought of disobeying. If I did so, I would be yelled at for sure when I got home.

Miss Brookshire began again to give instructions. "Go around the room in a circle using these dance steps and singing this song:

Jump! Jump! And jump, Jim Crow! Take a little turn and away you go. Slide, slide, and point your toe! Then you take another partner and you jump Jim Crow!"

"Her head's crooked, too," confided Ellen.

She had a point. This game wasn't nearly as much fun as dominoes, especially the part where you lined them all up, knocked one over, and made the others fall.

We all got lost on "Take another partner." Some of us ended up with different partners, some with the same person. You could always tell whether you had a girl or a boy. The girls hung on to your hand as if they were strangling it and the boys twisted and jerked with all their strength trying to get away.

"Tommy!" Miss Brookshire zeroed in on another target. "Who's your partner?"

"I don't know."

"Your partner is Ronnie. Pay attention and remember that."

"Yes, Miss Brookshire."

"Betty, who's your partner?"

"My partner is Danny Amina, Miss Brookshire."

"Good. At least someone is awake this morning. Judy, who's your partner?"

"I don't know, Miss Brookshire."

"For goodness' sake! Don't you people even know how to exchange names? Judy, say, 'My name is Judy Dent. May I have your name, please?'"

I wondered if even Emily Post's kid actually said, "May I have your name, please."

"But they might get insulted and punch me and call me an old maid if I said that, Miss Brookshire."

At that moment Miss Brookshire made me think of stories Uncle Martin had told me of small birds that fluffed out their feathers when they were upset or afraid until they were twice their normal size. "Are you questioning my authority? Are you calling me an old maid? It isn't even lunch time on your first day and I've already had to tell you over and over not to be a smart aleck. I don't want to have to keep telling you. Get out of the circle and sit at that desk in the corner and think about how disrespectful you've been and what you plan to do about it in the future."

What I wanted to do about it was thank her profusely for kicking me out of that horrible game, but for once my better judgment prevailed and I kept my mouth shut.

The game droned on. It wasn't much less boring to listen to than it had been to play. I had been all excited about going to school, but this was the pits. My parents had expounded with great enthusiasm about the joys of school, especially Mother, who was interested in science, and Grandma Dent, who loved books. "You will learn all about how the earth turns and how the planets move, and how the sun is cool outside and hot inside like a pie," said Mother.

"And about Shakespeare and Milton and the Greek gods," added Grandma.

Dad had bought me a three-dimensional puzzle map of the United States. Each state was a plastic cutout that you could take out and put back. Dad would take my hand and trace the places on the map where we had been on vacation. Mother had made me a model of the Solar System with different size Christmas ornaments for the sun and planets. She attached them to wires and they actually moved in their orbits. None of this was anything like "Jump, Jim Crow." I felt colossally let down.

"All right, class," Miss Brookshire's sharp voice, like a saw on metal, interrupted my thoughts. "Let's all pretend we're kangaroos and hop to our places. Judy, get up and join the circle. Let's all hop. One! Two!"

That morning dragged on for at least a week. The highlights were cookies and milk at ten and nap time at eleven. Miss Brookshire magically produced canvas cots out of a closet and we stretched out on them, a welcome relief after all that hard play. The lowlights were blocks, Tinker Toys, a futile attempt to make a rabbit out of construction paper, and going to the bathroom.

Bathroom Blues

The cubicle was small and claustrophobic. I almost said "dark," which shows how well trained I am in using the language of sight, even though I am trying to avoid it while describing my true experiences. I had the exact feeling a sighted child must have when trapped in a small, dark place. "I want to get out of here!" I screamed. I wasn't sure how I got in, but I knew I wanted out. I know people will ask me how I got inside and locked the door, but I don't remember. I only remember I couldn't get it unlocked.

"Crawl under!" I heard the voice of one of the big girls instructing me.

I wasn't sure what "crawl" meant or what "under" referred to. I felt the part of the wall that jiggled a little, which must be the door. I rattled it but couldn't get it open. I cried louder. There was considerable noise and confusion, but no one could get across to me how to open that door. Finally someone had to get a maintenance man to come and take the door off to let me out. All this was followed by a brutal dressing-down from Miss Brookshire.

"For heaven's sake, Judy, haven't you been in a bathroom before? Don't you know how to pull a hook out of an eye?"

Even though it was my first day of kindergarten I already knew it was better to let Miss Brookshire yell until she tired herself out than to try to answer her rhetorical questions. I knew what a hook was from going fishing with Uncle Martin. I knew what an eye was and that mine didn't work. Even so, the idea of putting a hook in someone's eye appalled and terrified me. I couldn't let this threat pass without comment.

"Are you going to do that to me, Miss Brookshire?" I had heard Dad speak of the Geneva Conventions, rules for how prisoners of war were supposed to be treated. Some of the rules said that when interrogating enemy prisoners, the prisoners were not supposed to be tortured. I knew that interrogation meant asking questions and torture meant inflicting pain to get people to answer your questions. I had figured out by now that Miss Brookshire was my enemy, and I couldn't leave school until Mother came to pick me up at 4:30, so I supposed that qualified me as a prisoner. "Isn't that against the Geneva Conventions to stick a hook in someone's eye?"

"What are you talking about, you defiant little devil? Anyone who can't even open the door of a bathroom stall shouldn't be citing the Geneva Conventions. You certainly have your priorities misplaced."

I felt around on the table in front of me and in my pockets. "I don't think I've misplaced anything, Miss Brookshire. Why are you always so mad at me, and what are priorities?"

"One of your priorities should be to stop talking back. Another should be to stop pretending you can't do things you really can, just to get attention."

"But everyone has been so angry with me all day, Miss Brookshire. I don't want that kind of attention. What am I doing wrong?"

"If you don't know, then you need to do some soul-searching."

Now was not the time to ask about soul-searching. Maybe Miss Brookshire thought I had misplaced my soul as well as my priorities.

I would work hard the rest of the day to make sure I didn't have to go to the bathroom, and I stayed away from the drinking fountain.

Through my hands like water

Then came lunch, where I drank only a few sips of milk, just enough to get the food down. It turned out to be something less than the welcome interlude I had expected. The lunch was a kind of beef hash without much beef in it. It had the consistency and flavor of greasy wood shavings. (I had never tasted wood shavings, but the hash tasted the way I imagined wood shavings would taste.)

During lunch an odd thing happened. I didn't understand it then and don't understand it now. I forgot how to feed myself. That part of my memory was gone, as if someone had taken a scissors and snipped it right out of my brain. All Dad's instructions for using a spoon—"Dip, slide, and into the mouth," and a fork, "Find, stab, lift," were as distant as the Civil War, the Renaissance, or anything else that had happened a long time ago and I had not learned about. The silverware slipped through my hands like water.

"Look at her!" another elderly woman's voice broke in. "She just sits there like a little bird with her mouth open waiting for every bite. For crying out loud, child, open your eyes and say something. Didn't your parents teach you any manners while they were failing to teach you to feed yourself?"

"Yes, ma'am," I said, not at all sure what I was agreeing to, but not wanting another confrontation.

The woman shoved a forkful of hash in the general direction of my mouth, getting most of it all over my face and down the front of my dress.

"Look at you!" she screeched on. "Food all over yourself! What a disgusting little pig you are! Say something, for goodness' sake! Didn't you learn to talk either?"

"Yes, ma'am," I said, throwing caution to the winds. Nothing I said or did was going to placate this horrible woman anyway. "I can talk. I can recite a poem my Grandma taught me. 'They call me Little Chatterbox. My name is Little May. I always talk so much because I have so much to say. I love my mother and my father and my grandma, too. And if you're very, very good, I think that I'll love you.'"

I felt a resounding slap that knocked my head sideways and made my neck hurt. "Did you just talk back to me, you sassy little vixen? If nothing else while you're here, learn some respect."

"Is that a subject people study here?" I persisted since I had already been informed twice that I needed to learn it. "Is it anything like reading?"

"You're hopeless," fumed the woman. "I'm taking you down to Mrs. Hubbert's office. She'll straighten you out. She's not as tolerant of children's nonsense as I am."

Grandma had told me a story about powerful women warriors called Amazons who killed anyone who bothered them. I had evidently bothered this Amazon quite a lot because she grabbed my arm with a fierce grip that convinced me my wrist was about to break like a toothpick and hauled me at a dead run down a long hall to a room that resembled all the other rooms I had visited in this school, except it was smaller and in addition to the other smells, there was paper and ink.

Mrs. Hubbert, the principal, was yet another of those formidable elderly women who seemed to be everywhere in this place, distinguishable only by their sameness: claws like eagles, voices like mynah birds, and a single-minded desire to whip bad children into shape with rigorous discipline.

Mrs. Hubbert was not the kind of person you could ask in a jocular tone if the cupboard was bare or if her dog needed a bone. I would have bet she didn't have a dog, or if she did, it wasn't a gentle, compassionate one like Tuffy. In fact, the students were so intimidated by her that not once during the six years she was principal while I was there, did I ever hear anyone refer to her as "Old Mother Hubbard," even in the relative safety of the dorm or the playground.

"Well, Judy," she began, and I had the feeling she was sizing me up, deciding which part of me to eat first, "I hear you've managed to get yourself into trouble on your first day of school."

For what seemed like the hundredth time that day, tears began to roll slowly, silently down my face despite my best efforts at self-control. "I hate this place. It's so big. I want to go home. This isn't anything like what Grandma told me about school."

"And what did Grandma tell you school would be like?" Mrs. Hubbert didn't miss a beat as she wound up for the inevitable reprimand. "Did she tell you we were going to feel sorry for you and coddle you all day? Did she say we would handle you with kid gloves? If so, Grandma was wrong. Your first lesson today is to stop paying attention to Grandma and start listening to us. We don't baby our students here. Life is tough, and you have to learn to be even tougher than it is. We won't spoil you the way your parents do. When you leave here you'll be an independent adult. For heaven's sake, stop crying and pay attention!"

The one phrase that had stood out when Mrs. Hubbert was talking was "kid gloves." My mother had an alpaca sweater. If I wasn't mistaken, the alpaca had to die to make it. I wasn't at all sure what an alpaca was, but Grandma had read me a book called The Wind in the Willows, where a rat, a mole, a toad, and a badger talked and lived just like people. I imagined that poor alpaca standing in the principal's office being terrorized as I was now.

I cried harder than ever, at the same time getting up my courage to ask the most important question of all. "Mrs. Hubbert, you said, 'kid gloves.' Do they make gloves out of kids who get in trouble here? Do you have kid gloves?"

"What kind of nonsense is this? Don't be stupid. 'Kid gloves' is just an expression. It means we don't take a lot of guff from obnoxious little hellions like you."

My head was reeling from all the new vocabulary words I was learning. I decided not to ask Dad what "obnoxious" and "hellion" meant; it couldn't be anything good, and might bring about unpleasant questions.

"Your preschool evaluation says you have a 160 IQ, so don't play dumb with me. You won't get away with it. What the test didn't show is that you're a smart aleck as well as smart. We don't put up with that at this school. I don't expect to see you back at this office any time soon. If I do, I'll whip you till you have something to cry about. Now go on back to class."

"I don't know where it is, Mrs. Hubbert. It's only my first day."

"Didn't you just come from there? What were you thinking on your way here?"

"I came from lunch," I mumbled.

"Right, you need to go to the dorm for siesta. I'll call Miss Temple to come and get you, but remember, you have to start learning your way around. People here have better things to do than escort you everywhere like you were the Queen of England."

What am I doing that makes everybody so mad?

Pretty soon another old woman with shriveled hands and a cracked voice came and dragged me off to a long room with twelve narrow, lumpy beds in it, along with some hard, wooden chairs and some metal dressers and lockers for clothes. I soon learned that the students lived here. They didn't go home at night. Many of them didn't even go home on weekends. Mother had said she was coming for me at 4:30 that afternoon. I wondered if she really would, or if she had left me in this awful place forever. Maybe this was a place to get rid of kids nobody wanted. This line of thought almost made me cry again, but I bit my lip and held it in. I was catching on quickly. Maybe school was a place to learn after all.

"Siesta," another new vocabulary word, meant stretching out on the hard bed and waiting tensely for a bell to ring. After that we went back to class and did more alternately difficult and boring stuff until gym class, the last period of the day. Before we left for gym, Miss Brookshire asked, "Who enjoyed kindergarten today? Raise your hands."

Dad had always taught me to tell the truth, so my hand did not go up.

"Who said they didn't like it?" screeched Miss Brookshire. "Judy, yours was the only hand that did not go up. What's wrong with you? What didn't you like about kindergarten today?"

I remembered again about Dad admonishing me to always tell the truth, and wished I could be on Pluto, which Mother had said was the farthest away of all the planets. "I didn't like any of it, Miss Brookshire," I slogged on. "I didn't like playing 'Jump, Jim Crow,' or stacking blocks, or hanging up my coat, or making a paper rabbit. I didn't like the lousy lunch or Mrs. Hubbert yelling at me. I didn't like that we didn't read any stories or listen to any music."

"Well, you are quite the little critic," snarled Miss Brookshire. "I'll be sure to talk to Mr. Johnson, the superintendent, and he'll put you on the curriculum planning committee."

"What's 'curriculum,' Miss Brookshire? What's a committee?"

"You're impossible, Judy. If I were your mother, I'd have you over my knee twenty-four hours a day, seven days a week. Blistering your smart-aleck little bottom would be worth the wear and tear on my knee. Now it's time for your treat, class. Nothing for you, Judy. You get a treat when you learn to show some respect."

"Everybody's been saying that all day, Miss Brookshire. What do they mean by respect? What am I doing that makes everybody so mad?"

"Shut up. That's enough out of you. Good news, class. Milky Ways today. I wish I could send some of you to the Milky Way and be rid of you."

I resisted the temptation to point out that the Milky Way was an imaginary place made up out real stars and planets and that she couldn't send any of us there because Einstein's Theory of Special Relativity said you couldn't go faster than light or you would arrive before you left.

That was something my mother had taught me, but I had a feeling Miss Brookshire wouldn't want to hear that.

"All right, future juvenile delinquents of America, off to gym class. It's time you did something besides just stand around and get fat! Out!"

I wondered what standing around had to do with getting fat, especially right after Miss Brookshire had just given everyone but me a Milky Way. I also wondered about Jim. Was he a nice man? Maybe so, since he evidently let people call him by his first name. Maybe Jim wasn't a man at all. Maybe he was an elephant. I had ridden an elephant at the zoo named Miss Jim. The zookeeper said that when they first got the baby elephant, they thought it was a boy, so they named him Jim. Later, when they realized he was a she, they changed her name to Miss Jim. Maybe Jim was a big, friendly animal like Miss Jim. Whoever Jim was, I hoped he would be kinder than all those grumpy women I had met today.

"Come on, I'll walk you to the dorm," said a familiar voice. A clammy hand grabbed mine, but it didn't feel creepy and scary to me; it made me feel glad and safe. At least one person in this terrifying place wasn't mad at me.

"Ellen!" Miss Brookshire got in one last attack. "Leave Judy alone! She has to find her way by herself. How will she ever learn if you keep coddling her? She got that at home, but it's not going to happen here."

We dashed out of the classroom, holding hands almost tight enough to cut off the circulation. "Never mind her," said Ellen under her breath. "Her head's crooked."

We rushed down a long hall and up an even longer staircase. Soon we were back in that long, narrow smelly room where we had taken our siesta. "This is your bed," said Ellen, who seemed to know everything. "Your gym suit is on it."

"Well, here come the celebrities, fashionably late!" Here was Miss Temple, the housemother, ready with yet another reprimand. "Hurry up, girls. Dress yourselves and get on down to gym class. And remember, no hanging onto one another. Every day is Independence Day at this school. Judy, you can find your way by following the voices and footsteps of the other girls. Now everybody get a move on. Judy, why aren't you changing clothes? Don't just stand there with your tongue hanging out like a big dog on a hot day."

I felt around on the bed. Apparently a gym suit was a top and shorts outfit stuck together. It had a narrow cloth belt hanging from some loops at the waist. But first I had to get my rest-of-the-day clothes off. My dress buttoned down the back and if Miss Temple had asked me to fly an airplane I wouldn't have known any less about it than I did about how to unfasten those buttons. I could hardly reach them, much less push them through those tiny holes. I tried turning around super fast, hoping they would move to the front. No dice. I tried wiggling and squirming to get them into a better position. That didn't work either. "Oh, Judy, for goodness' sake! This is only January, but at the rate you are going, you won't be ready by next Christmas. Well, I don't have time to teach you now, so I'll have to do it for you, but you better have it learned by tomorrow."

I got another barrage when I couldn't tie the belt. The ends slipped uselessly through my fingers as most things did when I tried to do something with my hands. I thought Miss Temple would have a heart attack, she was so angry with me by the time I was ready to go.

"All right, girls, you can go now. Remember, Judy, follow the sounds."

So I tried to follow the sounds, which seemed to move away from me with lightning speed. I put my feet down slowly, first one, then the other. I was scared almost to paralysis, sure that any moment I would fall into a bottomless abyss. Then I really was falling, not just imagining it, but falling, falling, falling, bang, crash, so much pain, dear God, what did I do to deserve such a bad day?

This nightmare was real. I lay in a bruised heap on the landing. My face was scratched. My knees were skinned. I could feel a big knot coming up on my head. All the pent-up rage and pain of the day came tumbling out. "Please help me!" I called to no one in particular, imploring anyone who heard, and there must have been a lot of them because I was being loud, an impulse I usually tried to restrain, considering the repercussions my noise brought on at home. I finally managed to scramble to my feet and stood there completely disoriented. That was another new word I had learned today. It apparently was Wilson School for the Blind language for being good and lost. I took a couple steps forward in what I imagined was the direction the other girls had gone. Bang! Crash! Head over heels, falling, falling, falling again, down I went, down more stairs to land hard on concrete.

I rolled into a ball, jammed my fists into my eyes, and screamed and screamed a crescendo of incoherent rage and pain. I prayed to God to open the sky and send me a wrecking ball to smash this building with its flesh-searing steam radiators, its lung-destroying smells, and its collection of evil old witches whose greatest pleasure was torturing children. I rolled around on the floor. Thank you, thank you—no more steps. I didn't care who yelled at me. However loud they yelled, I could yell louder. Forget how the earth rotated on its axis and turned in its orbit, forget the names of oceans and rivers, forget George Washington and Abraham Lincoln and Joe Blow. Mother, Dad and Grandma had always insisted I tell the truth, but they had lied about school. School wasn't a place to learn at all. It was a horrible place to be abused and hurt and belittled.

"What are you doing down there, you big crybaby?"

"I fell down the stairs."

"No kidding! I thought you were whipping up a batch of ice cream. You yelled so loud I bet the students at the Illinois School for the Blind in Jacksonville could hear you. They were probably shocked out of their minds. They know their way around school. They aren't spoiled brats like you. I'm Mrs. Caine, the gym teacher. Get up right now and come join the others. You should be ashamed of yourself for wasting time in my class. Come on!"

Hands like eagles' talons grabbed me and yanked me to my feet. I threw caution to the winds, or I would have if there had been any air in that dank hallway. "Is it alright to waste time in someone else's class, Mrs. Caine? Miss Brookshire's is pretty boring."

Whack! My head whipped around and a sharp pain ran up my neck.

"It's never all right to waste time in class. Everything you learn here is important. I've heard some pretty bad things about you today, but this is the worst I've seen in all my years of teaching. Now come into the gym and maybe you can learn something about good behavior from the other girls."

Mrs. Caine dragged me into a large, moldy-smelling room which she said was the gym. Along one wall was a long line of low stools, which she called "stall-bar" stools. I wondered where the stalls were. I neither smelled nor heard horses. What else would you keep in stalls?

"Sit down on one of those stools and wait. I'll be back to show you what to do."

One thing was clear: No kind man, elephant, nor any other creature named Jim was going to teach this class. This was a totally different kind of gym, a kind I had never heard of. I still did not know its meaning. Maybe that was another thing I was supposed to listen and learn from the other girls, right up there with good behavior.

None of the other girls had spoken to me so far except Ellen, who seemed to be an outcast like me. The other girls seemed to move in an alternate universe—they didn't notice me; I didn't notice them. They didn't seem to have trouble surviving, the way I did. They didn't fall down the stairs. Everyone else seemed to know how to get where they were going. They didn't get slapped around. I listened for signs of that good behavior Mrs. Caine had said I was supposed to imitate. Some tinny organ music came on, probably from an old 78 record player. We had an Atwater Kent radio at home that had belonged to Grandpa Dent. It had a 78 record player in it, but Grandpa's player sounded much better than this one. I heard an irregular whirring noise. It sounded like some little cars I had at home called "friction toys." You rubbed them back and forth on the floor and they ran on the friction they had built up. They never ran very long, so they never got so far away that I couldn't find them when they stopped. If I sat in the middle of the floor, they didn't roll under the furniture.

"All right, Judy, it's time to roller skate."

"What's roller skating?"

"Heavens to Betsy! Every child in the world but you knows how to roller skate. I wouldn't be surprised if even blind children in the Amazon jungle know how to roller skate. Take this key and screw the skates onto your shoes. Skate around the gym in a circle. Turn when the music gets louder. I hope you fall on your head and knock some sense into it."

There was that circle again. When we had played "Jump Jim Crow," it had felt like a straight line, but Miss Brookshire had said we were in a circle. Now Mrs. Caine had told me to skate around this big room in a circle. If I had to guess, I would have said the place was long and narrow. Mother had told me that medieval monks had argued endlessly about how to square the circle; they never found the answer, but these people seemed to square the circle all the time, or at least they rectangled it. I know medieval monks had some screwy ideas, like believing that the universe was shaped like a whirling stack of pancakes with the earth in the center like a giant dollop of maple syrup, but could those monks really have been as dumb as the grown-ups at this awful school?

Back to the matter at hand. I was quickly learning that at this school you had to appear to be doing something, anything but thinking things through. I examined the small metal platforms with wooden wheels that Mrs. Caine had handed me. Mrs. Caine said to use the key to screw the skates onto my shoes. I knew that keys unlocked doors, but nothing around here felt like a door. Mother kept her keys on a chain attached to her wallet. I could tell when she was coming by the rattling of the keys. I shook the key Mrs. Caine had given me. It did not rattle. Let's try a different angle. I had held screws when Dad showed me his toolbox. A screw had a round head on one end and a point on the other. There was something else called a nut but I couldn't find anything like that on the roller skates. The one thing I remembered about nuts was that a long time ago when I was a child, at least two years before, I had put one in my mouth. It didn't taste anything like a peanut or cashew. Back to the screw. Between the point and the head it was squiggly like some kinds of macaroni and cheese—the macaroni, not the cheese. Dad had a little saying he used to help him know which way to turn the screw, "Righty tighty, lefty loosey." If I could find the hole in the skates, maybe I was supposed to put the key in it and turn it to the right. Just as I had worked out this brilliant deduction—"deduction" was a word I had learned from Grandpa telling me stories about a famous detective named Sherlock Holmes, who I wished were here right now, because there sure were a lot of mysteries that needed solving—I heard an angry voice I was to know only too well over the next eleven years.

"What in the world do you think you're doing, you lazy little lummox?" Dad, always the editor, would have said Mrs. Caine was a little heavy on the alliteration. I wished I had a red pencil to scratch her words out the way Dad did with his writers at the Globe-Democrat Sunday Magazine.

"You are the most helpless child in the history of this school. Now pay attention. This is the last time I'm going to show you how to put these skates on." But Mrs. Caine did not show me how. She yanked and jerked my legs as if they were enemies she wanted to strangle. "Now get going. Pay attention to your circles. If you fall, pick yourself up. Don't whine and wait for someone to help you."

I stood up shakily and pushed off from the wall. This was the strangest sensation ever. If cars could feel, this must be what it felt like to be one. I remembered that Mrs. Caine had said to pay attention to my circles and turn when the music got louder. Turn which way? Louder than what? The music was loud always and everywhere. It washed over me like the waves of the Gulf of Mexico when we were in Florida on vacation. Nothing Mrs. Caine said made sense.

Boom! Down I went. My head made a noise like someone dropping a watermelon off a roof. I had a knot on my forehead from falling down the stairs; soon I would have a knot on the back of my head from falling while roller skating. Don't cry. Don't cry. I put my hands on the floor and tried to push myself up. I felt dizzy and fell back down. Up down. Up down. Several times more.

"Judy! What did I tell you about trying to make people feel sorry for you? You should win an Academy Award for that performance. Now get up and go back to your skating. And your circles are atrocious. You wouldn't know a circle if it jumped up and bit you."

That 45-minute gym class seemed longer than the rest of the day put together. In all the years and all the hundreds of times I skated around that gym, I never learned to guide myself by that music. When Lions Clubs or anyone else who might become a big donor came to visit the school, that was one of the highlights of which the adults were most proud. They went on and on about how totally blind children could listen to the music and use the sound as a guide to roller skate around the gym in perfect circles. I don't know if other kids did it; I never could. We never talked about it, and it wouldn't do any good to ask.

Even in kindergarten we were all so driven, so pressured to outperform one another in physical tasks like finding our way around, which was called "mobility;" things like bathing, dressing, making beds, tying shoes, and fixing our hair, which all together were called "A.D.L." for "Activities of Daily Living;" and athletic activities, which were called "gym." Sometimes they lumped all these together in the impressive phrase, "Expanded Core Curriculum," which is to say, not the regular curriculum. It seemed to me that we were extravagantly praised or blamed for our performance in the expanded subjects, and the academic subjects just limped along and took care of themselves. I heard years later from former students who had not done well in academic subjects that the situation was exactly the reverse. The policy of the school was to badger and browbeat the students, emphasizing tasks, some of which we would never accomplish if we lived to be a hundred, thus accenting our disabilities rather than our abilities, but I didn't come to this conclusion on the first day of school. It took years of this treatment.

Somehow I made it through the rest of gym class, somehow got back to the dorm, somehow my gym suit was off and my dress buttoned up the back. These things got done, but someone must have helped me. I did not do them myself. All was a swooshing blur, like when you have ringing in your ears.

Ellen

"Judy, stop dilly-dallying and get downstairs. Your mother is waiting for you. Honestly! You can tell the day students every time. They're all spoiled brats."

I didn't remember hearing this voice, so probably had never met this woman before this moment. How did she know I was a spoiled brat? "Downstairs where?" I asked, terrified at the prospect of having to search at least two floors of this gigantic building. What if there were more stairs to fall down? Where else on my head could I get a knot?

"Don't get smart with me," came the new voice, new in tone quality, familiar in reprimand.

"I'll walk you down." Magically, there was Ellen again. "Your mom's probably at the Spring Avenue door or the front desk. We'll find her."

I thought the day was almost over—the pain, the horror, the abuse. Mother would soon be here to take me home, home to Tuffy, to Jacko the monkey, to Grandma Dent and Grandma Loehr, who loved me. Maybe there would be an earthquake during the night and I would never have to come back here at all, but the day was just getting going. Just as a decadent chocolate dessert tops off an outstanding dinner, making what came before it exquisitely better in remembrance, the end of this day was a kind of dessert in reverse; it was so bad that it made what came before it seem like comparing a mosquito bite to a war wound.

Mother was at the front desk, although after that day we met at the Spring Avenue entrance, because that was the door nearest House C, the dorm where I changed out of my gym suit.

"Oh, there you are," came a voice I had never been so delighted to hear. Then a stunned pause, a moment of suspended animation, followed by "Judy, why are you playing with that little colored girl?"

Ellen did not cry. She did not make a sound. She just wasn't there any more.

I cried, though; I howled, great sobs that came all the way up from the tips of my toes. Mother grabbed me so I wouldn't fall.

"What's the matter, Judy? Why the tears?"

"Oh, she had a little fall today and she's making the most of it."

There was Mrs. Caine again. She seemed to pop up everywhere, like weeds in the backyard.

"What's wrong with Judy, Mrs. Caine? She looks all bruised and banged up."

"That's just one of the occupational hazards of being blind. We teach our students to take such things and move on. We don't baby them."

"We signed Judy up to go to kindergarten, not Marine boot camp."

"That's an idea," said Mrs. Caine. This place was a bottomless pit of sarcasm.

"I think it's about time I took Judy home." Mother was never comfortable in a verbal duel.

I continued to cry softly, every once in a while choking down a big sob. "Mother, what's a colored girl?" I asked when we were safely in the car and I had pulled myself together enough to speak.

"Put your head back. You're blocking my view. They have black skin. They smell funny. They look like they never wash. Why, of all the girls in that school, did you have to pick the one colored girl for a friend?"

"She was nice to me," I mumbled. I dissolved into silence. This was way too bad for tears, for sobs, for conversation. Something had happened, something too awful to talk about. Ellen was the first friend I had chosen for myself, or rather, Ellen had chosen me. When Ellen said, "Your head's crooked," we had established the desperate bond that can only come from recognizing a fellow outcast, although I couldn't have put it that way at the time. This was my first experience with race, but I knew as certainly as if I had a Master's in sociology, that it was a canker sore, a cancer, a disease like the one that made people say with tremors in their voices, "We don't have the facilities" when Mother asked yet another school to accept me. If Mother said, "What facilities are those?" they usually became agitated and found a quick way to end the conversation. All my life my friends had been chosen for me, which is to say, I didn't have any friends. My cousins were chosen by God; the neighbor kids were chosen by real estate agents; the children of Mother's bridge club members were chosen because our moms liked to play cards together. Anyone else who happened to come into my life was chosen by my parents. Ellen and I had chosen each other. When I was having trouble, all the others had ignored me; only Ellen had defied the authorities and helped me. She had done what Dad would have called the politically unpopular thing.

Once Grandma Dent had given me a black baby doll with tight curls of hair glued to her head.

"Be nice to black people, Judy," Grandma had said. "They've had hard times." Then she sang a little song she said she had learned as a child down in Reynolds County, Missouri, which began:

Little nigger baby,

Black face and shiny eyes,

Just as good as anybody else in the sweet by and by.

Why were they only "as good as anybody else" in "the sweet by and by"? Why not now? Who was "anybody else"? I asked Grandma these questions and she hugged me tight. "I don't know, Honey," Grandma answered. Her voice broke and I could tell Grandma was crying. I had never heard Grandma cry before.

"What's wrong, Grandma?"

"I don't know why things are the way they are. They just are. But remember, God loves everyone: you, Dad, Mother, little nigger babies. Some people don't understand that."

Was Ellen a slightly older version of one of those little babies Grandma sang about?

This was all too much for me. I was quiet the rest of the evening. When I went to bed I forgot all about "Dear God, if it be thy will, please give me sight." I prayed "God bless Grandma Dent and Grandma Loehr, Mother and Dad, and especially Ellen, and God, please let Ellen still want to play with me tomorrow." I climbed into bed, counting the people I had met today whose heads were crooked and, I have to admit, not praying for them.

That was my first day of school, the first of thousands, of eleven years' worth. Ellen continued to play with me at school, but we were never allowed to visit in each other's homes. I remembered what Grandma Dent had said, and I always tried to imitate her because everyone loved Grandma Dent. I wanted them to love me, too. The rest of my school days, with a few outstanding exceptions, were pretty much like the first.

So if that was The Day My Childhood Ended—the first day of kindergarten—what was my short childhood like?

Chapter 2

Early Memories

My eyes and the full moon

The crystals hung, long and smooth. They tinkled when bumped together. I stood on the kitchen table, fascinated. "Chandelier! Chandelier!" I cried in delight. Those crystals, my mother called them "teardrops," were the most beautiful things I had felt in my eighteen months of life. They were smooth and I loved smooth things. The big chandelier was the centerpiece of our kitchen and my mother often stood me on the table to touch it. "Chandelier" was one of my first words, right up there with "Mother," "Daddy," and "cookie," that last being one of my favorite words today. I loved anything that stimulated the senses—smells, sounds, textures. I loved anything soft or smooth or that had an interesting shape. That hasn't changed from my earliest childhood.

That chandelier is my first memory, probably because it was such an intense sensory experience. If I concentrate hard, I can almost imagine I feel the smoothness of those dangling crystals and hear them clinking together. I would love to have a chandelier like that in my home now, although climbing on a table to touch it might be a problem.

In the same way, most aspects of my life are related to an excess or lack of sensory experience. An episode I don't remember—but which was often recounted to me—set the tone for my early life. Again it was about sensory experience.

The first inkling my parents had that something was wrong with me was when I showed no interest in my bottle until it touched my lips. I never looked at nearby objects. I was evaluated by several pediatricians and clinicians whose common refrain was, "She doesn't respond like a normal child." This comment made my folks furious because, as Dad often pointed out, "I didn't need them to tell me that. Why don't they tell me something I don't already know?"

When I was four months old one of the doctors suggested that they have my eyes examined. I don't know why it took these professionals so long to come up with this recommendation unless my parents just needed that long to get used to the idea that there might be something wrong with my vision. At last they took me to an ophthalmologist who had office hours at night so both parents could take me without missing work. As the new doctor asked for my medical history, all the evidence came out, intriguing the doctor and upsetting my parents almost to the point of hysteria. I was born on October 18, 1946, ten weeks prematurely, weighing two pounds, seven ounces. I was only eleven inches long. When I came home from the hospital after six weeks in an incubator, Mother crocheted me a cap. As a model for my head she used a small orange. The cap fit perfectly. One parlor trick she enjoyed showing off to friends and relatives was to put her wedding ring on my wrist like a bracelet and to put my baby bracelet on her finger like a ring. She loved to tell anyone who would listen that the nurses at the hospital had called me "Miss Littlebit" and said I was their miracle baby. When my parents brought me home the doctors said I had only a one in a thousand chance to live, so they shouldn't get too attached to me. When the ophthalmologist heard all this and examined me he pronounced my diagnosis—gleefully, my dad insisted, because I was the first case this doctor, and most others we visited, had ever seen. I had retrolental fibroplasia, RLF. It was the result of too much oxygen in the incubator, which caused, the doctors believed, fibrous tissue to grow behind the eye, blocking light from reaching the retina. The doctor explained to my parents that it was like pulling down a window shade to keep out the light.

This explanation was later changed to the hypothesis that the oxygen had burned out my retinas. Accordingly the name of the diagnosis was changed to ROP, "retinopathy of prematurity."

I don't know much about the anatomy of the eyes, except that mine don't work. Nor do I understand the true nature of the "opacity," "whiteness," or "fibrous tissue" that obscured my vision and so fascinated the many doctors and medical students who poked and prodded me over the next ten or twelve years, who put drops in my eyes that burned like molten lava, who said, "Look up! Look down! Look right! Look left! Can you see my finger? How many fingers do I have up? What do you mean, you can't move your eyes? Of course you can! They're moving around all over the place."

As my parents carried me out of the ophthalmologist's office there was a full moon. Mother looked up, began to cry, and said, "Just think, George. She'll never see the moon."

That juxtaposition between my opaque eyes and the full moon I would never see became the defining moment for my early years, if not decades. I felt circumscribed by my limitations, identified by what I was not. I had to try harder than everyone else, accomplish more than everyone else. I worked endlessly for a vague concept rather than a specific, achievable goal. I heard it every day until it rattled in my brain and echoed in my sleep. "You have to be twice as good to be half as good." Dad said it; Mother said it; my teachers said it; it seemed that those who did not say it thought it. Twice as good as whom? Half as good as what? I did not know then and I do not know now. I do know I have not achieved it.

"One foot, the other foot"

My first memories fall into two categories: sensory experiences and being different. Until I was four we lived in a rented house on Sappington Road in Glendale, Missouri, a suburb of St. Louis. Although my sensory experiences were intense to the point of being exhausting, it never occurred to me to ask what my neighborhood, or even my house, looked like. I experienced the world with my ears, nose, mouth and fingers. When my parents wanted me to touch a new object, they would say "See this!" or "Look at that!" or "I have something to show you." There were many things to show me—an old robin's nest vacated by its former owners, interesting pebbles and rocks, all kinds of worms, insects, flowers and leaves. One day my mother put a butterfly in my hand. Its legs felt sticky as they clung to my finger and its wings fluttered like eyelashes. To this day when I touch eyelashes I think of butterfly wings. Our family must have struck terror into the hearts of the non-human inhabitants of our backyard. They must have lived in fear that they would become specimens in our private natural history museum.

One of my favorite living creatures was the earthworm. It felt like spaghetti, only much more interesting. Spaghetti didn't wriggle the way the worm did. We had a large compost pile in our yard and it was always full of worms. I didn't much like putting my hands in the dirt—dirty hands gave me a distinctly uncomfortable feeling, like listening to someone squeak chalk on a blackboard. It sent creepy chills down my back. But I loved the feel of the earthworms; they had life in them, although I wouldn't have put it that way at the time. I would hold the worm, transfixed by its movement, until it didn't wiggle any more. It took me a long time to understand that the worms stopped moving because I was killing them. Realizing that dampened my interest in touching living things. Years later when I read Steinbeck's Of Mice and Men, about a man who loved to touch small, fragile living things until they died, I remembered the earthworms and the butterflies, and I felt a profound sadness.

Walking, or rather the lack thereof, was another of my defects that perplexed and upset my parents. I didn't do it. Apparently walking as a naturally occurring activity is yet another magical power possessed by "normal" people. I didn't know I was supposed to walk, or crawl, reach, point, or wave bye-bye. These were only a few of the myriad forms of self-expression I simply did not get. Our family history was rife with lore about the things I did do, exceeded only by the things I didn't. I talked in simple sentences at nine months, complex ones at fifteen months. One of my first sentences was, "How long have I been living?" I don't remember why I asked that question, but I do remember asking it. People were always shocked at my vocabulary and at the sophisticated questions I asked; they were equally if not more shocked at my failure to walk and perform gestures, at my inappropriate facial expressions, and worst of all, at my failure to imitate people.

One of the refrains I heard years before I understood it was, "She doesn't respond like a normal child. She lacks imitation." When I was three or four I asked about it. "Dad, what's imitation?"

"It's when something isn't the real thing," Dad explained. "Mother's handbag is imitation needlepoint. It was made by a machine instead of by a person with a needle and thread. Margarine is imitation butter."

This explanation was no help whatsoever. If imitation was such a good thing, as the doctors and social workers said it was, then why was it better to be fake than real? This exchange with Dad was typical of all my conversations with my parents. We never faced blindness head-on as an issue. I had to learn gradually that I was blind, and even more gradually what it meant.

Many of my questions were answered in the wrong context or with evasion. Once Mother read me a story about a little girl being sent to the grocery store by her mother. "Why don't you ever send me to the store?" I asked.

Long silence. "It's too far away and there are no sidewalks."

I could tell Mother was struggling for a reply. She had that sad tone of voice again and the reading session, now spoiled, soon ended.

The store wasn't the only place I never walked. I didn't walk around the house until months after a "normal" child would have been into everything. Mother talked forever to anyone who would listen about what an exercise in frustration and heartbreak it was to bring up a blind child. Then in the same breath she would say what a good baby I was. "Judy never gets into anything," I often heard her say. "When I put her somewhere, she never moves. She just stays right where I put her." I don't know at what point my parents began to figure out that my always staying in one place wasn't an unmitigated asset. I didn't reach for food or toys, especially if no one mentioned they were there. If someone shook a rattle near me, I would stretch out my hands toward it but not make a move in that direction. Mother had first begun to suspect that something was wrong with me when I failed to reach for the bottle. After a while what had been a source of pleasure for my parents became a major frustration.

Instead of praising me for being calm and placid as they had in the past, they found in my behavior yet another occasion for yelling. "You are the laziest, dumbest child I've ever seen. Use your hands, for crying out loud!"

I never knew what they wanted; the more they would reprimand me the more I would cry. I don't remember a specific incident that precipitated a change in tactics, but at some point they deduced that no amount of hand-wringing and aspersion-casting was going to elicit the responses they wanted. They began to place my body in the desired positions. I remember one event in particular that must have had the same effect on my parents that Helen Keller's famous pump handle incident had on hers.

Anne Sullivan, Helen's teacher, ran water over one of Helen's hands while finger-spelling w-a-t-e-r into the other. This was the first time Helen was able to make the connection between words and objects. I learned to walk in the same way. Mother strung a rope from one end of our long, narrow living room to the other. She put my hand on the rope then guided my feet through the walking position, placing one foot forward, then moving the other one ahead of it, chanting, "One foot, the other foot, one foot, the other foot." Learning to walk didn't happen in a sudden eureka moment. It took dozens of attempts over many days. The drama of walking was more like a soap opera than a magic trick. We practiced every day for weeks with apparently little results. Eventually the idea clicked in like a lamp being plugged into a wall outlet. This strange motion could get me from one place to another. Over and over again my parents stood one on each end of the room, taking turns calling me as I held the rope and walked from one of them to the other.

After a while I began walking on my own, which presented a set of challenges far beyond holding a rope and walking from one parent to the other. I quickly discovered that furniture had sharp corners, many of them level with my face. There was a sharp-cornered coffee table in the living room that I'm convinced was out to get me. In fact, inanimate objects are usually out to get me. If there's a half-open door within miles, my head will find it; if there's a small, rolling object on the floor, it will end up under my foot; if an ice cube falls on the kitchen floor or a drop of grease detectable only by a microscope, my foot will find it. I have never skied or ice-skated. I get enough slipping and crashing adventures right in my own home.

It didn't take me long to learn that walking straight ended in a fall or a collision. There was one place, however, that I could walk without getting hurt: the middle of the floor. I could find the middle of a room, where there was no furniture, and twirl in circles. As long as I didn't stray too far to one side I was safe. Sometimes I would get carried away and go too fast, wander out of my confined space and hit something, but the odds of not getting hurt were much better twirling than walking straight. Walking left me always tense and usually bruised; twirling left me relaxed and exhilarated. Spinning rapidly in a small circle is the most exhilarating form of movement I have ever experienced. I get high from it the way I imagine people get high on drugs. I feel a kind of heightened awareness when I twirl, an almost trancelike state where all my thoughts are clear and I seem to have an unlimited supply of good ideas. I like to have a good twirl before I write, preferably about a half hour's worth with music. For me rock and country are the best twirling music. Classical and jazz require too much attention. Walking on a treadmill does not produce this effect; neither does riding a stationary bicycle. Walking with a sighted person or a guide dog certainly doesn't. I can understand why Sufis, often called whirling dervishes, use this movement to put themselves into a meditative state. I feel closest to God when I twirl.

"I'll play the harp for you."

Fingers press hard. Holes drill deep in my skull. Needles everywhere. Caustic slime covers my face. Eyes burn. Hair pulled. Stretched. Struggle. Scream. Stop! Stop! Stop!

"Hold still. For heaven's sake, I'm not killing you."

"What's going on in there? Whatever it is, it better stop now." Will Dad come to my rescue? Will one of the grandmas?

The pain is tremendous. A great tide of water pours over me. More rubbing. More pain. The slime goes away and becomes water. Acid. Dry burning now. Wet and dry. Sour.

"For crying out loud, Judy, stop screaming. I'm only washing your hair."

Not noticing, or caring what kind of example she was setting for me, Mother was screaming now. "I can't do a thing with you. You won't even let me touch you."

"Let me try." I stopped screaming, hearing Grandma Dent's soothing voice. "Try to be gentle, Erna. You're scaring her half to death. When I came out here and heard all that racket, I thought something really bad had happened."

"That's just it, Ida, I'm barely touching her. Every time I come near her she screams the way Pop's hogs used to scream at butchering time. I used to shampoo her hair every week, but now I only try every two weeks. She has a fit every time I pick her up. I can't stand this. I'd like to walk out of this house and just keep walking until I fall over dead. Nobody needs me around here anyway." Mother began to cry. She sounded almost like me when she was washing my hair.

"Oh, Erna, that would make us so sad. We all need you."

"What's going on here?" Thwock. Dad put down his newspaper and stood in the door. "Can't a guy read his newspaper in peace without all this ruckus? Judy, knock it off. What the hell's wrong with you? Erna, leave her alone and come in the living room. I saved the bridge column for you. It's about a guy named Tommy something who made seven no trump three times in one evening using some obscure strategy or other."

Mother, still sniffling, went off to the living room. Grandma rinsed and dried my hair. "Let's not put those awful pins in it tonight. Let's let your hair hang straight down. It will look more natural and relaxed. Come in the bedroom and I'll play the harp for you. Maybe we can sing some songs together."

The harp was a diatonic harmonica, which some people call a mouth harp. Grandma Dent played with so much skill that I didn't know until after she was dead and I tried to play it myself that the instrument had no sharps or flats. She got sound out of that little mouth harp that I can't produce even after years of trying. Grandma could play lots of old country songs. Sometimes she put down the harp and sang in a voice that sounded like feather pillows and hot chocolate. She would hold me on her lap and bounce me up and down in time to the music. Tonight she played "Oh, Susanna," then made up her own words.

Oh, dear Judy, oh don't you cry today,

For God and Grandma love you. We'll fix it right away.

She played "The Wabash Cannonball," complete with long, lonesome train whistle and short, quick notes to depict the chugging of the locomotive. "The harp is getting tired, Judy, as I imagine you are. Listen. It wants its mama." The harmonica let loose a long, slow wail, ending with, "I want my mama." I only had to use my imagination a little bit to understand the words.

"Can you make it say 'I want my grandma?'"

"No, little Sweetmeat. The G is too far back in my throat. I can't make that sound and play the harp at the same time."

"But I don't want my mama. I want you, Grandma." I began to tear up again, burying my face in Grandma's warm, soft lap.

"Shhhh." Grandma stroked my back. "Don't say that. You'll hurt your mother's feelings and make her cry. Your mother loves you, Judy. It breaks her heart that you can't see. Erna relies on her vision so much that she can't imagine anyone living a happy life without it."

"But she's always so mad. And she hears voices. None of the other girls at school have mothers who hear voices."

"Some of those girls don't have mothers at all. Some have mothers who don't want them."

"Does Mother want me, Grandma? She's always so sad."

"You need to be patient with your mother, Judy. She's afraid when she hollers at you, just like you're afraid when you have a bad dream."

"But why does she hurt me and scream at me?"

"You know how you have trouble dressing yourself and tying your shoes? Sometimes Mother has trouble with her brain. She gets confused and scared. When you scream, she gets even more scared than usual. That's why you have to be patient with her, just as you want her to be patient with you. Now let's think about something more cheerful, and I'll help you get ready for bed. Soon you'll be able to say, 'Good night, all, I'm going to bed.' You'll be able to go to bed all by yourself."

"But who will read me a story and kiss me good night?"

"Someone who loves you will be there to kiss you good night. When you get older it will be your husband, then later your children. Later your grandchildren will kiss you good night and that will make you feel loved, just like I feel loved when you kiss me good night. As for stories, they have machines now that read stories to you. Soon you will have one."

"I'd rather have you than a machine, Grandma. I love you."

"I love you, too, Sweetmeat. Now let's go to sleep." Grandma pulled the covers over me and kissed me goodnight. I had a lot to think about. I had to be patient with Mother? That was a hard one to get my mind around. Mother was hardly ever patient with me, but Grandma was almost always patient. Usually no one needed me to be patient; no one ever asked for my help, not even Grandma; but being patient was something I could do for Mother. Maybe then she would stop being so disappointed in me. I went to sleep thinking about how much I loved Grandma Dent.

Mother continued to wash my hair; it continued to hurt; I continued to scream. Dad, from time to time, kept yelling, "Knock it off! What the hell's wrong with you?" Mother sang a little song as she rubbed the soap into my scalp. "Hippity-hop, hippity-hop, hippity-hop to the beauty shop." Actually Mother didn't use shampoo. She used a bar of smelly stuff called "tar soap" that stank like hot pavement so I suppose it really had tar in it. When Mother used regular shampoo my head broke out in flaky, itchy sores. I cried and screamed and scratched until I bled. At last the doctor suggested the tar soap. The itchy sores went away, but the stuff felt and smelled awful.

I got all kinds of infections, especially strep ear and throat. I got a recurring itchy pain deep in my vagina. The doctor said it was a yeast infection, but it was nothing like the fragrant bread Grandma Loehr made. Instead, the washcloth smelled like stale beer. I knew what stale beer smelled like because school was near the Anheuser-Busch brewery and sometimes, when the wind came from a certain direction, the fumes blew into our classroom.

Hoeing sweet potatoes

Squeak burn. Squeak burn. I was trying to eat something called "salad." In a way I couldn't quite grasp, it reminded me of Mother washing my hair, but this hurt was inside, though, much worse than having my hair washed. I screamed proportionably louder. "It hurts. It hurts. Make it go away."

"What hurts, Judy? Make what go away?" Grandma Dent, as usual, tried to sooth me. "Tell me what's wrong."

"The squeaky vegetable has battery acid on it."

"Knock it off, Judy. If you want us to understand you, you have to speak English."

For a moment I was distracted from my pain by wondering what Dad would say if I said the same thing in Spanish or French. If I said it in German it wouldn't help, because he spoke German fairly fluently. He would probably have the same trouble understanding me in German as in English.

"Eat your salad, Judy," said Mother. "Then you can have the rest of your meal."

"Battery acid!" I slammed down my fork for emphasis.

"Now, Judy, let's be reasonable." Dad was trying hard to practice what he preached. Being reasonable was not something Dad found easy, at least at home. When his coworkers came over they always maintained he was kind and fair at work. Were they talking about the same George Dent? Did he say "Knock it off" to the magazine writers when their stories were unusually long-winded or boring?

Discreet questioning indicated that Dad never behaved that way at work. Was that because he respected his coworkers more than his family? He never yelled at the two grandmas. When Grandpa Dent was alive, Dad didn't yell at him. Mother screamed at everyone all the time; Dad yelled at her every day. Maybe screaming hurt him the way this battery-acidy, sharp-pointed, squeaky salad hurt me. The lettuce squeaked against my teeth the way chalk squeaked on the blackboard when the teachers wrote explanations for the sight saver students. The vinegar dressing excavated the inside of my body from the tip of my tongue to the bottom of my stomach. Maybe screaming assaulted Dad's senses in the same way sharp-pointed, acidy food assaulted mine. Although my throat and stomach still hurt, I was able to stop screaming when I focused on psychology instead of salad. I felt a little more peace, a little less pressure.

"Judy, for crying out loud, stop meditating and eat. The rest of your food is getting cold. You're just staring off into space. Who do you think you are, the Buddha? You're getting as fat as him."

"Is the Buddha fat? I thought he only ate vegetables."

"Don't argue. Eat your salad." Dad was getting impatient again.

"It hurts. I don't want it."

"You don't have to want it; you have to eat it."

"Why? It hurts."

"Every time you don't want to do something you say it hurts. The rest of us hurt too, but we don't cry and scream about it."

"What hurts you, Dad?"

"None of your business. Eat your salad."

I took another bite. Squeak burn, squeak, burn. "Enough!" growled my stomach. I jumped up from the table and hurried to the bathroom, retching all the way. I threw up in the pot, but didn't get the seat up in time and got vomit all over it.

"Look what you did!" Mother was standing at the bathroom door screaming. "Now I have to clean you up and clean up the bathroom. Can't we ever have one peaceful dinner? Yuck. I wish I didn't have to touch you. You stink."

I wanted to say, "If you didn't give me poisonous food that made me sick, this wouldn't happen." I caught myself just in time.

"Take off that dress. It's a mess." Mother yanked off my dress and threw it on the floor. Washcloths and towels thwacked me from all directions—wet, whack, whack—dry, whack, whack. "Now get out of here and stay out of trouble for a few minutes."

"Erna, don't scream at her. Where do you think she learns that?"

"Ida, you have to stop interfering with the way I bring up my child. You spoil her. That's why she's such a whiny little crybaby."

"Erna, she's sick. That happens with little children. It happened with George. It happened with me. It probably happened with you."

"When I was sick Mom just smacked me and sent me out to the field to hoe sweet potatoes. One day she shoved me out the door barefoot and I accidentally sliced off part of my big toe with the hoe. Mom just washed it, slapped a bandage on it, and sent me back out. My sister Quinetta was always sick and got all the attention. She was premature like Judy. She was also a little wimp who couldn't do anything."

The implication hung in the air. "A little wimp who couldn't do anything … just like Judy."

"Erna, for goodness sake, she's listening to every word. You want her to love you, but you scream at her and say things like that."

"This is my home, Ida. If you don't stop causing trouble, you'll have to find another place to live."

While they were arguing I slipped away to the room I shared with Grandma Dent. I hoped no one would disturb me. There was so much to think about, all of it scary and confusing. Had Grandma Loehr really sent Mother out to the fields to hoe sweet potatoes when Mother was sick? Had Mother really chopped off her toe? Had Grandma really made her go right back out and keep hoeing? Would Grandma Loehr do those things to me? Worst of all, could Mother actually throw Grandma Dent out of our house? If Grandma Dent left, and Grandma Loehr started being mean to me, I wouldn't have anyone to love me but Tuffy. I was too afraid to cry. "Wimp." "Crybaby." I was trying so hard, but it wasn't enough, not enough at home, not enough at school.

Meanwhile sharp needles were boring holes in my stomach. "Please God, don't let me throw up again."

Why did so many things hurt so much? Why did so many things that were supposed to be good for me make me sick? Milk, cheese and ice cream made me feel good, so did mashed potatoes, noodles, most meat, and chocolate. Oatmeal, also supposedly good for me, was disgusting with lumpy, gritty balls floating in it. Tapioca was even more repellent. Almost all vegetables except peas and potatoes made me gag. Marinara sauce, simply called "tomato sauce" when I was growing up, burned like fire. Most fish upset my stomach and tasted like metal. Raspberries and blackberries felt like grit in my mouth, and their tiny seeds cut my gums and made them bleed. Citrus and vegetable juices burned like toxic chemicals in my throat. They felt like battery acid. Dad would say, "But you've never tasted battery acid. How do you know what it's like?" I tried patiently to explain to Dad that these things tasted like I would imagine battery acid would taste if I tried it—caustic and poisonous. I couldn't eat anything made with vinegar for the same reason. To this day the popular abomination raspberry vinaigrette salad dressing makes me feel ill just thinking about it.

Part of this was the synesthesia that makes my senses hop around like Mexican jumping beans. Synesthesia is a neurological condition in which the experiences of one sense lead to automatic and involuntary experiences in another sense; at this time, it was decades away from serious consideration by the scientific community. To me, at first, the word "Oklahoma" tasted like cinnamon rolls, but when Grandma Dent read me The Grapes of Wrath, and I learned about the Oklahoma dust bowl, the cinnamon rolls became gritty and the dust ground around in my teeth and Oklahoma began to taste like cinnamon rolls in a bad way, and cinnamon rolls began to sound like Oklahoma. Wallpaper smelled and tasted like bananas and bananas felt like catfish—not cooked catfish, but raw just after it has been caught: catfish don't have scales like most other fish, and bananas tasted smooth and wet, like catfish felt. The word "raincoat" smelled like dirty socks. Sounds, smells and textures conflated and coalesced until I wasn't sure what I was tasting, hearing or touching.

Until I was twelve I was lactose intolerant and had to drink a milk substitute called Starlac. I don't know what it was made of, but I'm sure in a pinch you could have used it to kill rats or remove old furniture polish. I was allergic to betacarotene, another thing nobody knew. I spent three Thanksgivings in the emergency room before it became clear that it was not a wise idea for me to try Aunt Quinetta's candied yams or Aunt Beverly's pumpkin pie. Tomato juice, orange juice, all those vegetables that were supposed to be so good for me made my stomach burn like fire. When things got stressful I alternated between vomiting and diarrhea, especially when I had to spend the night at school. The school nurse, the housemothers and the other kids would sneer at me and tell me to stop pretending to be sick and get back to class. My body would tense up with rage. I felt helpless. I got yelled at at school and at home. There was no place to be safe. I knew both grandmas loved me, and sometimes I believed Mother and Dad did, but I was never completely sure. The teachers at school valued all the things I couldn't do, but didn't seem to care that my braille skills were outstanding, both reading and writing, that I could do arithmetic quickly and accurately in my head, or that I was the best speller in the school. None of that seemed to matter. When I bumped into something or fell, it hurt like power drills going through my body. People just told me not to be a baby.

Chapter 3
Grandpas and Grandmas

Grandpa Dent
George Beauregard Dent, 1865-1948

Smooth. Hard. Cool. I squeezed a little to enjoy the crystalline feel, like the chandelier, but not hanging. Hard was good sometimes, but not usually; soft was good usually, but not always. This hard was the good kind: no sharp points. It had a cool aliveness, like Uncle Martin's baby alligator, not a warm aliveness, like Aunt Leona's cat. Slither. Slip. Slide. Crash. Mother had told me that if you dropped a light bulb it would make a funny noise. I had tried it last Christmas. It was a very small light bulb; it didn't make a really satisfying noise, more like a sad kernel of popcorn that didn't know its place. The one who made the loud noise was Mother. "You did that deliberately, Judy. I don't know what to do with you. What were you thinking?"

I spoke clearly and in complete sentences, something everyone but my parents said was a remarkable feat. I didn't know what was so remarkable about my feet. It was my eyes and my words that got me in trouble. "I wanted to hear the funny noise."

"You what? You'll hear a funny noise all right, and it won't be a laughing matter. I'm taking you in the living room, and you stay there until I clean up this mess."

Mother held me on her shoulder and flipped me over like a pancake. Pop! Pop! The two whacks on my bottom were much louder than the light bulb. The noise was more frightening than the pain. I added to it by screaming with all my lungpower. Mother carried me into the living room and put me on the couch. Like a good little blind person, I did not move.

Today it wasn't a light bulb going pop, clink, splash; it was a glass of milk, or what used to be a glass of milk. The result was the same, though, and right on cue, Mother began to scream.

"Now look what you did, you stupid individual!" Mother was in full throttle. "Judy, can't you just pick up a glass and drink out of it? And what's wrong with the rest of you people? You're all sitting there like you paid to gawk at a sideshow! Why doesn't somebody get up and help?"

I was terrified when Mother yelled like that. It gave me a deep-down, animal fear of being hurt, of being abandoned, of never belonging anywhere. Of course I could not have put any of this into words at two years old, but I felt it in a raw, visceral way, like drinking acid. I screamed louder than Mother.

Someone did get up to help. It was Grandpa Dent, but he did not get up to help Mother clean up the mess; he got up to help me. Grandpa was blind, too. It was a bond between us that I didn't think about until years later. I was not old enough while I had Grandpa to talk to him about our shared blindness; it was just there, like being wrapped up together under a big, soft blanket. I can't remember anyone yelling at Grandpa the way they yelled at me, but I can't remember him breaking and spilling things, either. Slowly, with great care and a kind of grace that I could not achieve even now, Grandpa plucked me from the puddle of milk and broken glass, held my wet, crying self high in the air like an athletic trophy, and walked us to the couch, where he held me, milk and all, in his warm, comforting lap. I stopped crying and enjoyed him like sunshine.

"Don't baby her, George Beauregard," Mother admonished. "She has to learn to behave."

Learning to behave was the farthest thing from my mind or Grandpa's as he cuddled me on the couch and let the chatter roll away like subsiding thunder. "They'll never understand, will they?" he whispered in my ear, "but we do."

I was sure, on some instinctive, wordless level, that Grandpa did.

Grandpa had developed cataracts in both eyes a few years before I was born. He always said he was more afraid of the treatment plan after the surgery, which at the time involved immobilizing one's head with sandbags for weeks, than he was of blindness. My parents never discussed how they felt about the extra help Grandpa needed because of this choice. I don't remember any pressure being put on Grandpa to accomplish household tasks or mobility. I remember how it felt to hold his hand, to sit in his lap, to listen to his stories. There always seemed to be a magnetic safety field around Grandpa; when he was present nobody got too angry or too loud or too crazy.

Grandpa loved to tell jokes. Grandpa's head contained a whole library of jokes—long ones and short ones, jokes with dialect and jokes with puns, one-liners and shaggy dog stories, but I don't recall him telling a dirty joke around the family. The first joke he told me went like this:

First man: I work on a farm with goats that don't have any horns.
Second man: But …
First man: There are no butts.

The first million times I heard it, I rolled on the floor laughing. Another of his favorites:

Grandpa: What has four legs, wags its tail, and barks?
Me: A dog?

Grandpa: Oh, you heard that one.

Sometimes I would try to show off when Grandpa told a joke. "Grandpa, you've told me that one a hundred times."

"Old jokes are the best," Grandpa assured me. "Then everyone knows when to laugh."

He was full of wise sayings that sounded silly until you thought about it. "The more I think of him, the less I think of him," he said about a politician he didn't like. "Never do today what you can put off until tomorrow, because tomorrow you might not have to do it at all." He usually lived by exactly the opposite philosophy, but the saying had a double meaning. If you couldn't work on a problem right away, time often made it less urgent. Grandpa's humor dispelled fear, relieved anxiety, and made it easier for everyone around him to face difficult situations. If he sensed that someone felt uncomfortable with his blindness, he would say, "You're feeling good, how are you looking?" Blindness never put Grandpa into a deep depression. I never heard him express anger or resentment because he could not see. I wish I could say the same.

I work hard to avoid inflicting pain on myself by endlessly questioning why I still scream with rage and frustration when I am misunderstood—which is by most people most of the time—while Grandpa's conduct never seemed less than loving, gentle, and open-minded. Now that I'm older and more cynical, I don't beat myself quite so hard on this subject. There were circumstances in Grandpa's life that were completely different from mine. In his youth and his two careers, first as a Morse Code expert for the U.S. Postal Service, then as a newspaperman, Grandpa did not have a disability. He did not grow up thinking of himself as damaged, as less than acceptable. He did not face social, educational or job discrimination, as blind people still do today. He lost his sight long after his retirement, when it was socially acceptable for him to stay home and be safe, not to have to face the irresistible force of the sighted world continually pushing back. He was considered a charming old eccentric with a remarkably analytical mind and almost total recall, brilliant, but not enough to be dangerous. His family loved and cherished him, so he never had to rely on help from strangers, paid employees, or, worst of all, volunteers. Knowing Grandma Dent as I did, she probably loved him more after he lost his sight, not less. I wish there had been more time for me to learn from his example.

Grandpa did me one favor for which I am grateful every time someone speaks to me or asks for my signature. Grandpa was George B. Dent. The B stood for Beauregard. Grandpa's father was on the side of the South during the Civil War and was a great admirer of General Beauregard, thus Grandpa's middle name. Mother called him "George Beauregard" to distinguish him from "George," who was Dad and was often referred to as George Junior, although he was not technically a Junior, because his middle name was Rayfield, Grandma's maiden name. When Mother found out she was pregnant after seven years of marriage, she and Dad were thrilled at the prospect of having George Dent the Third. It was a complete surprise to my parents when I was not the Third they had hoped for. Trying to make the best of a disappointing situation, Mother came up with a compromise: name me GeorgeAnn. If I had known about that I would have cried while still in the womb. Soon after my birth, my family met to consider what name would go on my birth certificate. Grandpa was adamant. "You will not call this child GeorgeAnn. Call her Judith Anne after my grandmother who came over from England." I became Judith Anne instead of GeorgeAnn. I like the 'e' at the end of my Anne. It feels elegant and French. I like to say it's the only thing I have in common with the saint. There are lots of things about myself I wish I could change, but Grandpa gave me a nice name.

When Grandpa lost his sight he did not lose his love of books. When he gave up his large home in St. Louis City and moved in with us he donated most of his extensive library to St. Louis University, but some of his favorites he could not bear to part with even though he could no longer see to read them. We had no room for his oversized bookcase, so it stayed in our garage covered by a tarpaulin. It was full of signed first editions and other rare books. He counted Mark Twain among his friends and mentors. Two of his prized possessions were signed first editions of Roughing It and Huckleberry Finn. He had the works of Shakespeare, Milton, Dickens, and many other English and American poets and novelists. He had the essays of John Locke, from whom he derived many of his ideas about freedom and democracy. Grandpa's literary tastes were cosmopolitan, although English was the only language he read fluently. His bookcase was full of world literature in translation, especially from French. His favorite French philosopher was Voltaire, from whom he learned the importance of arriving at reasoned conclusions by thinking for oneself. He had the complete works of Victor Hugo, including a copy of the first English translation of Les Miserables, which was his favorite Hugo novel. He had all Jules Verne's novels. My favorite was Journey to the Center of the Earth, which, along with a story by Voltaire about a trip to Saturn, inspired my interest in science fiction.

Grandma spent hours reading aloud. She and Grandpa always had several books going. He was like a child in that he could hear his favorites over and over and never get tired of them. Grandma read to us whenever she could. We read together: grown-up books for Grandpa or children's books for me, but always together. Grandpa was patient when we read my books; he taught me to be patient when we read his. It was not unusual for us to go in one session from Read to Me Storybook to Aristotle's Nicomachean Ethics. Grandpa would hold me in his lap, his warm, gentle hand folding around mine. I was tiny when we started reading together, less than three years old. The reading was a cocoon of white noise that wrapped me up and kept me safe. Gradually I began to understand the stories. As I grew older, I started asking questions. Grandpa never told me to be quiet so the reading could continue. He could boil difficult concepts down into easy ones, as when he described Ptolemy's cosmos as a spinning stack of pancakes. He went on to explain that Ptolemy made the mistake of believing the earth was the center of the universe; human beings had to learn that we are a tiny, insignificant speck in the universe, just as I had to learn that I wasn't the only member in the family. For example, we spent some time reading what I wanted to hear and some time reading what Grandpa wanted to hear. We read and discussed Greek and Norse mythology, Shakespeare, Milton, and the Bible. I had no idea, until both Dent grandparents were gone, that I was reading-impaired. I didn't realize I was not a normal reader until first grade when I was hit by the cognitive dissonance between "To be or not to be" and "See Dick run," between parents and grandparents reading to me from intellectually stimulating if difficult works of philosophy, literature and history in print, and reading babyish non-stories to myself in braille. For years I struggled with the tendency to evaluate books based on their format: braille was boring, but I could read it myself; print was interesting, but no matter how hard I tried, I could not read it. Print was disorienting for me, blank, empty, the way I felt when I was lost at school or in the yard at home. I still panic when I reach out expecting to touch a landmark and my hands hit air, or my body hits a sharp object. My grandparents tried to keep me safe—safe from inaccessible reading and safe from danger in the environment.

Grandpa's other favorite diversions also involved listening. His old-fashioned Atwater-Kent radio held an honored place in our living room. It had a row of buttons from which you could select AM radio, short wave radio, or a 78-rpm record player. He liked to hear the news from various countries and discuss each country's point of view. The most objective news, Grandpa maintained, came from the BBC World Service. The most contrasting versions of the news came from Radio Moscow and the Voice of America. After every newscast Grandpa would explain to me how each country slanted the news to promote its own interests. That's why you had to hear as many sources as possible and try not to shut out points of view that differed from your own.

He had a large and varied collection of records, mostly classical. His favorite was opera. He was well-versed about the stories of the operas and the lives of the composers. Before we listened to a record, Grandpa told me as much as he could about it. Maria Callas was his favorite singer; he had all her recordings. Every Saturday afternoon we listened to the Live from the Met broadcast on KFUO AM. The announcers were pompous and stuffy. They sounded, as Grandpa often observed, as if they "had a mouthful of mush."

"Much too much mush!" I would respond, and Grandpa would laugh as if that were the funniest joke he had ever heard and he was hearing it for the first time.

One Sunday morning after one of these performances, Mother actually served cornmeal mush for breakfast. I filled my mouth as full as I could and announced, "Today we will hear a performance of Giuseppi Verdi's Aida." I started laughing so hard that all the mush flew out of my mouth and splattered everywhere, including down the front of my church dress.

"Oh, for heaven's sake, Judy. Can't I ever get you ready ahead of time? Now I'll have to clean you up and find something else for you to wear. What will God think if you come into His house looking like a slob?"

"God loves slobs too, Erna," said Grandpa, who had been laughing quite a bit himself. "Do you think that with all the garbage and camel dung and other junk people had to walk through back in Jesus' time that they all looked like beauty queens?"

"George Beauregard, don't encourage her. Her behavior is bad enough already."

"Try to take things easier, Erna. Life is more than a business."

"Fine. You clean up then."

Mother clattered and banged as she carried the dishes to the sink. The rest of us finished breakfast and got out of there as quickly as we could, not saying a word, as if we all expected at any moment to be ordered to stand in the corner. I wasn't entirely clear on why standing in the corner was such a bad thing, except that grown-ups liked to put you there when you made a mistake. Dad said kids didn't like it because when they were standing in the corner they couldn't see anything but the wall. What was so bad about that? I couldn't even see the wall.

Grandpa did not like to go out socially. Both grandmas, Mother, and Dad all enjoyed parties and family get-togethers. Grandpa said they were too much trouble, too devoid of intellectual stimulation. "I don't want to take the chance on knocking my coffee cup over if I can't balance it with good conversation."

It was years before I understood what spilling coffee had to do with conversation, but Grandpa always seemed to take for granted that I would know what he meant, even though I could not articulate it. I was too young when Grandpa died to discuss blindness with him, but his wisdom lay in finding humor everywhere, making the best of a bad situation without denying its existence. Grandpa did not deceive himself with positive thinking, but neither did he indulge in self-pity. Grandpa was never mawkish or sentimental; he applied therapeutic irony liberally and often. If Mother got upset when one of us knocked over something or made a mess, Grandpa would say, "Let's turn on a light. It's so dark in here." By the time I understood what he meant, Grandpa was gone.

I was only three when Grandpa Dent passed away. My parents believed in exposing me to all the realities of life, the harsh as well as the pleasant. That exposure included funerals and wakes.

By the time Grandpa died I felt like an old hand at communing with corpses; Grandpa's was not the first wake I attended. Grandma Loehr's older brother, Adam Wertman, died before Grandpa. I believe I was not quite three, but I'm not sure of the date. This was my first visit to a funeral parlor. The experience was so ghoulish and terrifying that I hardly knew how to write about it until this morning, when my husband asked me, "What will you be writing about next?"

"Uncle Adam."

"Who's Uncle Adam?"

"Grandma Loehr's older brother."

"Was he a nice guy?"

"I don't know. I only met his dead body."

That was one of my usual snarky, throwaway wisecracks, a reflexive way of distancing myself from the inexplicable scariness of life, of defying difficulties I have not figured out how to surmount, of giving my sense of powerlessness the finger or, as my smart-aleck self likes to say, pumping irony.

I have not one memory of Uncle Adam as a living man, but an indelible mental picture of a hard, cold object under a sheet. The sheet was starchy and smooth, the way sheets always felt right after Mother changed the beds. The thing underneath reminded me of nothing so much as a plaster statue, but much harder, much colder. The cold oozed out from under the sheet to grab me. I wanted to scream and get out of there. Notice I did not say "run." Even before my third birthday, I knew that running could get me into serious trouble.

"That's Uncle Adam, Judy. This is what a corpse in a casket feels like."

Mother's voice was so calm, as if we were discussing what was for supper. My mind fixed on the word "casket." A tisket a casket. Blow a casket. Fruit casket upset. A casket case. Then a new question occurred to me. "Mother, is he the Adam of Adam and Eve?"

"No, don't be silly. That was thousands of years ago. Our family is old, but not that old."

"If that's really Uncle Adam, why is he so hard and cold? When I climb into bed with you and Dad after a bad dream, you are both soft and warm."

"Will you be quiet? That's enough silly questions. We're in a funeral parlor. That's not Uncle Adam; it's his body. It's hard and cold because he's dead."

"What does it mean to be dead?"

This conversation was getting way too deep for Mother.

"Come over here. I want to show you something else."

Mother guided me toward the plop, plop of water dripping. "Look, they have a fountain with goldfish. Here's one of the fish." Mother put my hand into the water, and sure enough, I felt a large, scaly fish. This was not like the tiny fish they had in pet stores, or the minnows Uncle Martin used to bait his hooks. This was a larger fish, like the bluegill he often caught. "Isn't that a nice, comforting sound?" said Mother. "It's so serene. People can listen to the waterfall and watch the fish, and maybe they don't feel so bad about the person who died."

I failed to see how a cold, wet fish was comforting, but the sound was calming. Since that time, whenever I hear the word "serene," I hear water plopping into a pool, and feel that slimy fish trying to escape from my exploring fingers. The comfort has an edge to it, as if the pillow might have a pin stuck in it, or the rose could have a thorn. Years later, when I was in a psychiatric ward and relaxation techniques were all the rage, and the facilitator would say, "Imagine yourself in a safe, serene place," I had trouble reconciling safe with serene; the quiet masked an element of danger, a shark lurking beneath the ocean sounds, or a bumblebee floating on the meadow breeze. So that was Uncle Adam whom I had never met in life: hard, cold body; soft, cold fish; plop, wet, and be quiet.

I knew how to behave, the questions not to ask, the noises not to make; what I did not realize was how different this ritual would feel when the dead person was someone you loved.

I went to Grandpa's wake and funeral with the rest of the family. Grandma cried softly throughout the service. Everyone seemed sad and spoke in hushed tones. The priest rambled on about what a nice man Grandpa had been, but I had the feeling he didn't know Grandpa from any other dead person.

Dead person! I had a baby duck named Quackie who had been killed by a cat. A few days later I asked Mother, "Where's Quackie?" She had started to cry and said, "Quackie flew away." I knew that wasn't so. Quackie wouldn't leave me and go off on his own. Had Grandpa flown away, too?

I cried in earnest now, not just because Grandma was crying. Why had Grandpa flown away and left me? Was this one of his jokes? If so, I wasn't laughing.

"I know, Honey." Grandma's arm was around me, her hand massaging my back. "I miss him, too."

"Will you still read me the books with big words, Grandma?"

"You bet, Honey. Soon you'll be going to school and you'll be able to read them yourself."

That thought consoled me; it consoles me still. It would take me years to learn the complications of braille, audio, and later, digital books, but reading has retained its preeminent place in my life, and no matter how many books I can read independently, I still feel a special camaraderie, an agape about being read to that represents close, loving relationships, a sense of continuity and permanence that I don't find in any other activity.

Soon it was time to go to the cemetery. We piled into a huge car that Dad called a "limousine" and drove slowly for what seemed like a couple of years but was really about an hour. The priest said more prayers in Latin while we knelt in the dirt and they put Grandpa in the big hole. My knees felt gritty; my hands felt gritty; grit was all around. Did Grandpa feel gritty? Would it be gritty in heaven or was the absence of grit part of what made it heaven? I hoped so.

"It's time to leave now," said Mother. "Say good-bye to Grandpa."

"Are we going to leave him here all by himself?" I could not contain my outrage. "Are you going to leave me here alone someday?"

"Grandpa's not alone," Grandma assured me. "He's with God. And nobody's going to leave you alone, not here or anywhere else."

None of this made any sense to me. I sat on the cold, on the wet, on the ground in the grit and yelled, at the top of my voice, so Grandpa would be sure to hear me, "Good-bye, Grandpa. We'll be back soon to take you home." I knew it wasn't true the moment I said it. "Good-bye, Grandpa," I called over and over until Dad picked me up and carried me away. Only the good-bye part was true. We would not be coming back to bring Grandpa home.

Grandpa Loehr
Herman W. Loehr, 1881-1949

I had another grandpa, too, Herman Loehr. He never lived with us as the other grandparents did. I met him only a few times and don't remember much. He was the stuff of family myth, a giant presence like Paul Bunyan, more real in legend than in life. He was an outstanding carpenter and cabinetmaker who built all his household furniture, though I never saw anything he made. He was a brilliant musician who could play three instruments at the same time: a harmonica with his mouth, a guitar with his hands, a drum with his feet, but I never heard him play. He was an amateur astronomer who could identify hundreds of constellations and stars; I cannot see stars. He was a young genius who became an old drunk; I never experienced either of these. He beat my mother several times a week throughout her childhood; I did experience that, not from my grandfather, but from my mother, whose rages were violent and unpredictable. If I disappointed her, she hit me. If I failed to go along with her delusions, she hit me. When she wasn't hitting me, she was screaming at me.

I have only one memory of Grandpa Loehr. One Christmas when I was a small child, a surprise package arrived in the mail. It was a basket of fruit and other goodies which Mother said was from Grandpa Loehr. Two of the items in it were fresh pears and Juicy Fruit gum. Now every time I taste pears or Juicy Fruit, I think of Grandpa Loehr, of what a complex man he must have been, of how odd it was that Mother loved him so much and resented him even more, of how she loved me so much and resented me even more. I don't chew gum now (my dental work does not allow it), but when I did chew gum, I never chewed Juicy Fruit.

Grandma Dent
Ida Elizabeth Rayfield Dent, 1878-1953

Life was more somber around our house without Grandpa Dent. Dad and the two grandmas could not ratchet down Mother's anxiety the way Grandpa could. She would get annoyed with his lack of seriousness, but in the end he could always make her laugh. I wish I could have learned his technique.

Grandma Dent was a woman of quiet wisdom, of gravitas without stodginess. Whether reading a thick book of philosophy, or waiting on a corner for a bus, Grandma never got hysterical over challenges. I don't remember hearing her cry except that one time at Grandpa's funeral. Now, to Mother, raising cane was a fine art. She never met a problem she couldn't yell about. Getting upset came naturally to Mother, like breathing. Grandma Dent handled everything with an easy grace that I tried, without much success, to emulate.

When I had a bad dream it was usually Grandma Dent who came to comfort me. If I lost one of my toys, it was usually Grandma Dent who found it. Grandma Loehr's skills leaned more toward the practical; Grandma Dent was adept at making me feel loved. Grandma Dent was the only one in the family, after Grandpa was gone, who could get me to stop screaming. She always treated me with respect, even when I was lying on the floor kicking and screaming. Grandma would pick me up and say, "Come on, Honey, crying isn't going to help. Let's see what we can do to fix the problem." She would hold me on her lap until I could tell her what was wrong. We both liked mysteries, in books and on the radio. "Let's be detectives and solve the problem together. Give me a clue, Judy." We would keep trying until we solved the problem together. One thing Grandma Dent never did was trivialize me. She never made me feel as if my needs were not important. She never said, "You're just trying to get your own way," or, "You are only doing that to get attention." She knew there was always a reason, and she worked diligently and lovingly to find it.

Only when the solution eluded us did Grandma try to distract me. She would bounce me on her knee and we would go for an imaginary ride, either on a train, horse or boat. The boat rides were the most fun. We didn't mess around with a noisy, stinky steam-engine or motorboat. We took float trips down the Missouri, the Mississippi, and many smaller rivers. Grandma described everything along the way; we stopped to see interesting natural or historic sites. Grandma could describe these places so vividly that I almost believed we really were on a float trip. Even my synesthesia got involved. When we stopped in Cairo, Illinois, Grandma explained that the name of the city was spelled C-a-i-r-o like the city in Egypt. In my mind, as I listened to Grandma's description, I touched a shaggy camel with a large hump and heard Middle Eastern music. Then Grandma explained that the name of the town in Illinois was pronounced Kay-ro, like the corn syrup. I vividly tasted pancakes. Soon I was no longer thinking about what had been bothering me.

Grandma Dent and I had many conversations. She never raised her voice in anger, even when Mother yelled at her. I couldn't understand what Mother and Grandma Dent disagreed about. Their differences seemed simple to me. Mother wanted to punish me more, Grandma less. Mother was always threatening to kick Grandma Dent out of the house and make her move down to Lesterville to live with Aunt Leona, her older sister. I would plead, "Don't leave, Grandma. This is your home."

"I won't leave if I don't have to," said Grandma.

The day after a particularly bad incident, I marched up to Mother and confronted her directly. "Why do you want Grandma Dent to go away?"

"She spoils you."

What a peculiar thing to say. I had heard of spoiled meat, or spoiled fruits and vegetables. Uncle Roger often called my cousins Bobby and ben "rotten kids." Could children go bad, like food? Did they stink?

"How is Grandma spoiling me? Am I a rotten kid?"

Sometimes," said Mother, "and Ida just lets you do whatever you want. Life is a struggle, and she isn't preparing you for it. You all just laugh and sing all the time instead of taking care of business."

"Business is when you have to do something hard and no fun, but you do it anyway?"

"Business is the important, necessary stuff, like right now I have to stop talking and clean the house before my bridge club gets here. All the rest is just silly."

"When the bridge club comes over and you play cards, is that silly?"

"I don't have time for this backtalk. Go talk to Grandma."

"But if Grandma went away, she wouldn't be here to keep me out of your hair."

"Go!" Mother had had enough.

Life was not a dichotomy for Grandma Dent the way it was for Mother. Grandma Dent could take "necessary" tasks and make them, if not fun, at least tolerable. She took the monumental challenge of getting me dressed, which, considered as a whole, would have been all but insurmountable, and broke it into small pieces. Grandma made these arcane procedures clear with what she called "magic words," small poems that told me what to do and kept me on track:

Put the button through the hole. Move it left to right. Grab the zipper by its tongue and pull it up tight.

Grandma's voice was always gentle and patient when she showed me how to do something. She never shouted or told me to hurry. She never put my hand over hers for me to observe how she performed a task, as the instructors at school did, on those rare occasions when they did any hands-on instructing. Feeling someone's hands while they work is complete gibberish to me, probably for the same reason a cane or knife and fork provide no feedback at all. When people try to write print in my hand it feels like an insect tickling my palm. Grandma understood instinctively that I could not learn a task by placing my hands on top of someone else's. To have any chance at all, I had to put my own fingers through the motions.

Learning nonverbal tasks by imitation was something I could not do, no matter how many times the instructions were repeated, or how loud the instructor's voice became when he or she was berating me, which usually happened early in the process with them, but never with Grandma.

There were instructions for washing as well as dressing. My favorite was the hand-washing song. Grandma sang it to the tune of the "Wassail" song:

Wash hands, wash hands, take your time and be calm,

The back and the thumb and the fingers and the palm.

Wash hands, wash hands all over the place,

And when you are finished it's time for your face.

Every holiday season, when I hear, "Wassail, wassail all over the town," and all year round when I wash my hands, I silently bless and thank Grandma Dent; she tried to reduce the sensory overload, to bring a modicum of order to the chaotic bowl of scrambled eggs that is my life.

I can understand, now that Mother and Grandma are gone, how hard it must have been for Mother, who often felt my frustrations and failures with actual pain. The grandmas, especially Grandma Dent, entertained me, read to me, helped me to learn the activities of daily life and, I knew, loved me, but Mother's love was tempered by fear. She knew the grandmas were not ultimately responsible for me. Mother believed she was. After both grandmas were gone, Mother would have to guide me toward independence, and I wasn't making much progress in that direction. I made no secret of the fact that I preferred the grandmas to Mother. She was always yelling at me, spanking me, making me do things I didn't want to do. My child's mind could not manage the contrast.

Grandma Dent took all the fear out of mobility long before I knew the word "mobility," before I knew it was a school subject and that I should be afraid of it. It wasn't strictly mobility, because there were no canes or dogs involved, but it was travel the way it should be: long walks and bus and streetcar rides all over St. Louis. At every destination there was something to touch or taste or listen to. Grandma showed me the world without hostility, without getting hysterical over details, without that relentless push, push, push, to learn and to do things that made my head buzz and churn like vegetables in a blender. Grandma never made me recite, "The northwest corner of the block is the southeast corner of the intersection," or, "We are walking north on the east side of the street. The parallel traffic should be on my left." Even now, as I write this, I'm not sure I'm saying it right. I wanted to give a more detailed example, one that would have more clarity and specificity, but nothing comes. Just thinking about orientation and walking and knowing where I am—although I know I'm in my safe chair at my safe desk, writing, which I do well, instead of navigating, which I don't—I feel as if I'm in a mixing bowl swirling in all directions at once. If I don't move on to another subject right now, I will be too upset and scared to write for the rest of the day.

Suffice it to say that Grandma Dent never made a chore out of any task. No matter how difficult or boring the job, she made it fun, and there was never the threat of punishment if I did not succeed the first time, or at all.

Once when we were in the yard, a cardinal was singing in a nearby tree. "Listen," whispered Grandma, "he's talking about you. He's saying, 'Sweet, sweet, sweet!'" Most of the songbirds are gone from our area now, but there are still cardinals, and I still hear them saying, "Sweet, sweet, sweet!" Thank you again, Grandma.

Grandma Dent loved college basketball. I'm sure if she were alive today you wouldn't be able to pry her away from television during the NCAA Tournament. Her favorite team was the St. Louis University Billikins. (I believe a billikin is a kind of leprechaun.) Grandma listened to every game on the radio. Grandma explained the rules of the game and she, Dad, and I would listen to the game on the radio. We did not have a television in those days. Neither Dad nor Grandma ever got annoyed at my basketball questions, especially if I remembered to ask them during the commercials. Grandma's favorite Billikin player at that time was Jerry Coke. I liked him, too, mostly because his name sounded like cherry Coke, my favorite soda fountain drink, one Grandma and I often shared during the long time lags between streetcar or bus connections. I still listen to Billikin games, and if Grandma and Dad are not physically with me, their legacies are.

Grandma Dent grew up in the Ozarks, but she started educating herself from the moment she began attending a one-room schoolhouse and learned to read. Grandpa exposed her to many more new books and ideas. She could talk like a country song or the BBC, depending on the situation. She always insisted on impeccable grammar from me, however. Never say "ain't." Never end a sentence with a preposition. If you finish a job, never say, "I'm done." Biscuits are done; chores are finished. When I was a college freshman and had to read The Elements of Style, it felt like review; Grandma was much more stringent than Strunk and White. If I prefaced a question with "How come" instead of "Why," Grandma caught me up short. The same if I said, "What for?" Sometimes I got really sloppy and turned it into "What fur?" Grandma would demand, "What fur? Cat fur to make kitten britches."

No pretend swearing was allowed: "dam" was a structure to hold back water, "darn" meant to mend the holes in socks, and "shoot" was done with a gun. Once I misplaced one of my favorite dolls. "Oh, gosh!" I complained.

Grandma instantly corrected me. "A lady does not say 'Gosh.'"

There were so many things not to say, I wondered how anyone could say anything at all.

Yet even Grandma's speech went native when she got excited. When one of her favorite songs came on the radio, or the Billikins made a noteworthy play, Grandma would exclaim, "Listen at it! Listen at it!"

If I had said "Listen at it," Grandma would have been right on hand with a grammar lesson. "You don't say, 'Listen at it.' You say 'Listen to it.'" "You look at something. You listen to it."

My Asperger's clamored to point out this inconsistency to Grandma, but she was so happy whenever she listened "at," that I was able to swallow my autistic tendencies to avoid making Grandma sad.

I work hard to control the weirdness the autistic spectrum imposes on me. I try to keep my mouth shut without appearing silent and sullen; nevertheless, I have noticed a direct correlation between how accepted and safe I feel and my ability to restrain the impulse to correct people's mistakes, to be a know-it-all, to sound like a walking, talking encyclopedia. I usually cannot hold it in in a hostile atmosphere. Many professionals who work with clients with autism invoke the "theory of mind" which suggests that persons on the spectrum have no idea what others are thinking, that they cannot perceive what other people want or need, and that's why we have so much trouble socially. Maybe that's true, maybe not; maybe I'm not as far down the spectrum as most people; maybe blindness has made me more vigilant, trained me to pay more attention, made me more keenly aware of the small, dismissive noises people make while they reject me as a lesser species, somewhere near the level of a sea slug. The words "You don't know what they were thinking, because you can't see the expression on their faces" resound in my head like a stuck phonograph needle. I have become hypersensitive to these body signals, possibly on occasion imagining them when they are not there, but most of the time my impressions prove correct. I am often asked how I know these things if I'm on the spectrum and I can't see. It's hard to describe to people who do almost all their learning through visual cues. It's a quick intake of breath, a physical shrinking away, a subtle alteration in tone of voice, a reluctance to speak directly to me and instead addressing the person with me and expecting him or her to translate. When I'm with people who make me feel as if they regard me with revulsion and contempt, it's all but impossible for me to keep from correcting what I perceive as their errors, the more pedantically the better.

All this was in my future, however. When I was with Grandma Dent, I never experienced this awfulness, never felt hatred, contempt, or fear from others. Grandma died when I was six, so

I was never with her after I had ceased to be a cute child, but I do not believe this was the only reason. Grandma was a thoroughly good person; I never met anyone who knew Ida Rayfield Dent and did not respect her. Dad told me that during the Depression, her house became famous among homeless people because they could come to "Aunt Ida" and receive something to eat. Sometimes she was sad, but I never heard Grandma Dent get angry or disparage anyone. She did not expect people to be cruel or negative toward her and, when I was with her, they never were—with the notable exception of Mother's resentment toward Grandma Dent, her jealousy of my love for Grandma.

New Year's Eve 1953 was the last good time I had with Grandma Dent. Grandma Loehr was staying with one of my aunts. Mother and Dad were invited to a huge New Year's Eve party for adults. Grandma Dent and I were home alone. We spent the whole evening together listening to music and eating cheese, crackers, and cookies, and drinking eggnog without the alcohol. There was never a question of my not being allowed to stay up until midnight, when we sang, popped some balloons and yelled, "Happy New Year!" Then we hugged and it was time for bed.

Soon Grandma began to complain of headaches. She would lie in bed and say, "Put your hand on my forehead, Honey. My head's throbbing." I always stopped whatever I was doing to help Grandma. I rested my hand on her head and prayed silently for her. I asked God to stop the throbbing and take away Grandma's headache, and as the days passed and she became worse and worse, I asked God not to take Grandma away.

God did not answer my prayer, but he gave her a moment of lucidity to help me set priorities before the lymphoma got the best of her. "Hold my hand, Judy. I'm so cold and your hands are so warm." I slipped my small, smooth hand into her veined, wrinkled one. It felt sticky and damp like the petals of a petunia, a flower I find so repulsive that I can't stand to have it around. Not only do petunias remind me of Grandma's death, but also they smell like dirty gym socks.

Grandma gathered her strength and said clearly, "Judy, always remember: it's more important to be happy and contented than to do a lot of things."

Those were Grandma's last words to me. I did not understand at the time what she meant, but I knew Grandma wanted me to remember. If I had heeded her advice, I probably would have stayed out of the psychiatric ward, probably would not have tried six times to commit suicide, but in the struggle to achieve, to be "twice as good to be half as good," I completely ignored it.

Grandma was gone. Dad, Mother and I were riding in a big limousine out to Calvary Cemetery where I had said good-bye to Grandpa. The day before we had sat in a funeral parlor. The books Grandma read me had talked about parlors. Grandma said they were living rooms where people went to visit with important company. Why was a living room used to host a party for a dead person? I was glad we didn't call our living room at home a parlor. "Come up to the front, Judy, and tell Grandma good-bye one last time. See, these are her hands. This is her face." Mother guided my fingers over something hard and cold. Plaster. Mud. Dirt. Cold, colder, coldest. Definitely no throbbing now. No fingers closing over mine. No whisper of breath coming from that stiff, still mouth.

"That's not Grandma! Grandma is warm. This is cold."

"It's Grandma's body, Sweetheart. Her soul has gone to heaven to be with God."

"Then I want to go to heaven and be with God, too."

"Someday you will, Judy."

"Not someday! Now!" My voice rose and squeaked the way it did when I couldn't keep the autism under control. "That's not Grandma!" I screamed at the top of my voice. "That's mud! Mud! Mud! That feels like mud! Mud! Mud! I don't want to be here. I don't want mud! I want Grandma!"

"George!" Mother's voice was almost as high and desperate as mine. "Please take Judy out. I don't know what to do with her."

"We'll take her home, George. You stay here and talk to people." Grandma Loehr put her arms around me. "You still have one grandma left, Judy. Things will get better."

Aunt Beverly and Uncle Martin were there, too. Mother and Dad stayed at the funeral parlor and the rest of us piled into Uncle Martin's car and drove home. The next day we were in the limousine. Would I have to touch Grandma's body again?

No body-touching occurred at Grandma's funeral, but that was the only good thing that happened that day. First we stopped at church, where a young assistant pastor who hadn't known Grandma mumbled some words in Latin, then other words in English about how wonderful Grandma had been, which sounded vague and unconvincing even to me. I was mad. What right did this person have to say anything about Grandma? I wanted to stand up in front of the congregation and tell everyone how kind, generous and loving Grandma had really been. Failing that, I wanted to stomp my foot and scream. Grandma had loved me; who would love me now?

I began to cry softly. "If you feel like crying," whispered Mother, "go on and cry."

That was the first and last time Mother told me it was all right to cry.

Eventually the Latin mumbling came to an end and we went home where there was lots of food nobody wanted to eat. When most of the company had drifted away Mother delivered the next blow of the day. "Come on, Judy. Let's get in the car. It's time to go back to school."

Back to school! I had taken for granted that I would have the rest of the day off to sit in my room with Tuffy and Jacko, to cry until I was sufficiently exhausted to sleep. Not today. Back to that horrible school, just in time for gym, the last class of the day. Why were my parents doing this to me, punishing me with Mrs. Caine, Marjorie Lowell, and the rest of my tormentors? As we walked through that dreaded Spring Avenue door, all the pain of losing Grandma, the cold, stiff body, the priest who talked about how terrific Grandma was without ever having known her, the need to behave in front of company, all caught up with me; although I was pretty sure Mother's permission to cry did not extend to school, I wailed like a two-year-old.

"Why is she crying?" one of the girls asked.

"Honey, her grandma died."

I cried harder, but felt no better. Nothing would have made me feel better except to turn around and head for home, but no matter how loud I screamed, Mother was, as usual, adamant. Grandma was gone and I was back at school. I wailed as much for my hypocrisy as for my loss. Grandma was in heaven now; would God tell her I was crying, not just because I missed her, but because I had to go back to school after the funeral? Silently I begged God not to tell her. That was the first of many choices I made that tore me apart with guilt. Nobody said a word to comfort me; Miss. Temple, the housemother, yelled at me to hurry up and get my gym suit on. God already knew what a fraud I was. Soon Grandma would know. I got my suit on as quickly as I could.

We had a jump rope contest that day. One by one we took turns practicing "continuous turning." The object was to jump over the rope 100 times while turning it continuously. This was an activity I always flunked. I was such a klutz that I couldn't jump over the rope once without stopping. Marjorie Lowell sneered in her usual helpful way. Others followed suit. While the others took their turns I crawled off to a corner of the gym. No one paid attention to me. I wondered if anyone would ever again pay attention to me in a good way. Grandma Dent had loved me. I had never felt as if I disappointed her. Everyone else seemed to see me as defective, as not measuring up. I had trouble dressing myself and finding my way around. I could not cut my meat or zip my zipper. (Now, sixty years later, I still cannot do those things.) I still did not have sight. None of the shrines and healers my parents had taken me to had helped. The Virgin Mary, Sainte Anne, and all the rest had not made me the kind of daughter my parents wanted. As for school, I had figured out on the first day that I was a flop there. I didn't think about Grandma Loehr. I'm glad she never knew that.

I lay on the floor in the corner and took one last deep breath. At six years old I did not know that you could not hold your breath until you died. No one loved me. It was over. Soon I would not be disappointing anyone. I probably would not be with Grandma, since Father O'Toole said people who killed themselves went to hell, but maybe I would be in good company among others who had disappointed those whose approval they desperately craved.

"Mrs. Caine! Mrs. Caine! Judy Dent fainted!" Marjorie Lowell's shrill voice dragged me out of, if not a tunnel of light, at least a state of blessed unconsciousness. God really must act fast. Was I in hell already? I thought there must be some kind of antechamber, or waiting room, like in a doctor's office, where you sat and sweated out God's judgment. Nope. I had died and gone directly to hell, to "the other place," as the housemothers delicately—or was that ghoulishly?—phrased it.

"Mrs. Caine! Mrs. Caine! Come quick! She might die!" Marjorie said this in the way one might say, "Santa Claus is coming!" Marjorie was almost beside herself with glee, as if she expected to win a Purple Heart for discovering my limp body.

"Take it easy, Marjorie. Thank you for pointing this out to me. There's nothing wrong with Judy. She's just trying to get attention as usual. Judy, stop this nonsense. What's wrong with you?"

"My Grandma died."

"Do you think the world is going to stop because of that? Stop this silliness right now. Everybody's grandma dies. Get up and jump some rope. It's time for the next event. It's your turn. We're all waiting for you. Maybe if you concentrate instead of feeling sorry for yourself, you'll surprise all of us and earn an I instead of your usual F."

I did not surprise anyone. The school had a grading system based on the letters E, S, M, I, F, for excellent, superior, medium, inferior, and failing. I may have flunked kindergarten, but I knew that I stood for inferior and F for failure.

That was my first suicide attempt. Knowing that I was not in hell, but at the Wilson School for the Blind, did not cheer me. How long would I have to put up with this treatment before I could die and see Grandma?

The rest of that day, and the next few months, passed by in a dreary blur. When life got to be too much for me, I retreated into the deep, safe place in my head where I took float trips with Grandma and heard the lonesome notes of the harmonica singing, "Oh, dear Judy, Oh, don't you cry today." I never told my parents or Grandma Loehr that I had tried to kill myself.

Grandma Loehr
Katherine "Kate" Wertman Loehr, 1884-1970

Grandma Loehr was more practical and decisive than Grandma Dent. I did not properly get to know Grandma Loehr until after Grandma Dent was gone. Grandma Dent entertained me with folksongs and lullabies, and with stories, both those she read to me and those she told. She almost never disciplined me—"no" was a word I used often; Grandma Dent, almost never. It was Grandma Loehr who handled the details, to make sure Mother took her meds, such as they were in those days. It was Grandma Loehr who made sure our meals were served on time, and that I was ready for school each morning when Dad was ready to drive me. I can't imagine, with Mother torn apart by schizophrenia, what would have happened to our family had Grandma Loehr not taken charge.

All this is my adult perspective, however. At six, all I knew was that Mother subjected me to endless educational experiences conducted with frenetic seriousness and intensity, which alternated with screams, slaps and scary stories about Indians, fallen archangels whose voices no one but Mother heard, signs and wonders in the stars I could not see. Dad fluctuated between being a gentle, tender, protecting presence, and a rigid, demanding dictator. I missed Grandma Dent so much my whole body hurt. I had vivid dreams that she was back, that her death had been only a bad dream. The nightmare part came when I woke up and realized that Grandma Dent's death had been real; her return was the dream. Compared with Grandma Dent, Grandma Loehr seemed harsh: not straightforwardly evil like Mrs. Caine and Marjorie Lowell, but unwilling or unable to shield me from everyday realities. Grandma Dent believed childhood should be as safe and long as possible; Grandma Loehr maintained that no one was too young to assume a few responsibilities.

Grandma Loehr came from a hard-working German farm family whose subsistence life allowed no room for unnecessary luxury. Grandma, whose maiden name was Katie Wertman, was the fifth of six children. Her mother died shortly after her younger sister, Leslie, was born. Her father had a farm to run; he had no time for sentimentality. He married again almost immediately after his first wife's death. Katie never understood why her stepmother preferred the others to her, especially Leslie. Grandma became emotional whenever she talked about her early life. At three she was doing housework; at five, field work. Her father and stepmother quickly had six more children, which added childcare to Katie's duties. Hard work was just normal.

Despite Grandma Loehr's hardscrabble background, there was a major difference between her and the militaristic faculty and staff at the school for the blind. They had certain physical standards based on the highest common denominator. Every student was expected, from the very first day, to get around with grace and precision, to look well-groomed within an inch of one's life, and to perform each task absolutely without assistance. Their standard for these achievements was measured against the highest-achieving partially-sighted student in one's age group. Braille students were separated from sight savers for reading, but beyond that, no distinctions were made for differing degrees of visual acuity, or for the age at which one lost one's sight. If you complained about any of these inequities, you were instantly and forever branded a crybaby and a whiner.

Some of these powerful grown-ups may have thought they were preparing the students for a brutal future in the "real" world; others, I believe, enjoyed working with children with disabilities to feel superior and exercise power.

Grandma Loehr never used her sight or her words to humiliate me. She encouraged me to learn all the skills I could. She continued Grandma Dent's project of using rhymes to help me learn personal care. I enjoyed lounging in my pajamas on Saturday mornings, but Grandma only allowed so much of that. After breakfast she would say, "Judy, it's time to get dressed."

"Aw, Grandma," I would moan, dragging it out as long as possible. "It's Saturday. I want to relax. Can't you read to me instead?"

"Reading comes after dressing." Grandma's voice was firm, but not angry. I did not scream; my strong sense of fairness knew Grandma was right. "Work comes before play" had always been a motto around our house. Grandma liked to say:

Whene'er a task is set for you,

Persistence pulls you through it.

Take one step and then the next;

Begin at once, and do it.

Another favorite saying was, "Once begun is half done."

Grandma Loehr was like the Parson in Chaucer's The Canterbury Tales: first she wrought, and afterward she taught. Grandma stayed with me the whole time I was getting dressed, always offering encouragement, but never physical help unless I was having so much trouble that I was about to go beyond my frustration tolerance and throw a kicking, screaming fit. She could take me to the edge, and pull back at just the right moment. We seldom had the yelling matches that occurred every day with Mother, whose illness seemed to increase in direct proportion to my trouble in school. Grandma lived with us most of the time, but occasionally had to get away for a vacation. Then she would stay with one of her other daughters, Beverly, Quinetta and Ida. After one or two weeks away she would come back refreshed and ready to plunge into the battle.

I could not run around as easily as my cousins, so I spent hours sitting with Grandma and listening to her stories. Grandma was a suffragette and had fought for women's rights long before it was fashionable. Over and over she told me how, in 1920, when women first got the vote, she had walked several miles to vote against Warren Harding, beginning a long tradition in our family of voting against rather than for a candidate. Grandpa voted for Harding, which Mother and all three aunts attested was a subject of long and loud debate. Grandma rushed home in high glee—a term rarely associated with her—and shouted as she came in the door, "Herman, I canceled your vote!" That was the first time Grandma didn't have supper on the table when Grandpa came home.

"Being one of the first women to vote was a proud day for me," Grandma would end the story, "but that was nothing compared to what you can achieve. If you persist in everything you do, the way you have in learning to dress yourself, you could be the first woman president of the United States."

I didn't tell her I wanted to be the first woman Major League baseball radio broadcaster. That wouldn't have upset Grandma, though; she loved all kinds of sports, especially baseball. She never missed a Cardinals' game unless it conflicted with her soap operas on television. She watched a lot of television and it was my job to sit and watch with her—after homework was done, that is. If I complained about it, Dad would say, "My job is to work on the newspaper; Mother's job is to take care of us and the house; your job is to entertain Grandma." Reading got the axe as well. I had to pay attention so I could discuss the programs with Grandma later, which wasn't too bad when we watched I Love Lucy or Father Knows Best, but what is there to say about somebody getting a custard pie thrown in their face on Truth or Consequences? The summer before seventh grade I was expected to watch six soap operas a day with Grandma: three in the morning and three in the afternoon. I resigned myself to three long months of crushing boredom. I was already a budding intellectual who read Shakespeare and Plato in her spare time; I considered myself way too smart to get hooked on Grandma's stupid stories. The first morning, at breakfast, Grandma filled me in on the backgrounds of all the shows. The only one that sounded mildly interesting was The Edge of Night, about a brilliant detective named Mike Carr and his resourceful wife Sarah. Before I knew it, I was rooting hard for them to get the bad guys. Then I began to follow The Secret Storm. After that it was downhill all the way. I treasured those days watching with Grandma; she always told me what was happening on the screen without my having to ask. She never made inarticulate noises like "ooh, ooh" at the most exciting parts. Grandma did video description long before it was ever thought of, making up her own script as she went along. I became so hooked that the first thing I did each evening when I came home from school was to ask Grandma what had happened that day in the stories. I even stopped calling them "soap operas."

Grandma liked real-life stories even better than the fictional ones on television. Every day when I came home from school, before I got the door closed or my coat off, she would say, instead of hello, "Tell me something." At first I thought Grandma was about to ask me a question. I would wait expectantly, only to discover that Grandma was anticipating a story. If Grandma asked, "How was school today?" I could never say, "O.K.," and let it go at that. I had to come up with at least one account of something that had happened—the more detailed the better—and Grandma listened. At the end of each recitation she would ask questions and offer trenchant advice:

"When the boys call you 'Fender Bender' and 'Grandma Dent,' remember that when little boys tease you, that means they like you."

"When the teachers and housemothers yell at you, don't talk back or ask too many questions. Learn which battles are worth fighting and which to let go. You know when you've done your best."

I quickly learned that every afternoon I was expected to have a story for Grandma. I began looking for the funny and unusual. I searched everywhere for inconsistencies, the way normal kids searched for Easter eggs, not once a year, but every day. It was Grandma's insistent demand—"Tell me something!"—that started me thinking like a writer.

I couldn't tell Grandma everything, though. One day I came home eager to give Grandma the latest newsflash. "Grandma, big news! I didn't fall down once today!"

Grandma was not as happy for me as I had expected her to be. In fact, she seemed upset. "That's big news? You mean you do fall down most days?"

"Yes, Grandma." This conversation wasn't going the way I had planned. "I usually fall down the stairs or get knocked down by the big kids."

Grandma was first horrified, then sad. "Does your mother know this?"

"No."

"We have to talk to the people at school about this. This is one of the battles we absolutely should fight."

Grandma did talk to Mother and Dad about my falling at school, but, as usual, nothing came of it. If my parents had talked to the teachers and housemothers, I would have been yelled at more for not paying attention to where I was walking, and for whining about it at home, so these after-school sessions with Grandma taught me to be both a storyteller and a censor.

Grandma enjoyed the stories I listened to almost as much as the stories I told, although I believe she would rather have had her fingernails pulled out one by one with pliers than admit it. Talking books, as they were called then, were for blind people. As Grandma's sight failed, she became less and less willing to admit she enjoyed listening to my books. She could never accept that the books I heard on records were the same books sighted people read in print. I would offer to help her to apply for her own talking books, but she would say, "Those books are for blind people. I'm not blind," her voice muffled behind the newspaper, which she was holding right in front of her nose because she was unable to read anything but the headlines. When I listened to a talking book in my room, Grandma insisted on sitting in the living room. One day I was reading Thomas Hardy's Tess of the D'Urbervilles for a book report for school. Trying to make a point, I waited for an exciting place in the story and turned the volume down so the words were audible only to me. "Turn it up! Turn it up!" yelled Grandma. "How do you expect anyone to hear it with the volume turned down so low?"

"But, Grandma, this is a talking book. You said talking books were only for blind people."

"Don't be a smart aleck."

I turned the book up. Often I ordered books I thought Grandma would like. She was interested in biographies, history, and current events. I ordered books on these subjects, which at first bored me out of my mind, but Grandma would discuss them with me, and I soon found to my surprise that I became interested in them, too. I ordered Newsweek with the same result, although at that time the magazine came on 12-inch records, about six weeks late. You could keep it only a few days, then you had to send it on to the next person on the list. I complained that the magazine should be called "Old News Week" because it came so late. Dad laughed and told me that old magazines were like old wine, they improved with age. He said old Newsweeks were better than any comedy on television because the pundits were so positive about how the future would turn out, and then, when their predictions turned out to be wrong, they would be equally positive in insisting they had known all along what would happen. The writers depended on the readers to forget.

In attempting to entertain Grandma I broadened my own reading interests. I still read Newsweek; I still enjoy books of biography, history and current events; but after Grandma was gone I stopped watching soap operas.

This is as good a place as any for a small but related digression. Reading is such a tremendous gift, those smooth print pages are so blank, that I can't understand why anyone would want to pass up a reading opportunity just because the material is in a format other than the one they are used to; yet I've known people who could not read because of learning disabilities or vision impairment, yet they fought tooth and nail against applying for services from the National Library Service for the Blind and Physically Handicapped. One woman I knew lost her vision as she grew older. Her son went to the public library for her each week to borrow audiobooks on compact discs from the limited selection of audiobooks most public libraries carry. At my suggestion, her granddaughter tried to persuade her to apply for NLS digital talking books, which would have arrived free in the mail. No more running to the library, no more trying to keep CDS in order. Nothing doing. That woman absolutely refused to consider applying for "blind people's books." I know another case of a high school girl with a touch of cerebral palsy. She also had dyslexia. This girl could not read her homework assignments, especially whole books for English class. She had trouble walking except for short distances. For longer travel she used a wheelchair. This girl loved to play wheelchair basketball, even though she used the wheelchair only a small portion of the time outside of basketball. I thought she might find equal pleasure in talking books. Both the girl and her mother emphatically declined when I suggested it; in fact, they became upset, as if they wondered how I could have the nerve to suggest anything so demeaning and stigmatizing. I absolutely do not understand this attitude. As soon as I learned about talking books—I was eight years old at the time—I called the library and lied about my age to get a talking book machine. You were supposed to be ten. The librarian had doubts about my squeaky little voice over the phone.

"How old are you, Honey?"

"Ten."

"What year were you born in?"

"1944."

"What grade are you in?"

"Fourth."

I brazened it out and got my talking book machine. I did not break it or drop peanut butter and jelly down the mechanism, or any other ridiculous thing the grown-ups thought a little kid might do. Grandma, on the other hand, although she listened to my books with rapt attention, never got them for herself. When I had to study, or she was staying with one of my aunts, Grandma had nothing to read. Worst of all, she never got to choose a book for herself, all because "talking books were for blind people." As years passed, I was to learn much more than I wanted to about exclusion, stigma, and that limbo of partial inclusion that goes, "You may be here, but don't say a word, don't try to participate, and don't cause trouble." I learned all this, and I could talk about it until the whole world dies of boredom, but I will never change my attitude toward braille and audiobooks.

Grandma Loehr awakened in me an interest in world affairs and foreign languages. Grandma was completely bilingual in English and German. She spoke both without an accent and we often spoke German at home. The family spoke no English until Mother and her sisters started school. Grandma Loehr entertained me with poems by Rilke, Goethe and Schiller the way Grandma Dent had entertained me with Milton and Shakespeare. She made the Vikings as real to me as the Greeks and Romans. She regaled me with the Norse myths, including thrilling tales of valkyries, women warriors like the Amazons. Many of these she probably made up herself. She told me the story of Wagner's Ring Cycle, adding two jokes that were almost certainly apocryphal. In Das Reingold, which of the Rhine Maidens is a dental hygienist? Flosshilda. The other takes place in Asgaard, home of the Norse gods. Thor is riding around yelling, "I'm Thor! I'm Thor!" Lochi, the trickster god, comes up to him and says, "Of course you're Thor. You forgot your thaddle, Thtupid."

In this way Grandma Loehr made stories that could have been terrifying and unpleasant, funny and accessible.

Each Christmas, Grandma regaled us with "Stille Nacht," "O Tannenbaum," and other German carols. She knew all the words to all the verses. I learned several of them, and though I have forgotten most of the lyrics as the preoccupations of academia and survival took up more and more space in my mind, Grandma Loehr taught me to love languages and to be interested in learning about other cultures.

Even though Grandma worked hard to make sure I learned to care for myself, she had a sixth sense that told her when I had reached the end of my frustration tolerance. I can't remember a single occasion when Grandma pushed me into a screaming fit. She never called me "stupid individual" or "God damn, such an idiot." She never made me keep on practicing a new skill until I cried or fell asleep. She practiced with me every day until I mastered the finer points of dressing myself, except tying my shoelaces and putting together the two ends of a zipper, neither of which I can do today. She let me help her roll out the paper-thin dough for her famous sugar cookies; Grandma never cheated and made them into thick, tasteless drop cookies the way Mother did. Grandma was bilingual in English and German, but for me she was trilingual; she became an expert at interpreting my body language. As soon as I started flapping my fingers and contorting my face she would bring the lesson to a screeching halt. As my imagination catapulted through anticipated and remembered events, rippled and coalesced, as memory and emotion flashed from play to rewind to fast forward and back to play like a warp-speed tape recorder out of control, Grandma could always take advantage of that moment of grace between inappropriate body movements and nuclear explosion. Most people can see my triggers dozen of times and still keep pressing, keep asking for information I cannot provide or tasks I cannot perform. Grandma Dent, who passed on when I was six, and Grandma Loehr, who lived until I was twenty-three, hardly ever did. My parents—whose fear increased exponentially as I, and they, grew older and the struggle with my limitations became more and more desperate—never saw my screaming as the stop sign it clearly was. The issue that had provoked it became lost in the new dynamic of authority and submission. The screaming was understood not as a cry for help, but as a rebellious political statement: rage on both sides was the inevitable outcome. Both grandmas, perhaps because they did not feel ultimately responsible for me, were able to see when the pressure was getting too intense and to pull back before the day was ruined for the whole family.

I was far from the only person Grandma Loehr helped. She was known for miles around as a practitioner of folk medicine. If the doctors failed, people came to see "Aunt Kate." She could tell at a glance which were mushrooms and which toadstools. I asked her how they got that name; she said frankly that she didn't know, since we never saw a toad sitting on one. I guess the name sounded mysterious and witchy, like "eye of newt and toe of frog," or "imaginary gardens with real toads in them." Before her arthritis stopped her, Grandma would dig in the yard and come up with all kinds of grimy-feeling roots and leaves. From these she made a tea which tasted like rusty nails and dead bugs, but which she claimed cured just about anything that ailed you. Dad was a confirmed skeptic until one day he caught a severe cold that made his chest feel as if elephants were walking on it and his nose run like a sugar tree. Over loud protests, Grandma made him drink a cup of the hot concoction. Dad's succinct testimonial: "First I swore at it, now I swear by it." During the influenza epidemic of 1918—which produced the dark saying, "I opened the window and in flew Enza"—Kate Loehr walked for miles from house to house caring for families who had the flu, all while taking care of her own husband and four girls, all of whom were down with the disease. All Kate's many patients recovered. When asked why she never got sick, Kate would reply, "I didn't have time." She confided to me years later that every morning before helping her flu cases, she drank a cup of her special tea with a shot of Grandpa's homemade whiskey. You can't get those simple remedies anymore. Nowadays when I hear on the news stories about the ineffectiveness or short supply of flu vaccine, I wish Kate Loehr could be here to hand out her special tea.

Kate performed another of her healing miracles on her niece, Gloria. Gloria was about Mother's age and they often played together. The families lived on farms quite a distance apart, so a visit usually lasted several days. On one of these visits Gloria became seriously ill. She had all the symptoms of pneumonia. There was no doctor within many miles of their home, so Kate went into action. She made Gloria the same drink that had protected her during the flu epidemic. "It's good for man or beast!" she maintained. After Gloria's recovery the cousins kidded her about whether she was a woman or a beast, but everyone was happy with the outcome.

The most astonishing miracle of all was the survival of Aunt Quinetta, a situation I could identify with because it closely paralleled my own. Aunt Quinetta had a twin sister named Jennetta. They were born prematurely about a year after Erna, my mother. Jennetta was about the size of a normal baby; Quinetta was small and sickly. Kate held them and walked round and round the room, talking and singing to them and praying for them to get well. It was big, healthy-looking Jennetta who died, however; tiny Quinetta lived and became Janice's mother.

Grandma admitted that Quinetta didn't exactly thrive. She had a chronic lung condition called pleurisy. I don't know what we would call it today, but it interfered with Quinetta's breathing and prevented her from doing the hard fieldwork the other girls had to do. Her sisters resented her so much that they complained about it more than fifty years later. "I was the youngest," Ida was fond of saying. "Q was the baby."

Yet I can understand Aunt Q better than anyone in the family. I wish I had told her that. I was too preoccupied with being young and blind and having something else mysterious and undiagnosed wrong with me to develop the necessary thoughts, theories, and empathy to have the discussion I should have had with her. It is sad that she is not here to read this. She was, as Mother and Ida would complain, "always sick." So was I. She was premature and underdeveloped at birth. From infancy to adulthood she was always a little behind her sisters.

Most striking of all, Quinetta was never able to learn to drive a car. It was not a philosophical problem. Kate trained her girls to believe that women could do anything men could do. None of them subscribed to the old-fashioned notion that women should not drive. The problem was much deeper and scarier than that. Quinetta said the traffic sights and sounds terrified her. They came from up, down, and all around. She also lacked the sense of direction that the rest of the family had. She had to memorize directions by rote instead of picturing them in her mind. Even when walking she had to use exactly the same directions every time to each place she went. For instance, Ida lived in East St. Louis, Illinois; Erna lived in Kirkwood, Missouri; and Quinetta lived in Florissant, Missouri, a suburb at the north end of St. Louis County, about 35 minutes by car from our house in Kirkwood. If Quinetta had wanted to travel from our house in Kirkwood to Ida's house in East St. Louis, she would first have had to go to her home in Florissant, then to Ida's. Of course she never walked those long distances, but she could never drive a car, and the highway terrified her even as a passenger. This annoyed everyone in the family, especially cousin Janice, who decided after Uncle Clive died that she was going to teach her Mother to drive or die trying. She and her husband bought Quinetta a big Cadillac, hoping the status symbol would motivate her. It only made Quinetta more afraid. Her sisters laughed at Quinetta, and Janice almost went out of her mind with impatience and disgust.

If I had been sighted, would I have been able to drive? If Quinetta had been blind would she have been able to travel with a white cane or a guide dog? I will never know, but the effects she reported that traffic had on her—the panic brought on by loud noise and bright lights—is exactly the same thing that happens to me, with the exception of the bright lights. Quinetta was able to hide her sensory integration dysfunction and orientation problems better than I could, because she had sight and did not have to depend quite so much on others. I did not know about Aunt Quinetta's problems until I was almost thirty, and now I wonder if there was something genetic or environmental that affected Aunt Quinetta and me. I have always felt, as Quinetta did, that life was a constant struggle to keep up. Quinetta became an alcoholic; I pray I never do.

Chapter 4

Noise is louder, pain is more painful.

Life has always been intense for me. I can't remember a time when I wasn't under maximum stress. Hold the cup straight. Don't cry when you fall. Don't cry when you get lost. Don't cry if it hurts. Share with the other kids even if they steal or break your stuff. Always do what the other person wants so they will be your friend. Don't wiggle your fingers. Don't flap your hands. Don't shake your head. Hold your head up. Don't stick your fingers in your eyes. On and on it went. Sometimes Mother didn't speak to me for days except to admonish me for some form of misbehavior.

I tried to find ways to release stress. I would push with my hands and scoot around the house on my rear end singing "Row, row, row your boat" at the top of my voice until my parents couldn't stand it anymore and yelled at me to stop. I enjoyed being on the floor. I couldn't fall off of the floor. I enjoyed the floor deep into the far side of middle age, until my arthritic knees wouldn't allow me to get up and down. As explained earlier, I figured out soon after I learned to walk that walking straight caused painful encounters, especially with sharp-cornered coffee tables. I learned to find the middle of the floor and twirl rapidly in circles. It was even better with music. With or without music, I would make up elaborate stories featuring myself as a famous explorer, mountain climber, queen, woman pirate, even a gang leader. When I studied about slavery, I imagined myself leading a slave revolt. I never pretended to be a plantation owner. My stories were always about power. I felt safe when I read, I felt creative when I wrote, but I only felt powerful when I twirled.

The other power I had only when I twirled was that of not getting hurt. I have what neurologists now call "sensory integration dysfunction." Noise is louder, taste is more intense, pain is more painful. Nobody knew any of that back in the '50s. My response to pain was diagnosed as a moral failing. "Don't be a baby" was a refrain I heard in my sleep. No matter how angry parents and teachers became with me, I was angrier with myself. When other kids fell down they picked themselves up and kept on playing. When I fell I cried and wanted to go off by myself to be alone.

I remember reading, while still in high school, a newspaper article reprinted in Dialogue Magazine. Dialogue at the time was the equivalent of Ebony for the blind. It printed how-to articles, advice on where to get independent living aids and technology, and reprints of inspirational stories about successful blind people. One of these was about a woman who had lost her sight from glaucoma. The article emphasized over and over the woman's skill in mobility. She attributed her success to her mother's refusal to comfort her when she hurt herself as a child. That attitude still bothers me. It exemplifies the way I was treated in school. From what I am able to glean from contemporary literature, it still prevails. That treatment discouraged me and made a shambles of my self-confidence and mental health. Dialogue came out every three months. I would read one issue and feel depressed for three months until the next issue appeared and the cycle started over. I believe it is imperative that we take the moral component out of disability. It's easy and lazy for teachers and rehabilitation professionals to attribute all failure to accomplish a task to bad motivation. "You never try" was another refrain I heard both at home and at school. I believe most people are doing the best they can at any given time. I know I did my best for years, but the accusation of never trying has dogged me all my life.

Both my parents could put their hands in scalding hot water, especially Mother. She had always worked with her hands, including a job as an illegal child laborer in a shirt factory. Her hands were hard and calloused and could withstand almost any punishment. When she touched me her hands were hard and rough and they made my whole body explode with exquisite pain. She yelled at me and yanked and pulled me into the position she wanted. I usually cried when Mother touched me because I didn't know what she wanted and had no idea how to comply.

Dad thought I didn't use enough pressure when using tools. When I was learning to use a knife and fork, Dad would grab my hand and press down and say, "Press harder, for goodness' sake. Cut the meat, don't stroke it like a kitten." He often pressed on my hand so hard that the knife handle cut my hand and I felt blood oozing between my fingers. He was always astonished and apologetic when this happened, but it didn't stop him from doing it the next time. My parents never abused me intentionally, but they could never understand an experience so far outside their own. I baffled and frightened them. They had grown up at the turn of the twentieth century when children were expected to be rough and ready. Survival depended on power. Even in 1946 most babies as premature as I did not survive. My parents couldn't accept me as different; they tried to use force to make me the kind of child they wanted. It was bad enough to have a blind child, but a child with blindness and autism was unthinkable.

Hair shirts

Clothes affected me the same way as food did. Mother found an old army blanket at a discount store and put it on my bed. I itched so badly that it was like being attacked by clouds of mosquitoes. I wiggled and thrashed all night and got up exhausted. When I was seven years old and had my first confession, I explained my problem with wool to Father Conrad, our assistant pastor. "May I offer the itchy wool to God and earn indulgences the way the first Franciscan friars did when they wore hair shirts? Wool is the hair of a sheep."

"Absolutely not," boomed Father Conrad. "That's blasphemous, trifling, shallow, and presumptuous. You should be ashamed of yourself. You are in a state of mortal sin. If you die right now you will go straight to hell and burn for all eternity. For your penance, say one hundred Our Fathers, Hail Marys, and Glory Be's."

Blasphemous. Presumptuous. Whatever those words meant, it must be something really bad. "If you die right now you will go straight to hell and burn for all eternity." Tomato sauce forever. I knelt to say my long, long penance.

"Hurry up, Judy. What's taking you so long? Dad and I have been ready forever."

"Father Conrad gave me a long, long penance because of the wool blanket and the hair shirt."

"Oh, God, not that again," said Dad, fearing that a scene was about to erupt in church. "Let's go home. You can tell us about it later."

When I explained to Dad what Father Conrad had said, I thought he would yell at me or even spank me. To my astonishment Dad burst into fits of laughter. "What a riot," he guffawed. "I bet that little squirt Father Conrad has never heard a story like that. You won't go to hell. You drive me nuts, and I still love you. I'm sure God has much more patience than I have."

I was loved again. It was funny how my aberrations were amusing when directed at other authority figures. Dad was the absolute monarch in our house, the teachers and housemothers at school demanded unthinking obedience, but when I had a confrontation with authority figures they didn't like, they thought it was hilarious. I'm a grown-up now, but I'll never understand grown-ups.

A few days later I came home from school to find that the wool blanket had disappeared from my bed, replaced by a flannel one.

Labels in blouses and dresses scratched my neck. Mother had to cut them out and sew in something smooth so I could tell the front from the back without irritating my skin.

I couldn't stand to get my hands dirty. Mud and dust gave me a sensation like goose bumps magnified hundreds of times. When we lived on Sappington Road I played in the sandbox with Sue and Steve only because they liked it and because their mom was especially nice both to

Mother and me. I would never have chosen to play in the sandbox on my own. I didn't like the outdoors or the beach or the mountains. As I got older, the kind of adventure I enjoyed most was reading the National Geographic, which was available in braille. It still is and I still read it, but as much fun as the great outdoors is to read about, I still don't like being hurt or feeling that crawly, gritty sensation like worms all over my body. When I was in fourth or fifth grade one of my schoolmates told me a joke: "Did you hear about the two maggots who were making love in dead Ernest?" Feeling the joke with my whole body, missing the point, I exclaimed, "Poor Ernest." I could feel with Ernest, feel those maggots partying under my skin, eating me alive, or not alive. This line of thinking became so vivid and scary that I cried out loud and attracted the attention of the authorities. You just don't tell the recess supervisor that you are hallucinating maggots.

I flunked Tinker Toys.

The diagnosis of autism was not created until 1943, just three years before I was born. I was always bombarded with the idea that I was strange and difficult. The more they said I never tried, the harder I worked. I could read before the end of my first year of kindergarten but I flunked anyway. When anyone asked me why, I said I had flunked Tinker Toys. When told to build a house with blocks I stacked them higher and higher. I had no idea how to make them look like a house. I had a pet rabbit at home. Miss Brookshire, in an attempt to reach me that was too little too late, told me to build a hutch for my rabbit.

"But, Miss Brookshire," I tried to explain, "I can't build a rabbit hutch out of blocks. I need wire. The rabbit could chew up the wooden blocks, dig under and get out."

"Judy, I don't know what to do with you." Miss Brookshire sounded older than ever. She walked away. The old fight was gone. I almost felt sorry for her; I almost felt nostalgic for the screaming, grabbing Miss Brookshire who had not given up on me, who still believed I could learn to tie my shoes, find my way around, do all the things the school valued. It almost made me nostalgic, but not quite.

Meanwhile, I had to get along at home. One of my prime strategies was to play by myself and try not to be noticed. I had a bookcase in my bedroom that had shelves with many small cubbyholes. I kept small stuffed animals in it and pretended that each compartment was a house where different kinds of animals lived peacefully together. The bookcase was a town. I would take out the smallest animals and line them up for school. Each animal had its own personality and its own favorite school subjects. None of my animals had to learn mobility or activities of daily living. They didn't have to worry about dressing or laundry because they had fur and didn't have to wear clothes. They didn't have to learn cooking because they ate their food raw.

None of my animals was blind. None was conspicuously behind the others in learning the skills needed to survive in the forest. They seemed to know what to do. There were not many problems, and when there were, the animals banded together to help one another. They were like the animals in "Winnie the Pooh," whose problems were easily solved in one play session. When the small animals were not in school, the larger ones were in church or in a meeting. The grown-up animals had lots of town meetings. When Presidents Truman or Eisenhower spoke on the radio, the animals lined up to listen. They knew, long before people did, that what went on in news and politics affected what went on in the forest. Daddy Bear was the town mayor. He delivered pronouncements in a deep, booming voice which I tried to portray in a squeaky falsetto that made even Grandma Dent laugh. At the imaginary town meetings the animals lined up on make-believe folding chairs. On Sundays all the animals, adults and children alike, went to church. Then the make-believe folding chairs became pews. It was a freewheeling church. Jacko the Monkey was the pastor. Sometimes he held Mass, sometimes a Protestant service. In either case, Jacko delivered a ringing sermon about the importance of wisdom and kindness, of tempering justice with mercy. Jacko never talked about hellfire and brimstone. He never said the animals were bad. The animals lived safe, peaceful lives. They loved one another, and most important, they loved me.

I didn't always make up sophisticated stories about my animals. When I first started playing with them I liked to line them up for no reason. I would lean their backs against the wall and enjoy how their shoulders lined up evenly. Then some grown-up would ask, "What are you doing?"

This question always annoyed and distracted me. What did they think I was doing, whipping up a batch of ice cream? Why did I have to have a reason? Why did I have to share it with them?

"I don't know," which meant, "Go away and leave me alone." "I don't know" was my all-purpose answer for when I felt threatened or didn't want to be bothered.

I liked things because I liked them.

It was hard to articulate as a little kid that I liked things that were smooth and safe and predictable. I liked small things I could hold in my hand. I had more than a hundred dolls; I could recite all their names, but my favorite was a small china doll I could hold in my hand. I called him "Old Ben" after my cousin. He still had his arms, but his head was a shapeless mass of adhesive tape which Mother had to renew from time to time. When he needed more tape I would pretend that Old Ben had to go to the hospital for a brain operation. His legs were completely missing. He probably was the dustiest, most dilapidated doll in the United States, if not the world. I loved him more than I loved my actual, living cousin Ben. Old Ben never played tricks on me or led me into situations where I got hurt. He had more disabilities than I did, and I loved him with a fierce protectiveness.

When I was three or four years old, Grandma Loehr, Mother, and I took the train to Chicago to meet Dad after one of his business trips. We had dinner at the Palmer House, one of the finest hotels in Chicago. Old Ben was right there with me, clutched in my hand. I couldn't leave him in the hotel room for gangsters to kidnap. As we ate, Grandma noticed that a man in an expensive business suit was watching us intently. Soon he left the dining room and came back with a package.

He walked over to our table. "Excuse me," said the man, holding out the package. "I bought your daughter a new doll. I noticed hers was old and broken."

"She has about a hundred dolls at home," said Mother, "but Old Ben is her favorite."

"Please accept this gift. Then Old Ben will have a new friend."

"Thank you," I said as the man handed me a hard rubber doll whose hard clothes were a permanent part of her body. I knew better than not to acknowledge it. I never played with that doll. It was hard and unfriendly. It didn't need me. Old Ben continued to go with me everywhere. I kept him in my nightstand drawer for years after I was too old to carry an old, beat-up doll.

I was fascinated by steps. Any time I found a stairway I climbed up and down, up and down, over and over. The house on Sappington Road had an attic with some nice, wide steps leading up to it. I climbed up and down steps so much that my parents became concerned for my safety. They discussed this one day with a kind, resourceful neighbor whose name I don't remember. He did woodworking as a hobby. He made me a set of three steps from some boards, which he sanded down to velvety smoothness. He also made me a toy escalator from two boards nailed together in such a way that I could stand on it, wiggle my feet, and it created a sensation of moving that felt like riding on an escalator. I have no idea how it worked.

I loved to count things. I counted the toys in my toy chest. I counted the books on my shelf. One year Mother bought several packets of seeds for a vegetable garden. I learned their names and counted them over and over, first forward, then backward.

When I was seven we took a trip to Western Colorado. On the way home I amused myself by memorizing all the towns we would pass from Bovina, Colorado, a tiny place with a school, a church, and a house, through most of Colorado, all of Kansas, and most of Missouri, all the way to Kirkwood, a suburb of St. Louis that is almost as far east as you can go before you end up in Illinois. When I first started asking questions about autism, several neurologists said things like, "You couldn't possibly have autism. Your language development is off the charts. You couldn't possibly have right brain damage. You're too good at math. No one as smart as you are can have developmental problems. You're a malingerer. Stop being a crybaby. There's nothing wrong with your brain. Get back to class and start working instead of making excuses."

If we had library books, I learned their names and counted them forward and backward. When someone read to me, I insisted that they read the books in the exact order that I had received them, except that if I got a new book I wanted to read it first. When I was old enough to have chapter books read to me, I insisted on knowing before beginning the book how many chapters and pages it had. Even today when I listen to an audio magazine I listen to the contents and memorize the number of articles in the magazine and the number of minutes in each article. For instance, there might be 33 articles; I might be on number 21, which is 38 minutes long with 19 minutes to go. These calculations give me a kind of brain massage, giving me a sense of accomplishment even when I am reading for leisure. If any one of these number systems was disrupted, I screamed and cried inconsolably. Dad would quickly get enough of this and say in an exasperated voice, "Knock it off. What the hell's wrong with you?"

That question dogged me for sixty years. Daily I confounded my parents and teachers. The questions I asked confused them and made them angry. I was so verbal, I read so well, wrote so well, did complicated math problems quickly in my head; how could I be so peculiar, so inept? How could I be so smart and have so few friends, such bad social skills? Yelling at me didn't elicit obedience, but crying or withdrawal. As much as my parents and teachers became upset by my aberrations, I was even more so. I alternately tried to obey and defy those who were punishing me. I did my best to comply with the wishes of those in authority while still remaining myself. This tug-of-war was the most difficult of all. I began to have terrifying dreams about being squeezed in a revolving door. I was pressured at home; I was pressured at school; there was no safe place to go. I lived in a world I did not understand, and it became harder, not easier, as I got older.

An attempt to catch up

My toys were educational. My dad was the feature editor for the Sunday magazine of the St. Louis Globe-Democrat. One of his jobs was to go to F. A. O. Schwartz in New York City each year for the toy show where all the toy companies presented their new products for Christmas. There weren't many toys a blind child could use in those days, but what there was always showed up at F. A. O. Schwartz. I loved it when Dad went to the toy show because he always brought me back several presents, all designed to teach me about the world I could not see. One year he brought a toy tractor complete with plow, harrow and disk. They were small enough to hold in my hands. I got to try them out in the yard and they really moved dirt. He also brought me a steam shovel, crane, backhoe and forklift. There was a well with a bucket on a string attached to a pump handle that actually went up and down, raising and lowering the bucket. When we read The Little House on the Prairie series, Dad found a tiny replica of a real covered wagon. Another time he brought home a village with small, three-dimensional wooden buildings—school, church, store, and several houses each with different architecture, a ranch house like the one we lived in, a bungalow, and a Cape Cod house. If that was the kind of house they had on Cape Cod I wanted to live there! It slanted up like the trunk of a Christmas tree and there was a small, special level on top near the roof. I would imagine I lived in that toy Cape Cod house. Whenever things got too stressful, as they often did, I would go in my mind to that safe, quiet room at the top of my Cape Cod house.

Every moment was a formal learning opportunity. My parents were determined that I would know as much about the world as my sighted peers. Every toy I played with, every book we read, every moment of every day was packed with my parents' frenetic attempts to make sure I didn't fall behind.

I did fall behind, however, and my whole life was an attempt to catch up. No matter how hard my parents tried, there were certain concepts I did not understand. My mother enjoyed looking at the stars, something she did with her dad when she was a child. She yearned to share with me that sense of adventure and excitement she felt while picking out and naming constellations. I knew the names of all the constellations and planets visible from our yard long before I started school. I learned them to please my mother, as I did so many things to please those with power—that is, sighted people. Yet I could never do enough to satisfy those around me, could never learn fast enough, work hard enough, even play with the abandon and intensity others demanded. I put all my heart into pretending that I cared about the stars. I would raise my hand above my head and ask, "Up there?" My mother would agree that they were "up there," but much farther. She would expound endlessly about how beautiful they were, only to have me get bored and ask a question about something else.

I was full of questions, just not the right ones. If ears were for hearing, noses were for breathing and smelling, hands were for touching, feet were for walking, what were eyes for? Why did I run into the furniture so often? Why did I twirl in circles in the middle of the floor when other kids didn't? When I played with our neighbors, Sue and Steve, in the sandbox, why did they move around so easily without getting hurt, while I fell into, and off of, nearly every obstacle I encountered? Why was I never allowed to go alone to the nearby candy store when other kids on our block did it all the time? Why did no one ever ask me to come out and play? Why did other kids love picture books and coloring books, while to me they were page after page of blankness? Above all, why did I have to work so hard to do the simplest things? Why was I so different?

When I tried to ask such questions my parents would say, "You'll understand when you're older. You're not different; you're just like everyone else."

My Uncle Clive, who thought he was the funniest man since Groucho Marx, would say, "You'll get it when you're sixty-five," yet another remark I didn't understand, made all the more annoying because the adults would roar with laughter at my expense.

"We're not laughing at you, we're laughing with you!" they would choke out between guffaws.

"But I'm not laughing," I would point out, reasonably enough, I thought, although it sent them into further eruptions of merriment. My dad would laugh the loudest of all. Sometimes he would laugh so hard he got the hiccups, which would set everyone off again. One time Uncle Martin laughed so hard he leaned back, tipped his chair over backwards, and bumped his head. Everyone howled, proving that my family derived equal enjoyment from everyone's misfortunes, not just mine. It was like getting out of prison when the ridicule shifted to someone else.

The snide comment was a weapon of mass destruction in our family. Cleverness and toughness were valued, and how clever and tough one was depended on one's ability to destroy another person with a devastating riposte. One time my mother got enough of it and said, "I wish I was as smart as you people!" My dad pulverized her with, "So do we!"

Another time we were driving late at night on a country road. There was a slight thump. "George," observed my mother, "we should go back. I think we hit something, and it smells really bad."

"We didn't hit anything," Dad grumbled under his breath, but loud enough for all to hear. "That's just your breath backing up."

Actually, as we soon discovered to our dismay, we had hit a skunk. The odor stung our noses for weeks afterward. We never completely got the stink out of the car, and when we eventually traded in the car the dealer knocked off several hundred dollars. Evidently he didn't like skunk either.

After all that, Dad wasn't the least chagrined that he had been wrong or that he had said a cruel thing to Mother. She never forgot this or any of the other demeaning remarks Dad tossed off without thinking. They grew and festered as a kind of psychological gangrene that took over her whole mind, until the hostility came oozing out like pus from an infected wound. The saddest part of this ongoing conflict was that it never occurred to either of them to apologize to each other or to me, never occurred to them to talk things out, to consider that the other person might have a valid point of view. Each was determined to be right, and to annihilate the other person verbally for having the nerve to disagree. These were the relationship skills I learned for forty years and am still unlearning today.

Chapter 5

"God will give you sight" (1948-58)

The rough carpet dug into my knees like tiny needles. "Say the prayer again, Judy," ordered my mother. "How do you expect God to give you sight if you don't ask him?"

"Dear God," I mumbled, as Mother had taught me so many times before, "if it be thy will, please give me sight."

I knew better than to ask Mother to define sight. Once when I had asked about it the question had made Mother cry and Dad get all surly and quiet. Whatever sight was, I must be awfully bad if I didn't have it. Apparently sight was something everyone else had that I lacked. I knew I hadn't been born with it; I assumed others must have worked hard to achieve it. If I tried really hard, then Mother would stop crying and Dad would stop being grumpy and I wouldn't have to kneel on the hard bedroom floor praying the Rosary three times a day and going to Mother of Perpetual Help devotions every Tuesday night. Maybe we could stop running to doctors in New York, California, and dozens of places in-between to find someone who could "fix" me. I remember one doctor who tied me down on a table and shone a hot sun lamp into my face, then said some words in an angry voice that made my mother cry again. I screamed in fear because I didn't know what that terrifying man would do to me. He had already put another kind of holy water in my eyes that made them burn like fire. I screamed because, although I tried so hard, all the grownups around me thought I was bad.

Children must have thought I was bad, too, because they liked to play a horrible game with me called "tag," in which I was "it." That meant I ran into trees, crashed into playground equipment, and tripped over roots while they ran away laughing. It seemed to be a game that "good children," children with sight, liked to play. My cousins and the neighborhood children, who didn't know one another, all liked to play it. I practiced and practiced playing tag, but never got any better at it; nevertheless, my clumsiness seemed an endless source of amusement to everyone but me. I never knew what the object of these games was, but they left me crying, often bruised and scratched. One particularly bad day I came into the house sobbing with a large cut over my eye where I had fallen.

"Jee-zuss Kee-rist!" boomed Dad. This was one of his favorite expressions and I was to hear it often, from earliest childhood right up until the day he died. "Can't you do anything about a problem but cry? I never saw such a crybaby! How do you expect to have any friends if you run in the house bawling every time you don't get your way?"

"They aren't my friends," I talked back, something I never did to my parents or anyone else unless things got absolutely desperate. "They just like to laugh at me when I fall down."

"That's enough, young lady," said Dad. "You can just go into your room and stay there until you think you can behave."

I sat on my bed and hugged my favorite stuffed animal, Jacko the monkey. He had a music box in his back and when I squeezed him he played "Brahms' Lullaby." He was my friend in a way that no human being could be. He never got impatient, never yelled at me, never expected me to do things I couldn't. A crucial misconception I had as a child and from which I am still recovering today is that I should be able to do everything anyone else could do in exactly the same way they did. I concluded that others had a mysterious, magical power called "sight" which I didn't have. In my view it had nothing to do with biology; sight was something you earned by working hard and being a good person. My parents talked on and on about all the wonderful things we would do when I got sight—a trip to Europe, a car for me when I turned sixteen, a mountain-climbing vacation in Colorado. As a confused child those things didn't have much appeal for me but it made my parents happy to talk about them. I wondered why we couldn't do some of those things now, but didn't dare ask unless I wanted a "discussion" with Dad. "Sit down," he would command. "We are going to have a discussion." When we had a discussion he discussed and I listened. Usually I didn't listen to his words, but to his voice, a rushing current of sound that washed over me and swept me away. It wasn't until much later that I began to understand and listen to what he said. My motive was survival. If I paid attention and followed each of his directives to the letter, maybe we wouldn't have so many of these discussions. It never worked out that way, though; when I was thirty-seven years old and he was eighty-two, three days before he died, he gave me detailed instructions on how to vote in an upcoming local election. To my annoyance, he was telling me to vote the same way I had planned to vote anyway. I don't know whether great minds ran in the same channels, or whether I was so intimidated that I agreed with him unconsciously.

My parents, especially Mother, were obsessed with begging God to give me sight. "Dear God, if it be thy will, please give me sight" was the first prayer I learned, long before the Our Father and Hail Mary. It certainly never occurred to anyone to teach me to pray in my own words. I never thought of God as a loving father; he was a monolithic being who was preoccupied with my defects, who had the power to remove them but chose not to.

We were always making Novenas—a prayer, usually a long one, that you say for nine days in a row, though our nine days stretched out into many years. No sooner did we finish one Novena than we started another. There were many Novenas to Mary, the Blessed Mother, most of them addressed to Our Lady of this or that—Our Lady of Fatima, Our Lady of Lourdes, Our Lady of Guadalupe, our Lady of anything you could think of.

We lived near a Carmelite convent. Every July, just when the St. Louis summers were at their hottest, we made an outdoor Novena to Our Lady of Mount Carmel. It was held in the evening so the weather was supposed to be cooler, but cool was in the sweat of the beholder. The service was an hour long for each of nine grueling nights. We recited the Rosary and some other long prayers. The meditations on the Mysteries were graphic and heart-wrenching. The priest assured us that every little sin was a thorn in Jesus' head or a nail in his hand. These Mysteries made me sad. They were nothing like "The Shadow" or "The Green Hornet," two of my favorite mysteries on the radio. Not only that, but there was another element of false advertising in this whole experience. The two words "Carmel" and "caramel" are spelled differently, but my parents pronounced them both the same way, "carmel." For years I attended these summer tortures in the vain hope that caramel sundaes, caramel candy, or caramel rolls would reward us for our aching backs and skinned knees. Evidently God, being all-knowing, didn't make spelling or pronunciation mistakes, especially about the Blessed Mother.

I have heard some people say that if they had a problem with their biological mother they prayed to Mary and thought of her as their mother. It seemed to me that my heavenly mother was even more demanding than my earthly mother since she needed so many Novenas to persuade her to throw me a crumb, much less ask her cold, distant Son to give me sight. Needless to say, I kept these thoughts to myself. In fact, I couldn't have articulated them in those days. They were more feelings than thoughts, a deep rage that this supposedly all-powerful God chose, for no good reason, to withhold sight, that elusive magic power that would make my parents love me.

We were Catholic but that didn't stop us from being rejected by God in ecumenical fashion. We went to all kinds of healers—Catholic, Protestant, and several varieties of non-Christian—quiet ones, noisy ones, some who spoke in tongues; we even went to one who fell into a trance, rolled on the floor, and screamed like a banshee. We went to Oral Roberts, who intoned, "Heal, Lord! Heal, Lord!" I got a picture in my mind of this terrifying, noisy man, careering pell-mell down the hallowed halls of his university, being pulled by a gigantic Great Dane and shouting at the top of his voice, "Heel! Heel!" The dog wasn't heeling and neither was God. I left that scary place just as blind as before I came, as was the case with every shrine we visited, every Novena and pilgrimage we made. God always welched, Mother got madder and madder, and Dad sighed in that annoyingly resigned way he had, as if to say, "How did I ever get into this mess?"

Sainte-Anne-de-Beaupré

The worst of these horrors came when I was four years old. That summer we took a long trip to Canada and spent the whole time visiting shrines. I had only a vague notion of what we were doing or why we were there, but I knew it had to do with sight. It was, as were most things in my world at that time, about getting rid of what was wrong with me. I didn't just imagine it was about me; it really was. The highlight, or lowlight, of the trip came when we visited the shrine of Sainte-Anne-de-Beaupré in Quebec. The place was a cacophony of sounds. People milled around like cattle in a stampede. I expected them to start saying "moo" any minute. For people on vacation, they didn't seem to be having a good time. There was an intense sadness everywhere, an intimation of urgency mixed with a kind of hope that was more like despair. Were all these people here because they made their families sad? As usual it wasn't a question I could ask.

"Listen, Judy," Dad pointed out. "They're speaking French."

I didn't know much about French except for French fries and French toast, both of which I liked. But in this place, where everything felt foreign, the new language added to the noise and confusion. I had never heard a foreign language before, unless you counted German, which Mother and Grandma Loehr spoke at home. I understood most of what they said, although they thought I didn't, a useful advantage to have when you're four and blind in a houseful of big, smart people with sight.

Here, though, the language blended into the other racket. We had just arrived and already I had had it. We had been away for so long, away from my grandparents, away from my toys, away from the familiar house I could find my way around. In all our traveling, God had said no to sight, which my parents wanted; He had also said no to what I had been praying for: a safe, quiet place to hide. I began to cry, not softly, not delicately, but at the top of my lungs, loud sobs that made me quiver and choke until I almost fell down.

"Don't cry," said Mother in that controlled, reasonable voice that always preceded a chewing out. "Saint Anne won't give you sight if you cry. Do you think Jesus cried like a brat when he went to visit his grandma?"

I didn't get the reference, as I missed most of what other people said when they were telling me I had done something wrong. I just knew they were mad. This time, as on so many occasions, that knowledge only made me cry harder.

"We've been walking a long time," said Dad. "She's probably tired."

I felt myself being scooped up and experienced the terrifying vertigo I always felt, no matter how many times it happened safely, when snatched up unexpectedly. Then I felt Dad's strong arms around me and knew I was safe for the first time that day.

Next we did the Stations of the Cross, a reenactment of Jesus' walk up Mount Calvary to Golgotha. It was the most realistic Way of the Cross I have ever visited, built on a steep hill that must have been a lot like the original Calvary. As Dad carried me, I could feel the sheerness of it, although I wouldn't have put it that way at the time. I imagined Jesus carrying himself and his cross up here, thinking, "If this is bad, just wait. I'm about to be in some serious pain."

"The first Station: Jesus is condemned to death." The priest's voice thunder-rolled over me in the tone the story lady at the library used when she read books, as if she didn't think we would understand or be interested unless she injected a whole acting company's worth of melodrama. "We adore Thee, O Christ, and we bless Thee."

"Because by Thy holy cross thou hast redeemed the world," we responded with rote obedience.

Then he said some French words, apparently repeating what he had just said in English. As we climbed up the hill, the priest told, in fourteen vivid chapters, the story of Jesus from his condemnation by Pilate to his burial in the tomb. He told each one twice, once in English, once in French. After each of these we said some Our Fathers, Hail Marys, and other prayers together, again alternating between French and English.

It really got bad at the Eleventh Station, "Jesus is nailed to the cross." "Consider how the soldiers stretched Jesus out on the cross, pinned his arms and legs, and drove long nails into his hands and feet," the priest declaimed. "Those nails went through his holy flesh, through ligaments and tendons, through the bone right into the wood of the cross. Never forget, fellow pilgrims, that every time you get angry, every time you gossip, every time you get drunk, every time you lie, cheat, steal, or commit adultery, and you children, every time you disobey or talk back to your parents, you are a hammer driving one of those long, sharp, rusty nails into the hands and feet of your Lord and Savior."

I wondered if the priest or God—and at that moment I wasn't sure that they weren't one and the same—would get really mad, madder than my parents had ever been, and drive one of those big nails into me. That thought was enough to convince me that crying was not an option.

I don't know how we got through the Stations of the Cross, but we did, only to climb the sacred steps. This was a splintery, wooden stairway that was supposed to have been climbed by Jesus. How, and under what circumstances, nobody seemed to know. The object of this ordeal was to climb these steps on your knees, stopping at each one to say more prayers and sing a song in Latin.

"I can't carry you this time, Judy," Dad said. "This is something you have to do yourself. When we're done, God will give you sight and you'll be able to read books and walk anywhere you want and see the beautiful world around you—birds, trees, animals, sunrises and sunsets, mountains and deserts, flowers and butterflies."

"And the stars," added Mother.

The prospect of being nailed to a cross was no longer a deterrent. "I don't want to do this!" I wailed. "I hate this awful place! I want to go home!" I cried in earnest now, so hard the tears ran down my face and over the corners of my mouth. I stuck out my tongue and tasted their saltiness, an anchor with the familiar, not as good as hugging Jacko the monkey, but better than thinking about those horrible steps. I hoped he would still be waiting for me when I got home, if I ever did.

"Hush," Mother hissed just loud enough for me to hear. "People are staring at us, not that they don't stare at us all the time anyway."

"Come on, Pieface, it's time." Dad always called me Pieface when he was being especially gentle and affectionate. Dad picked me up again and held me close for a moment. Something wet, not my tears, hit my forehead. Dad was crying, too. This was by far the scariest thing to happen in a day full of scary things. I couldn't imagine that Dad had ever cried. I must have done something dreadful to make him feel so bad, perhaps to make this whole crowd feel bad. Dad placed me on the bottom step on my knees. When he let go I started to fall backward and caught myself with my hand, which began to hurt. A light gust of wind came up and blew my skirt out from under me and there I was, skin pressed firmly against rough wood. They began the songs and the prayers. The voices washed over me like the ocean, or like the stinky vinegar rinse Mother often used on my hair for reasons known only to her. Every once in awhile, Dad would lift me to the next step. There were probably ten or twelve steps, but it seemed like at least a hundred. I was long past crying. My whole attention, what was left of it, was on not falling back down the steps so I would have to do this all over again. I had to get to the top so Dad would stop crying. I did get to the top and Dad carried me again. Somehow he must have brought me down, but I don't remember it. As soon as his arms were around me I fell into a deep stupor. I did not see any stars or sunsets.

When I woke up we were in the relic room. This was a kind of museum, full of small containers that supposedly held pieces of the dead bodies of saints—bits of bone, locks of hair, fragments of finger or toenail. The object was to kiss these relics in the hope that the saint would be flattered and grant you a miracle. I doubted if there was any point in my starting now to save hair and nail clippings, as there was not much chance of my ever becoming a saint.

"This is a relic of Saint Anne," explained Dad. "Here is what it feels like." He placed my hand on a round, metal box with a glass front and a starburst of sharp points around the edges.

"Kiss Saint Anne and ask her to give you sight." I had to reach up to touch my lips to the cold surface.

"You are Saint Anne's special child," said Mother. "That's why your middle name, Anne, is spelled with an 'e'."

There were lots more relics to kiss. Most of the saints had regular first names and strange-sounding last names, which Dad said were towns in France and Italy. I thought how odd it would be to be called Judy Kirkwood, the town where we lived at the time and where I still live today. There was one native American saint named Tekakwitha. A priest we met there said it was pronounced "take it with you." I wished I had been named after her. The idea of taking her with me, of having a friend everywhere I went, was appealing. I didn't have many friends at home.

Kissing so many relics had made my lips raw and sore and my neck ache from stretching, but the saints must have been pleased with me; I did, at last, get my miracle: my time with the relics ended. Soon this trip would end, we'd get home, and Jacko the monkey would be waiting for me.

But on the way back to the motel after the ordeal at Sainte-Anne-de-Beaupré, my mother saw one of her visions.

She often saw visions and heard voices. They spoke to her with a clarity and conviction that demanded absolute obedience. Mother obeyed her voices with the same unflagging devotion with which I was expected to obey my parents. I lived in fear that someday one of her voices would tell her to hurt me a lot, as they daily advised her to hurt me a little. Most of the time her hands were rough and harsh when she touched me, as she pulled and pushed me into the positions she wanted me to assume for the baths in therapeutic mineral salts that reeked of rotten eggs, the shampoos in a witch's brew of jojoba juice, tar, and other caustic, smelly liquids, followed by the ever-present vinegar rinse. Then there were the wool blankets and clothes that itched like millions of biting bugs crawling under my skin. Later she switched to cotton, which was almost as scratchy. I can't wear cotton or wool to this day. She used all kinds of exotic soaps and creams on my skin. Far from feeling good, they made me break out in exquisitely painful rashes. Worst of all were the olive-oil enemas three times a week. I don't know what perverse medicinal purpose they were supposed to serve, but they gave me excruciating stomach cramps and kept me occupied on the pot for hours. During all these ministrations I would scream and cry at the top of my lungs hoping she would stop or that someone would come and rescue me.

All these abominations were the results of Mother's visions, one of which she had on the ride back to the motel from the shrine. "George!" she suddenly exclaimed in a yell that caused Dad to slam on the brakes and send me plummeting to the floor from the backseat where I had been sound asleep. "Did you see it?"

"For crying out loud, Erna, what is it?" Dad was, as I might have observed if I had the sight everyone wanted me to have, visibly shaken. "This better be good. You almost made me wreck the car."

"The light." Mother's voice was getting higher and louder, moving into that otherworldly mode it adopted when, as Dad put it, she was "tuning up for a big one."

"Didn't you see it? God is right in front of our car! Don't you see it? Stop, George, stop! God has something to tell us!"

"Give me a break, Erna." Dad sounded like he was tuning up for a fairly big one himself. "Those are the headlights of a truck. Are you trying to get us killed?"

"I don't care what you say." Mother was adamant. "I saw God's face and I heard His voice. He says that if I convert to Catholicism Judy will get her sight. That's what He has been trying to tell me all along. That's why we came here, for me to learn to stop being an unbeliever. I've been selfish and blasphemous all my life. No wonder Judy can't see. I was being punished for my sins, but now that I've seen the light, things will be better."

"Fine," said Dad. "Let's get some dinner and go to bed. I'm exhausted."

Meanwhile I had scrambled back onto the backseat and was pretending to be asleep again. If there was ever a time to feign unconsciousness, that was it.

Years went by. We continued to visit shrines, make Novenas, and consult doctors. Mother did convert to Catholicism with great fanfare and hubbub about hell and damnation. The doctors continued to say I was hopeless, "didn't respond like a normal child," and that my parents should think about placing me in an institution. During all this time we never talked about blindness. It hung like a pall over our family. When my cousins started bringing friends to our family get-togethers I was introduced as "the blind girl" more often than by name. Mother and Dad never seriously considered putting me in an institution, but my blindness broke their hearts and their hearts stayed broken until the day they died.

The patron of hopeless cases

When I was eleven we made one final pilgrimage to Quebec. The last shrine we visited was dedicated to St. Jude, the patron of hopeless cases. It was a hot August day. That cold front weather forecasters in St. Louis were always saying was about to come down from Canada was stuck somewhere up around the North Pole. If doing penance would persuade God to answer our prayers, He would have to answer this time. I could imagine how Jesus must have felt when he said "I thirst" while hanging from the cross. It was comforting to acknowledge that Jesus wasn't holy-Joe perfect all the time, that he occasionally had doubts, that he felt fear and pain like the rest of us. I was no longer praying for sight, but for an end to this perpetual struggle to make me into something I could never be. I fished in my pocket and pulled out a piece of gum. The noise it made as I unwrapped it seemed deafening, like the crackling of the hellfire in which I would probably be consumed for my irreverence, but the sun was hot right now and my mouth was as dry as a Sunday sermon; I decided to take my chances now and worry about the consequences later.

"Judy, put that gum away right now!" Dad's voice interrupted my reverie. "How do you expect St. Jude to give you sight if you chew gum at his shrine?"

To my amazement I heard my own voice, trembling with unaccustomed audacity. "Dad, St. Jude isn't going to give me sight and neither is anyone else." There they were, the words that would put an end to all this and would forever liberate me from hope.

I don't know why my parents stopped the pilgrimages after that; I only know they stopped. It remains a mystery what changed my parents' minds. I'm sure it wasn't my brief moment of rebellion. Maybe St. Jude convinced them of the hopelessness of the situation. In any case, although my parents never accepted my blindness, they at last resigned themselves to it. Mother never forgave God for welching on his end of their contract and she never missed an opportunity to slam the Catholics in particular and religion in general. Whatever Mother did, whatever her enthusiasm of the moment, she pursued it with the fanatical zeal of a wrecking ball knocking down a tall building. Religion was just one of many ferocious pursuits. She forced me to swallow noxious, homemade tonics every day, the worst of which was a vile concoction of lemonade mixed with crushed persimmon seeds and various boiled leaves and grasses from the yard. "Squirrels eat persimmons," she reasoned, "and you never see a blind squirrel."

I made the mistake once, and only once, of observing that blind squirrels probably crawled off into a hollow tree to die of starvation, whereupon she hit me hard, something she often did when I confronted one of her delusions. Meanwhile, the drink made me throw up violently, after which Mother would make me force down another cup and the cycle would start over again until she got tired of cleaning up. During all this time I would alternately scream and retch.

Years later, after Mother was dead and I no longer had to drink persimmon lemonade, I derived a certain ghoulish pleasure from thinking about those healthy, indomitable blind squirrels, bravely feeling their way from branch to branch with their squirrel-sized white canes. It's a shame Walt Disney never knew my mother. The company may not have missed a financial opportunity, but Sammy Squirrel might have done more for the disabled community than the cloyingly perfect Mickey Mouse.

Mother approached all her interests—religion, medicine, astronomy, sewing, gardening, knitting, playing bridge—as if she were about to slaughter a powerful enemy. My blindness was just one more of those enemies. She was like Hercules killing the hydra by chopping off one head at a time. Whatever monster was there, Mother was prepared to slay it. My mother was usually on, and sometimes over the verge, of mental collapse. Fighting off all those evil foes, all day, every day, was emotionally draining for her. Ogden Nash published a book of poems in the '60's called There's Always Another Windmill. That's the way my mother was. When she finished tilting at one windmill, there was always another. The one windmill that knocked her down every time, the one she could never overcome, was my blindness. She tried to eradicate it—no luck—she tried to deny its existence—even worse—she even tried coping with it from time to time without much success; but she never tried accepting it. She didn't want me with blindness; she couldn't have me without it.

Chapter 6

Frere Jacques Nursery School (1949-52)

I stood perfectly quiet, perfectly still, the only quiet and still thing on that vast playground. As a savvy three-year-old I knew that a head-on, or even a leg- or shoulder-on collision with playground equipment was not a good feeling. Coming too close to the swings could result in a hard whack on the head by some other kid's shoe. I did not know much about climbing on the jungle gym or sliding down the slide. I never got close enough to them to find out what they were. Playgrounds were a mystery to me, an enigma characterized by anxiety, dread, and a vague sense of guilt mixed with bewilderment. Other kids seemed automatically to know what to do on a playground. They did something called "play," which evidently meant to make noise and run around. It was supposed to be fun, but I didn't know what was fun about it. Grownups were always astonished at my big vocabulary, but I was almost as confused about the meaning of the word "fun" as I was about "play." Often when adults said they were having fun, they were laughing at me. I wasn't having fun.

My dad was a newspaper editor. One of his jobs was to correct the vocabulary of grownup writers, so naturally when I had a question about a new word, I went to him. "Dad, what does it mean to have fun?"

"It means to have a good time."

"But what does that mean?"

"Having fun means doing something that makes you happy, something you like so much, you don't want to stop."

I thought this over, but as usual the answer raised more questions. Eating a chocolate ice cream cone was fun, so was being read to by Grandma or listening to Grandpa's old 78 records. I especially liked an album called "The Grand Canyon Suite," my favorite part of which was called "Donkey Serenade." The music made the sound of mules' hooves as they climbed down into a big hole called "The Grand Canyon" in Arizona, which Dad said was the most beautiful thing he had ever seen, and where he said he would take me as soon as I got sight.

The playground, however, was not fun, at least not by Dad's definition. Being out there didn't make me happy, and when I was on the playground, I wanted to be somewhere else immediately, if not sooner.

Anyway, this playground had all the qualifications for a place I didn't want to be. I had also heard people say that children played together. I was an only child and as far as I could recall, no other kids had ever played with me, so I didn't have a clue what everyone was talking about. Maybe my cousins had played with me sometime in the past, but if so, it hadn't left much of an impression. If being in this big, loud place with these children with no names was playing, I didn't want any part of it. It never occurred to me to make the connection that when I used the shovel and built castles in the sandbox with Sue and Steve, I was playing. The sandbox was a small, safe confined place where I never got hurt. Sue and Steve, imitating their mother, called me "Judy," not "the blind girl," as other kids did. They never laughed when something bad happened, although I don't remember anything bad happening when we were together. Their mother, whose name was Mrs. O'Neill—my mother called her Louise—had a calm, gentle voice and she never got mad. She never screamed that saints or witches or Indian chiefs were telling her to do horrible things. As I did not realize until decades later, Mrs. O'Neill was not afraid.

Back on the playground I wondered what Sue and Steve were doing and when I would see them again. I hoped it would be soon. These thoughts distracted me briefly from the hubbub and racket around me, but it seemed to get louder and louder, drowning out the quiet place in my head. I was perplexed, a new word I had heard on the radio a few days before that perfectly described the way I was feeling. Why were all this noise and confusion so much fun for everyone else and so painful and terrifying for me? My head felt as if someone were slicing it into small pieces with a chainsaw. Was this the way Mother felt when the voices were in her head? Was this why they scared her so much? Speaking of Mother, would she ever come back for me? Would we ever go inside where I could hear walls?

I began to cry. I choked and gagged trying to hold in deep, hard sobs that made me shake like Jell-O. It was never a good idea to cry at our house.

"Knock it off! What's wrong with you?" Dad would demand. "Why are you such a crybaby? Your cousins don't cry at every little thing."

"Am I going to have to give you some castor oil?" Mother would add. Castor oil was a foul-tasting children's laxative, popular at the time, and one of the advertising jingles was, "Babies cry for it." I was reminded of this over and over.

Now here I was in a strange place, already breaking one of the all-important rules my parents had given me before putting me on the bus to the Frere Jacques Nursery School. "Do what your teacher tells you. Don't talk all the time. Say 'Please' and 'Thank you.' Play with the other kids instead of staying off by yourself, and above all, don't cry."

"What's wrong, Honey?" A kind, soft woman with a gentle voice was hugging me.

"I don't know." I cried harder. It wasn't that I didn't know why I was crying. I wanted to leave this scary place and go somewhere small, safe, and quiet. The "I don't know" I was talking about was an overwhelming, cosmic not-knowing that gripped me nearly all the time then and overtakes me at least once a day now. Only it's a sure bet that if I cry now, especially out in public, nobody's going to hug me.

"We'll be going inside for lunch soon," said the hugging woman, sensing what I needed although I couldn't tell her. "Then you can meet some of the other children."

That prospect didn't thrill me, but going inside and having lunch sounded good. I don't remember my new friend's name, but she was one of the teachers at the school, and she seemed to materialize like magic whenever I was headed for a major meltdown. She made sure I got lunch every day and that I didn't fall or bump into anything and get hurt. She found creative ways for me to participate in what the other children were doing without feeling like a dummy. Left to my own devices I would have sat in a corner by myself and rocked and poked my fingers in my eyes. My favorite teacher always stopped me from doing those behaviors, but she never got angry and reprimanded me about it, never made me feel that I was bad.

One day we were doing artwork, an activity that would later become the bane of my existence and the first subject I would officially flunk in school, except kindergarten, about which more later. I had only a vague idea what was going on and I began to feel anxious as I always do when I feel disconnected from what's happening around me. I started to grind my knuckles into my eyes. I don't know why; I'm sure there's some obscure, neurological reason for it, but this actually feels good. I've heard some sighted blindness professionals theorize that blind people press their fingers into their eyes because the pressure makes them imagine they see light specks. I don't know about that; I never saw anything, imaginary or otherwise, when I poked my fingers in my eyes. In fact, it strikes me as incredibly arrogant for anyone to suggest that sight by its very nature is so wonderful that seeing a useless illusion of light specks should give me such a big thrill, as opposed, for instance, to seeing something useful, like a curb I'm about to trip off of. I only know that pressing my eyes was great for reducing anxiety until I got eye prostheses, after which it hurt like crazy. In a way this is a good thing, because I no longer have to fight a continual battle with myself to keep from doing it.

These stereotypical behaviors—rocking, eye poking, head shaking, swinging from side to side, finger flapping, jumping, twirling and others—are often called "blindisms" when performed by blind children. I learned early that they are not socially acceptable and that "normal" people don't do them. Many blind children have taken untold emotional battering by well-meaning parents and teachers trying to get them to stop these behaviors. That only makes it harder to give up these activities. I still haven't completely conquered them—a mortifying failure to admit, considering I've been struggling to eliminate them for over sixty years. Most people would never notice this because I fight mightily to keep them under control; most people wouldn't know that from a casual acquaintance with me. In fact I am often complimented on my lack of stereotypical behaviors. When this happens, my mouth says "Thank you," but my heart sighs ruefully and says, "I wish." Anxiety brings them on. As soon as stress comes, it's safe to assume that blindisms will not be far behind. Then I have to take valuable emotional energy, energy I don't have, away from the problem and spend it on controlling the blindisms. I no longer do them when I'm lonely or bored, but when I'm flipping out on the inside, there's a strong possibility I'll be rocking on the outside.

For whatever reason, this day in art class I was feeling particularly disconnected and left out, and my fists were in my eyes, grinding away to beat the band.

"Do you want to paint?" My teacher friend was at my side again, where she always seemed to appear when anxiety, and with it the blindisms, overtook me.

"I don't know." That poor woman worked like a slave to draw me out, and most of the time all I could think of to say to her was, "I don't know." I did know some things: I knew she was always there when things started to get bad; I knew she had a gentle, kind voice which she never raised at me the way most other people did; I knew I wanted to tell her how much I appreciated her patience, her not whispering or laughing at me, her never making me do anything that hurt or made me feel stupid. I can tell her that now that I'm older, now that she has probably been dead for years and may never have had an inkling of how much she did for me or how much I liked her. This day she took "I don't know" to mean "Yes," and unclenched my fingers enough to slip the paintbrush into my hand, which she gently guided. "Let's paint a picture of a bear. What color would you like him to be?"

"Red." I mentioned the first name of a color that popped into my mind.

"OK," she agreed with her usual enthusiasm. "Let's paint a red bear." She didn't point out scornfully that bears come in brown, black, or white, but never red. She didn't sigh, adopt a sad tone of voice, and say, "Oh, Honey, there's no such thing as a red bear. If you could see you would know that." She just went ahead and moved my hand and pretty soon we had what she informed me was a red bear. Maybe it wasn't a red bear; for all I knew or cared it could have been a blue fire engine or a purple pancake or maybe just some squiggly black lines. In my mind it was a red bear, and I was not alone, struggling to keep up with something I did not understand.

I was usually happy at Frere Jacques. Being a Montessori school, it was always full of things to do and learn. There was always something new to touch, taste, smell, or listen to. The environment was pleasant and I don't remember ever getting hurt there. The other kids moved on a parallel trajectory close to but apart from me. There were a girl named Marcia and a boy named Jimmy with whom I played from time to time, but mostly the other kids ignored me and I them, but I didn't feel ostracized. They simply did not penetrate my awareness. I knew they had sight, that elusive, magical quality again, but it wasn't a source of pain at Frere Jacques the way it was at home. The word "blind," if it came up at all, never was mentioned in a negative or problematic way. They wanted me there, just like they wanted all the kids. No one was conspicuously left out or picked on. I don't remember that hitting or bullying were allowed.

The most important thing I don't remember about Frere Jacques was whether I could find my way around. Nobody cared. It simply wasn't the big deal it would become the minute I started real school. I was neither praised for getting around by myself nor punished for failing to do so. Nobody had a fit about how I used a fork and spoon or whether I spilled my food or got it on my fingers. Even today I'm terrified to eat in front of certain people, especially other blind people with sighted companions, because they do care. I know that after the meal their companions will give them a play-by-play description of every molecule of food that touched my finger or every crumb that missed my mouth. If I have a sighted friend at the gathering, I will beg them to do the same, and if they tell me the other blind person was a messy slob I will be delighted, and if they tell me they ate like Emily Post I will be heartbroken. That's the kind of intense pressure the blind subculture puts on us, but there was none of that at Frere Jacques. When I was there I never felt, as I so often did afterward, that I was on probation.

My parents were as impressed with Frere Jacques Nursery School as I was, mostly because it was the only pre-school in the entire St. Louis area that would let me in. I remember only one detail of the exhaustive search. My mother was on the phone over and over, saying things like, "She's blind, but she's really smart and she never cries. She won't cause you any trouble."

Then there would be a long silence and my mother would hang up and cry.

Once I tried to hug her and asked, "What's wrong? Why are you crying?"

Mother pushed me away, said, "You wouldn't understand," and walked out of the room.

I did understand, though; I understood that Mother was crying and didn't want to hug me, and I suspected it had something to do with that magic bullet, sight.

I failed in many places after that, and I continued that pattern until, decades later, I learned to repudiate those failures for the sham that they were, but I did not fail at Frere Jacques.

They had plans to expand the school by adding a grade each year until they reached sixth grade. They begged my parents to let me stay there with my class. The superintendent offered to hire a teacher to come in and help me learn braille. My parents said no, because they thought I would get a better education at the school for the blind. Knowing what I know now about mainstreaming, a word that had barely been invented in those days, I believe my parents were correct, if you only consider academic education, but for years after I left Frere Jacques, I looked back wistfully on that time and wished I had not had to leave there.

There is one more salient point. Not long ago I had dinner with a friend who was a Montessori teacher. I was reminiscing about what a happy time I had at Frere Jacques, how free and relaxed the Montessori experience had been compared to the entire rest of my education, including graduate school. She thought she remembered the place, and asked me if the school had been located in a big, old, rehabbed house on Clayton Road. I had to tell her I didn't remember any details about the building, except that I hadn't fallen down any stairs. She was astonished that I could remember so many details about the place but nothing about the appearance of the building. I tried to explain to her that what the building looked like was not important to me, either then or now. She didn't get it, yet another example of someone trying to fit me into a sighted mold. I don't remember the building at all, but I do remember their kindness to me. I remember my favorite times of the day were storytime and lunch, something that hasn't changed a bit. That's why I became an English major. Most of all, I remember that they wanted me, not as someone they hoped to force into an unnatural pattern, but as myself; not as the person they hoped I would become, but as the person I was right then. I will always be grateful to them for giving me that early experience of complete acceptance. I was not to feel it again for a long, long time.

Mother: Different Languages

Mother and I always seemed to be speaking different languages. My questions baffled and confused her. One day at nursery school we learned the alphabet song. "Where did we get the alphabet?" I asked Mother as soon as I got home.

"You learn it from your teacher." Mother was ready with a reply.

"No!" I was emphatic. Mother had answered a question I had not asked. "Not how do we learn the alphabet. How did we get the alphabet? Where did it come from?"

"You learn it from your teacher." Mother was already getting exasperated and I had been home less than five minutes.

"But how did the teacher learn the alphabet?"

"She learned it from her teacher." Mother was really getting annoyed now. This could go on forever. I wondered if there were grandteachers, great-grandteachers, and great-great-grandteachers, like grandmothers, where the family tree went on for hundreds of years. Why was it called a tree? Family members were called parents and children, not limbs and branches, and what were leaves? This was not the time to ask these questions, however. Mother was in full throttle. "I've already explained to you. You learn the alphabet from your teacher, and she learned it from her teacher. I learned it from my teacher. Grandma learned it from her teacher."

"But somebody had to invent it, didn't they?"

"Oh, for heaven's sake! I don't know who invented the alphabet—probably somebody trying to balance his checkbook. Go pester somebody else. I have work to do."

Being dismissed like that, coupled with Mother's complete inability to understand the question I had been asking, sent me into a spectacular rendition of a Judy Dent screaming fit. Grandma Dent had to rescue me and provide an extra long harp concert with lots of hugs before I felt better. With all the books she read to me, it's a shame Grandma didn't know about Rudyard Kipling's Just So Stories. Years later, when I encountered it, I remembered arguing with Mother about the origin of the alphabet and wished I had been offered that whimsical hypothesis. I'm still intrigued by the prospect of cave people scratching pictures on walls and Phoenicians scrawling trade information on clay tablets, and how scrawls began to represent sounds and eventually ideas.

Chapter 7

The House on Cranbrook (circa 1951)

The noise throbbed in my head. Bang! Bang! Bang? My brain hurt. The bed I was in felt like my bed, but everything else was confusing and unfamiliar. The room sounded bigger than my room at home, as if a tornado had picked up the walls and moved them farther away. The window was open; I could feel a warm breeze and smell wood. I couldn't hear any voices or the usual sounds of my mother sewing or doing housework, but I could hear the hammers. They went on and on and they seemed to get louder with every blow.

I felt for Sally, the doll I usually slept with, but she was gone. I began to cry, something I did often when there was a lot of noise, and still feel like doing sometimes. New things scared me. My mind was then and to some extent still is on a continual Easter egg hunt for theories and patterns to account for everything. Chaos completely turns me upside down. One of my favorite games as a child was to take all my toys out of my toy box, count them and put them back. For me that was almost more fun than playing with them. I keep ideas and events in little boxes in my mind and I like to take them out to anticipate or analyze them. I love to know that church is at 11:00 a.m. on Sunday morning, that "Law and Order" is on television at 9:00 p.m. central time on Wednesday night (or at least it was on at that time before they canceled it, something that really bothered me at the time), that at 4:00 p.m. every day the familiar theme music for "All Things Considered" will come on NPR and it will be time to listen to the news. I don't like it when things are stirred up and fail to go as planned. Spontaneity is a quality I admire in others, but haven't mastered for myself.

So on this terrifying morning, in this strange place, with hammers pounding outside the window and in my head, I cried long and loud. After what seemed like forever I heard someone walking into the room. "Hi, Honey!" It was Grandma's cheerful voice. "You dropped Sally. She's right here on the floor." Grandma sat down on the bed and put her arms around me. "Remember where you are?" she continued. "This is the first morning in our new house."

I stopped crying instantly, as I usually did when Grandma was around. Slowly the events of yesterday began to come back. They were not good memories; all my toys were taken away and packed in big boxes, along with all the rest of our stuff. A big, noisy truck came and took everything away. Then we got in the car and drove out into the country. I had never ridden on such a bumpy road. There was no pavement. It was just dirt with lots of big holes. The car bounced up and down like one of the rides at the Forest Park Highlands, an amusement park we had visited a few weeks before.

"Here we are, home at last," said Dad with a slightly rising inflection, as if he wanted to pump us full of enthusiasm. He pulled the car into a small, enclosed space which I learned later was a two-car garage. "This is a door that goes right into the house," Dad continued. "That way we won't ever have to get out of the car in the rain."

We went in. Dad's voice droned on, patient, reasonable, explaining and expecting me to remember every detail. At four years old all I cared about was when my toy box would be unpacked and when we were going to eat. "This is the screened-in porch," Dad went on. "Feel how smooth and cool the floor is? It's asphalt tile. Every room in the house has a different kind of floor. That way you'll always know where you are."

Sure enough, the floor was hard, cool, and smooth—not damp and rough like concrete. Every room had its distinctive feel. Each bedroom and the living room had a carpet with a different texture. The kitchen had another kind of tile; I don't remember what it was now. The hall had rubber tile. My playroom right next to the kitchen, where Mother could watch me as she worked, had cork tile. "It will be nice and warm when you play on the floor," Dad explained.

I still like to spend time on the floor, to do yoga, watch TV, or listen to the radio or a talking book; but as much as I enjoy the floor now, I liked it even better as a child. The floor had a safe, anchored feeling. On the floor I was always touching something. I couldn't fall because I was already down. I didn't feel stranded in a vast, shapeless space, as I so often did when walking or standing.

Now it was the next morning and all Dad's instructions were a jumble. His journalist's mind had almost photographic recall; he expected me, even at such an early age, to remember every detail after he had told me once. If I forgot anything, although it might be weeks later, he would say in annoyance, "You'd make a lousy reporter!"

"She's not a reporter, George, she's a little girl." Grandma's voice was mild, calm, and reasonable as she tried to divert him. "You're at home, not at work."

"She's not too little to learn." Dad was adamant. "She has to learn to be accurate. Sloppy thinking can get her a permanent place in the unemployment line. It's hard enough for a person without a handicap to get a job. She has to be twice as good to be half as good."

"What's a job, Dad?" I wanted to get him back into instructional, out of preaching, mode. At least then he would stop yelling.

"It's what I do every day when I go to the office to work on the magazine. It's how you are able to eat all those nice meals."

"Do they have food at the office, Dad?"

"Don't be a smart aleck."

Many people, not just Dad, told me not to be a smart aleck. I had no idea what they were talking about until years later when I began to take a certain pride in it. It was fun to insult people who were mean to me, and to do it in such a way that they knew they had been insulted, but had no idea how.

That morning and for many weeks afterward, I spent time trying to learn my way around the house. I was surprised at how hard it was. I had recently learned a new word, "elliptical," and that's how everything felt, in both a metaphorical and literal sense. Shapes confused me. I had no sense of what the rooms looked like. I believe they were rectangular, a word I didn't know at the time, but they seemed round, like endless circles, except that they had corners Mother made me stand in when I mouthed off or cried. The corners seemed completely discrete from the process of getting around the house. I knew only two shapes, round and square; I walked around things and bumped into square corners with sharp points. In the bathroom I walked around the sink to get to the pot, around the pot to get to the bathtub. Yet they didn't feel symmetrically lined up. The kitchen was the same way, stove and sink on one side, refrigerator on the other, table and chairs in the middle. I think. That's how it felt to me.

I lived in that house 36 years, from ages four to forty. That's all I can tell you about the decor of the house. The living room was so large and confusing, I continued to get lost in it for as long as I lived in the house. I quickly learned to find the easy chair that was nearest the door and it became my chair. I guarded it with Archie Bunker-like protectiveness. When we had company and someone sat in it, which they always did because it was comfortable and handy, I felt resentful, especially toward Uncle Clive, who always sat there and whom I didn't like much anyway because he was big and rough. It annoyed me that my parents wouldn't stick up for me and either ask him to sit somewhere else or help me find another chair when he sat in mine. I hated blundering around the room in front of company. I still do. To this day I make sure I'm where I want to be before the company comes in and my husband Blair opens the door, so the first thing the company sees isn't me stumbling around.

If the house was difficult to navigate, the yard was like being lost in outer space. I have no idea of its shape. It was half an acre, but it felt like half a world. If I was out in the yard, I couldn't come in when I wanted to, but had to wait for my parents to remember I was there and come out and get me. There were 38 large, old-growth trees on our lot, all waiting eagerly for me to run into them. As I grew taller the low branches would reach out like malevolent fingers to grab me. The scariest thing about the yard was that our area had a zoning ordinance against fences. The idea was not to obstruct the view. Our yard joined several others. I could get lost and wander into someone else's yard. Once a grumpy lady came out of her house and asked me what I wanted. I didn't even know I wasn't in my own yard.

There were good things about the yard but I needed supervision to enjoy them. Before we moved there my parents prepared me by rhapsodizing eloquently and at length about the wonderful big yard I would have to play in. My inability to enjoy it alone never ceased to disappoint and annoy them. They hired a top landscape artist to turn the yard into a fragrance and texture garden long before fragrance and texture gardens were even heard of. There were linden trees, lilacs, one lilac bush right outside my bedroom window, a magnolia tree, a sweet bay tree, a metal trellis with many kinds of fragrant roses, a grape arbor with different types of grapes, seedless and otherwise with a large swing hanging in it, several varieties of apple, peach, apricot, pear, and plum trees, spearmint, peppermint, sage, basil, oregano, and other fragrant and flavorful herbs, and my favorites, lambs' ears, a snowball bush, and pussy willows. There were tulips and jonquils for shape, narcissus and hyacinths for fragrance. We had Easter lilies and various other kinds of lilies. I loved it when Mother or Dad would take me around and point out these garden delights, but I couldn't find them when playing by myself.

Tuffy

The puppies, like the earthworms from years before, were full of life, but that was where the resemblance ended. The earthworms had been cold and gooey; the puppies were soft and warm. The earthworms died when I touched them; the puppies seemed to enjoy it. They wiggled and jostled one another in their large box and they seemed to be having a good time as they licked my hands and sniffed my fingers with their cold noses.

It was my fifth birthday. Dad had taken me to visit a friend of his who was a breeder of purebred Collie puppies. We were going to select one for my birthday. "This one is my favorite," said the breeder, placing my hand on one of the puppies. "He's so big and strong."

I examined the puppy. He seemed playful and full of energy. He nipped my finger in his enthusiasm. "Ouch!" I quickly pulled my hand away.

"He didn't mean to hurt you," said Dad. "He was just playing. He didn't break the skin. For heaven's sake, don't cry. If you want to get along in this world, you have to be tough."

Suddenly I wasn't having fun anymore. Did everything, even getting a puppy, have to have a big, moral lesson, one involving how worthless and inadequate I was? I sat back quietly, trying to pull my thoughts together. If I had a meltdown here, in front of this nice man who was trying to help me pick out a puppy, Dad would never forgive me.

I felt a gentle nudge on my hand. One of the puppies, not the one that had bitten my finger, was crawling out of the box into my lap. I felt a wet tongue on my cheek. It was almost as if this puppy were trying to comfort me. He was much smaller than the one Dad and the breeder had wanted me to choose. In fact he was so skinny that I could feel his ribs through the soft fur. He didn't try to bite me. He lay quietly while I stroked him, as if my lap were the place he had always wanted to be. I hadn't had to pick him out; he had chosen me.

"I want this one." I exclaimed in delight. All thoughts of a meltdown were long gone.

"You don't want that one," the breeder assured me. "He's the runt. Look how tiny he is. He will probably die."

"Listen to the man, Judy," Dad advised. "He knows a lot about dogs."

"No!" I was adamant. "It has to be this one. He needs me."

"Why do you want him?" Dad wasn't going to give up without an argument. "He could die tomorrow or next week and then you wouldn't have a puppy."

"He won't die. I won't let him. You said I was little and I didn't die."

Long pause. Even the puppy was quiet. Either he had gone to sleep or he knew our fate hung in the balance.

"How can you argue with that?" Dad's voice was resigned, a tone I had never heard before. "That's just what I said when the doctors wanted me to put Judy in an institution."

"I'll give you a discount," the breeder said. "He really could die."

"I don't think so. He has Judy to love him."

"Dad," I asked in the car on the way home, "what's an institution?"

"It's a place you'll never have to go." Dad's answer was evasive as usual, but this time his evasion felt reassuring rather than frustrating.

Dad hurried to change the subject. "What are you going to name your puppy?"

I had the answer ready. "His name is Tuffy. He's little, and if he's going to get along in the world, he'll have to be tough."

Tuffy did not die. He lived quite a few years after that. Our friendship continued to develop as I learned to feed and care for him. Once when I was feeding him, Tuffy licked my hand. "That's his way of saying thank you," Mother explained. "He appreciates all the nice things you do for him."

I had been telling people "thank you" for years, but this incident with Tuffy taught me what it really meant. Until then "thank you" had been a kind of echo for all occasions, something I was supposed to repeat mindlessly when an adult handed me something or said I was smart or cute. "Thank you" had been a source of frustration and embarrassment. If someone handed me something, before I had a chance to figure out what it was, or get my thoughts together, one of my parents would demand, "What do you say?" "Thank you," I would respond like a robot, often not sure what had been done or given that I was supposed to be expressing gratitude for.

My cousins and the neighborhood kids soon learned about this ritual and got a huge kick out of using it to make me look stupid. They would hand me old candy wrappers, used chewing gum, half-eaten hard candy, once even a long, slimy booger my cousin Bobby had pulled out of his nose for that express purpose, and then howl like hyenas when I said "Thank you." Some of the things they gave me were even grosser than that. Most of the time even the adults would laugh. I don't know if dogs can laugh, but I do know that Tuffy never laughed at me. It was from him that I learned that "thank you" had a meaning other than that someone had put something into my hand. Tuffy taught me that saying "thank you" was a way to acknowledge something nice. Tuffy never humiliated me; he never said, "What do you say?"

I had heard about guide dogs but had no idea how they worked. I didn't know until years later that a guide dog wore a harness that the person held onto as they walked through streets and sidewalks. Tuffy and I had our own way of walking. Whether we figured this out for ourselves or my parents taught him, I don't know. Tuffy would hold my hand gently in his mouth like a retriever holding a small bird, and guide me carefully around obstacles in the house. Even on those rare occasions when Tuffy became startled, he never once bit down on my hand. I always felt completely safe walking with Tuffy, something I can't say for most human beings. We never hit the furniture or tripped down the basement steps. I never bumped my head on a half-open door. We didn't go fast—it wasn't a power walk for exercise—but I felt safer and more loved walking with Tuffy than I had ever felt praying to all those saints in Canada. Tuffy never tried to make me better. He loved me the way I was.

Changes were coming. School was a looming inevitability, a trauma so profound I am still recovering from it today. But when I came home Tuffy was always there, more constant than the sunrises and sunsets everyone was almost angry with me for missing out on. I did not know then nor do I know now what a sunset is, and I don't care. I spent years caring about things like that, trying desperately to adopt everyone else's priorities so they would love me. Let sighted people get all worked up about sunsets and stars and mountain views. I'm glad they have them to enjoy, but I learned about love from a dog who was tough, but not with me; who was gentle when everyone else was rough; who took his time when everyone else rushed; who stayed quiet when everyone else yelled; whose vocabulary contained the words "Sit," "Down," and "Stay," but never "Sight."

Judo the Great

Our yard on Sappington Road had been too small for the luxury of playground equipment, but on Cranbrook I had a swing set, jungle gym, and slide. The teachers at Frere Jacques had sent a progress report stating that I withdrew and didn't play with the other kids on the playground.

Dad asked me about it and I answered, as I often did, "I don't know." What I should have said was, "I don't know how." Then Dad did something for which I will always be grateful, something my parents were often unable to do. He figured out that I couldn't watch other children and didn't know what to do on a playground. As soon as we moved into our new house, up went the swing set, slide and jungle gym. Dad worked nights so he was often free in the daytime. Weather permitting, almost every morning before work, Dad would take me out and literally put my body through the motions of playing on my new equipment. "Hold on tight," he would say, and pushed me on the swing. The higher I went, the happier I felt. The wind on my face was exhilarating, and I felt free and strong kicking my legs and pulling with my hands.

"As you go up, kick with your feet, pull back with your hands," Dad instructed. "As you come back, push with your hands, bring your feet in."

Come to think of it, I may have that wrong. I believe I still know how to swing; it would be great to have the chance to try again; but Dad's directions were long and complicated, and my orientation problems are here just as much as they ever were. All I know is, the instructions eventually became, "Out, in, pull, push."

Recalling Dad on the playground still brings back good memories. Dad was infinitely patient as he taught me to use the playground equipment. He placed my feet and hands carefully on the bars of the jungle gym and showed me how to climb and, equally important, how to hold on. We pretended I was a famous trapeze artist named Judo the Great. I wasn't especially great with anything connected with climbing bars, but Dad's believing I was made me feel strong, powerful and happy, even though we were just pretending.

As the finishing touch, Dad taught me how to use the slide. I was afraid of it at first, but soon it became the most fun of all. The scary part was moving from the ladder to the slide. I felt that same sense of vertigo that I always felt when launching off into unknown space.

"There's nothing to hurt you," Dad reassured me. "I'm here. I won't let anything happen."

Knowing Dad was there protecting me was enough to convince me to keep trying.

So I was just as delighted with the slide as with the swing. The wind resistance felt good on my face, only this time I was speeding down. I don't remember getting hurt on the slide at home, which can't be said for other slides and other times when the kids were mean, rough, and in a hurry, and pushed and shoved me out of the way.

I knew a family who hired a high school girl to take their blind child to a park and teach him how to use the playground. Years later I became friends with this former high school student who informed me, somewhat smugly, I thought, that this boy was a fast learner and that playing in the park with other children had been a watershed experience in beginning his extremely independent life. The implications were obvious, but my Dad knew, and I shall always thank him for it, that learning to play was a long, slow process for me, and he gave me the time, space, and above all the safety to do it.

Much as I enjoyed playing on the equipment when Dad or Mother was around to keep me from getting hurt or lost, playing by myself was all I learned to do. Other kids terrified me, especially on playgrounds, even my own. I still would rather be alone, unless I am with someone I've known for a long time and trust completely.

The swing brought about one sad incident, though. Shortly after he came to live with us, Tuffy was out in the yard, standing near me as I swung higher and higher. I didn't know he was there, however. I soon found out, much to my dismay. Whack! As I was pushing off I heard and felt a horrible thump followed by a high, thin cry of pain. The horror of what I had just done made me shrink from myself with revulsion. If I had known the word "atrocity" I would have been convinced I had committed one. I wailed much longer and louder than Tuffy had.

"Judy, what on earth is wrong with you? You sound like a screaming banshee. What's the matter with that dog? He looks like he's lost his last friend." Mother had come rushing from the other end of the yard where she had been pulling weeds in the vegetable garden.

I cried even harder. That was exactly what had happened; Tuffy had lost his last friend. "I kicked Tuffy!" I sobbed. "I didn't mean to!"

"How many times do I have to tell you? Pay attention to what you're doing!" Mother chided. "Tuffy likes to stand near you because he loves you and he wants to be close to you."

"But I didn't know he was there."

"That's no excuse. You should have been more careful. Tell Tuffy you're sorry."

I reached out my hand and said, "I'm sorry Tuffy. I didn't mean to hurt you."

He licked my hand. Then he climbed up on me and licked my face. All was forgiven, at least by Tuffy.

Spot's kittens

A similar incident occurred about a year later, shortly after I acquired a stray cat named Spot. I have no idea what color she actually was. I just thought Spot would be a cool name. One morning Mother hurried into my room. "Guess what! Spot has five kittens."

It was a warm spring day and Mother had placed the kittens' large cardboard box on the screened-in porch so the kittens could get fresh air. Spot meowed nervously as I put my hand into the box, but she didn't hurt me or try to push me away. "They're so soft!" Now I understood how the pussy willows in our yard got their name. "Mother, can we keep them forever?"

JUDITH ANNE DENT, PH.D.

"I don't know about forever, but we can keep them until they're old enough to leave their mother."

"How old is that?" A pang of fear crawled down my back like cold rain. How old was "old enough to leave your mother"?

"We'll see." Mother brushed me off. "Now it's time to get dressed for school."

Everyone at kindergarten was delighted to hear about the kittens and the class spent some time thinking up names for them. I don't remember the names now, but I do recall that that was one of the few times I felt accepted at school.

A few weeks later, on a Saturday, I was outside playing with Spot and the kittens. I was having a great time sliding down the slide. Then I got the bright idea that if I liked the slide the kittens might like it, too. I picked up one and put it as high up the slide as I could reach. I could hear its feet sliding on the metal as the kitten slid down. Soon all the kittens were climbing up and sliding down, having a great time. I got tired of this game before the kittens did. Listening for a time when it was quiet, I climbed up the ladder and slid down.

Mother had come out and was watching, laughing at the kittens on the slide. I didn't realize at the time how rare that was. Mother seldom laughed. Suddenly she wasn't laughing any more. She was screaming. "How many times do I have to tell you? Be careful and pay attention! You just knocked four kittens off the slide." How many times do I have to tell you? Pay attention to what you're doing. You could have hurt those kittens."

"They didn't seem hurt," I defended myself. "They just slid down a little faster."

"The point is they could have been hurt, all because of your carelessness. You'd better go inside and think about what you've done. When you think you can behave you can come back out."

"I can't go by myself," I mumbled, wishing I could crawl into a hole like one of the earthworms I used to play with.

"Oh, cheese and crackers!" said Mother, an expression she used when she was really mad but considered herself too refined to say "Jesus Christ."

"And to think instead of having you I could have gone to Hawaii and become a photojournalist."

"What's a photojournalist?"

"Will you be quiet for once in your life? Come on. Let's go in!"

Mother grabbed my arm and hurried toward the house with me stumbling in her wake. Her voice went on and on, washing and breaking over me like tidal waves. It reminded me of one of our trips to Canada, when we had visited Nova Scotia and listened to the tide come in at the Bay of Fundy. Crash, crash, crash! The noise rumbled and roared and thundered over everything.

I just wanted Mother to stop being angry with me, to stop that shrill screaming, to stop dragging me.

"What's the matter, Honey?" Grandma came out onto the porch. "Can I help?"

"Leave her alone, Ida." Mother was in no mood to have her authority questioned by her mother-in-law. "Don't interfere. She has to handle this herself."

"She's only a child, Erna."

"No one ever let me get away with that excuse when I was her age. If I behaved like that Pop would have taken the razor strap to me. Sometimes he beat me so hard I bled. I wasn't allowed to mouth off like that. You coddle her too much, Ida."

"That's what grandmothers are for."

"I don't remember my grandmother." Mother's voice took on a wistful note.

"I just made some lemonade," said Grandma. "Let's have some."

Mother: Amazing things in the sky

You never knew what Mother was going to do next. It was as if there were a monster raging in her head that would come out any moment and make her say and do horrible things. If I said the wrong thing she would hit me or start screaming. Often I could feel the wind on my face from her waving her arms around as she talked. Dad said her eyes got wild and scary at those times. I know she scared me when she was like that.

At other times Mother was just as kind and loving as anyone else's mother, only more so. She would read to me for hours or sing old songs from the 1920's when she was a teenager. She taught me all kinds of card games, including the intricacies of bridge. "When you think of finesse, you have to think of entry," she would intone like a mantra. Years later it struck me as ironic that someone who was so careful about finesse in cards should be so lacking in it in real life.

I never quite knew how to feel about Mother. Sometimes she wanted me to be independent and do things for myself; other times she seemed to resent every time I tried to exercise some initiative. When I was learning to dress myself, if the zipper got stuck or I got a button in the wrong hole, she screamed and yelled her disapproval in a way that convinced me that not trying was better than being yelled at. "Stupid individual! How can you be so smart and so dumb at the same time? I've shown you a million times how to button clothes! You could probably count to a million, but you can't button your pajama top. What am I going to do? I don't have anybody to help me! Your father spoils you; your grandmothers spoil you. I wish you were more like your cousin Janice. She isn't a genius, but at least she can dress herself." On the other hand, she would suddenly, inexplicably, decide I had to do things for myself.

One day Mother was watching me play on the jungle gym. I was feeling adventurous and climbed higher and higher. It was like climbing up to the sky that Mother was always talking about. She often told me about the stars and then cried because I couldn't see them. I wondered, if I kept going higher, would I be able to touch one? Did they have five points like the ones they gave us at school for good behavior? Would Mother be happy if I brought one back down to her? Up and up I went, hands first, then feet. I had never been all the way to the top before. I imagined that the jungle gym went on and on forever. Abruptly I reached for the next bar and found, not a star, but air. I held on with one hand and felt around with the other for all those amazing things Mother said were supposed to be in the sky—stars, planets, the moon, birds, airplanes—and there was nothing. I felt vertigo descend like a bag over my head. Nothing was all around me. Emptiness engulfed me. Space was everywhere. It filled my chest, my lungs, my head. It hit me like a body blow. I didn't like where I was. I wanted to be somewhere, anywhere, else right now!

"Mother!" I yelled. "Please help me down!"

"You got up, you can get down."

Mother was mad again, and I hadn't been able to get her a star. It felt as if I never did anything but upset her. I clung to the bars locked in fear, fear as much of Mother's wrath as of falling.

"I can't," I insisted.

"Can't is a sluggard too lazy to work."

"What's a sluggard?"

"A lazy dumbbell. Now will you stop asking questions and come down from there? I don't want to be out here arguing with you when your father comes home."

"Erna, you're mean!" a strident voice interrupted. "For heaven's sake, help that child down. Can't you see she's terrified?" Mrs. McConnell, our next-door neighbor, had come into the yard. Mrs. McConnell saw so much that she could have shared half her sight with me and still had 20/20 vision. She knew when you went out, she knew when you came home, she knew when you had an argument, sometimes she even knew what you were thinking.

"I am helping her, Fannie," replied Mother, with uncharacteristic calm. "If she doesn't learn to take care of herself now, she will just keep getting into trouble and not be able to get herself out."

"Well, she's your child, Erna, and you can do what you want, but if I were you, I'd help her. She could fall and crack her skull, and then how would you feel?"

I began to cry loudly, partly because the prospect of cracking my skull scared me even more than being up on the jungle gym, and partly for dramatic effect. If Mother didn't listen to one of us, she would have to listen to both.

I was wrong. Mother didn't listen. She was so quiet that she could have walked away for all I knew, except I didn't hear footsteps. Mrs. McConnell stomped off in annoyance, probably in search of another neighbor with whom to share this juicy tidbit.

I was alone with my hands, my feet, and my fear, holding onto those bars for dear life, unable to move up, afraid to move down. My foot slipped. I hung on tight with both hands, flailing for a place to put my foot, certain I would instantly fall to my death. I'm sure if I had known that old saying about your life passing before you at the moment of death, mine would have. I had no idea where the ground was, except that it seemed far, far away. There was no place to go but down. I stretched out my foot, hoping to touch something, anything, but empty air. To my astonishment the foot found a bar, not the one it had been on before, but a lower one. Maybe this was the key. I hung on with one hand, moving my other hand to meet my foot. Slowly, foot hand, foot hand, I moved down. After what seemed a long time there were no more bars and my feet hit the ground.

"Well, it took you long enough," said Mother.

"Did I do a good job?" I asked, hoping for once to receive a word of encouragement after my ordeal.

"You did what you had to do. That's what we all do every day, and what we have to do right now is go in the house and fix supper."

Life for my parents was never about thoughts or feelings; it was about getting things done. You didn't discuss it, you didn't analyze it, you just did it.

That summer on Cranbrook was ending and so was my time at Frere Jacques. It would soon be time for real school and real responsibilities.

Chapter 8

Bathroom Blues for Life (1952 and beyond)

When I got home from that first day of kindergarten at the school for the blind, I couldn't wait to run into the house and make a mad dash for the bathroom.

"What's the big rush, Honey?" called Grandma Dent from the living room where she and Grandma Loehr were listening to the radio. "How was your first day of school?"

"Be there in a minute, Grandma." I hurried into the safety of the bathroom, closed the door and lowered myself gratefully onto the seat. "Thank you, God," I prayed. "Thank you, thank you, thank you."

I recalled a Greek myth Grandma Dent had told me about in which Zeus had turned himself into a waterfall. Zeus may have been the king of the gods, but as a waterfall he didn't have a thing on me. The sound was like a flash flood. Water poured out of me like air out of a balloon. I wondered if I would be able to make it home every day and seriously doubted it. Oh, well, I was safe for now. "Sufficient unto the day is the evil thereof," as Grandma Dent loved to quote from the Bible.

I resolved to hold it all day, every day. Never again would I allow myself to be locked in that little cubicle. Of course my plan didn't work. Several times during the ensuing weeks I wet my pants. At last Mother sent a pair of clean underwear along every day in a bag. The first morning I marched up to Miss Brookshire's desk, feeling like that proverbial lamb going to slaughter. "Mother said to give you this," I mumbled in acute embarrassment.

"An extra pair of pants in case she wets them," boomed Miss Brookshire in a voice that couldn't have been any louder if she had been using a bullhorn.

Derisive snickers came from the back of the room. "Wassa matter, baby? Didum wetums witto panties again?" sneered one boy. The whole class had heard. I had just learned a new word: mortified. Grandpa had told me about a magician named Houdini who could make himself disappear and escape from anywhere. I wished I knew some of his tricks now.

That night I came home upset and told Mother about it. "That was so awful. What am I going to do?"

"Why do you wet your pants at school, Judy? You never do it at home."

"I can't find the bathroom," I sobbed, "and those stalls scare me. I got locked in one and a man had to come and get me out and Miss Brookshire threatened to stick a hook in my eye."

"What?" Mother's voice went up several registers. "I'm going to get on the phone right now and clear this up."

"Please don't yell at Miss Brookshire. She's so mad at me already. If you upset her any more she might kill me."

"Does Miss Brookshire know you can't find the bathroom?"

"I don't know."

"Why can't you just say, 'I don't know where it is, Miss Brookshire?'"

"What's going on in there?" Grandma Loehr came into the room, ready to defuse trouble if necessary. Mother told her about our conversation. "Let me call her, Erna," Grandma said. "You might flip out and make things worse." Grandma Loehr had many virtues, but tact was not one of them.

Soon I heard Grandma's voice, muffled and indistinguishable on the phone. When she came back into the room both her walk and voice had a steely determination that bespoke her German heritage. "Come on, everybody. We're going for a ride." I wondered if I should click my heels and say, "Heil, Grandma!" but prudence won out and I waited to see what would happen next.

"Wait just a minute." Mother wasn't about to embark on a mystery tour without knowing where we were going, especially since she was the only one in the family who drove except Dad, who was at work. "Where are we going?"

"Back to school to teach Judy what those so-called professionals should have taught her on the first day. Miss Brookshire will be at the Spring Avenue entrance in half an hour to let us in, so we can't dillydally. She won't wait forever."

When Grandma spoke in that tone of voice it was time to obey. She had made up her mind and would put up with no argument. Even Grandma Dent went with us out to the garage and we all piled into the faithful old 1949 Dodge for the ten-mile ride to school. It felt strange to be going to school in the evening. I hoped this wouldn't become a trend. Grandma Loehr was of the firm opinion that you shouldn't discuss your problems unless you were working on a solution. She had a little jingle that she recited for me every time she caught me putting off a hard job:

Whene'er a task is set for you,
Do not lament and rue it,
But persevere and see it through.
Begin at once and do it.

That verse echoed and rattled around in my head almost all the time. I heard it when I woke up, I heard it when I went to sleep, I heard it when Grandma said it, and I heard it in my imagination, but most of all I heard it when I was hesitant, when I was afraid, and when I wanted to slack off, and that was just about always since I started school.

"I hope you people appreciate how much I'm going out of my way to do you a favor." Miss Brookshire sounded more querulous and grumpy than usual, if that was possible. "I'm not being paid for coming back here after hours. I hope this practice session pays off. I don't want any more wet pants in my class. Remember, if you open the door, you can get out but you can't get back in."

Miss Brookshire left and we began a grueling, two-hour practice. First we worked on finding the bathroom, counting five doors on the right, starting with the first door to the kindergarten room. Mother showed me the large raised print letters on the door that said "women." I was able to make out the letters because I had three-dimensional alphabet blocks at home. There was no noise in the hall, no pushing and shoving, so finding the bathroom was fairly easy, but we were always supposed to walk on the right side of the hall. I was fine as long as I approached the bathroom from the kindergarten room, but I could not find it from the dining room, the offices, or anywhere that required me to find the bathroom door on my left. I either had to follow the wall on my left, strictly forbidden and guaranteed to get me yelled at and crashed into, or not find the place at all. What I could not do then, and cannot do now, was find a landmark directly across from where I wanted to be, turn my back to it, walk straight across, and find my target.

After an hour of hall practice, we entered the bathroom and worked on finding a stall. This was always problematic because in real life you never knew which stalls were vacant. All I ever learned to do was flap my hand around in the general direction of where I thought the stalls were. When I felt a door hanging open I made a grab for it and if I was lucky and no one pushed in ahead of me that was my stall. Grandma Dent advised me to ask God to help me find my way. Sometimes He helped, sometimes He didn't. The results seemed completely random to me, although I never told Grandma that.

Now came the tough part, locking and unlocking the stall door. "This lock is a hook and eye," explained Mother. "Miss Brookshire didn't mean she was going to stick a fishhook in your eye. She meant you have to take this hook and put it in that hole."

"These eyes can't see. They don't have eyeballs. I have eyeballs, but I can't see either. Are these special eyes they use at the school for the blind?"

"It's a different kind of eye, Honey," said Grandma Dent. "It's called a homonym, two words that are pronounced the same but have different meanings. Sometimes the words are not spelled the same, but these eyes are both e-y-e-s. I guess technically they are not homonyms, but you get the idea that the eye on the stall is not the same as the eyes in your head. Tuffy wags his tail. I tell you a tale, a story, at night to help you go to sleep."

Grandma had long since discovered that I was not confused by detailed explanations like this. I found them reassuring. They made me feel anchored in a way I didn't often feel. "I wish you could tell me a tale now, Grandma. I feel like I'm about ready to go to sleep."

"Let's not get off the subject, folks." Grandma Loehr was always the practical member of the family. "Back to the matter at hand. Do as your mother says, Judy. Put the hook in the hole."

I worked hard trying to put the hook in the hole. The door was like a living thing, swinging away from me just as I was about to capture it.

"Here, let me show you something." Grandma Dent whipped off her blouse and undid her bra. "This is my bra. It has hooks and eyes, too, only much smaller. It works the same way as this door."

I practiced with the bra for a while and eventually figured out the concept. The bra did not escape from me the way the hanging door did.

"Now try the stall door." Grandma Loehr was determined to keep us on track.

While Grandma Dent put her clothes back on, I worked with the stall door. Lo and behold, it locked and unlocked.

"At last we can all go home," sighed Mother.

"See what happens when you keep trying?" Grandma Loehr pointed out.

I wasn't aware that I had ever stopped trying. Before Mother and the grandmas came to help me, I didn't have a clue about any of this. I hoped I could remember it when the room was crowded and noisy.

"Let's stop at the drugstore on the way home and have a malt," suggested Grandma Dent. "We've all worked hard and this calls for a celebration."

"It's late," said Mother. "We have to go straight home. No story tonight, Judy. You have to go right to bed. Tonight is a school night."

Don't remind me, I thought. All at once the day was too much. The humiliation of wetting my pants and being chastised by Miss Brookshire in front of the whole class. Coming back to school in the evening for hours of practice. No ice cream, no story. I had worked hard and endured some horrible experiences. I wanted at least to be hugged and told I had done a good job. I pitched a fit, screaming and crying all the way home. It did no good. I had to go straight to bed and get up the next morning as if nothing had happened.

A few days later I was in the library, hiding to recover from the latest awfulness of the day. Miss Trahan, who doubled as librarian and Spanish teacher, was talking to her class of high school students. They were in the midst of a digression, and they were definitely not speaking Spanish. "Some students are so helpless when they come here that they haven't been toilet trained."

"Ooh, how disgusting!" said one girl.

The boys came out with some of the kind of gross bodily sound effects at which adolescent males are such experts.

Was Miss Trahan talking about me? I wanted to drop dead right there in the stacks. Then I wanted to run right up to their table, face down these jeering goons, and say, "You guys don't understand anything. I was toilet trained since my first birthday. It's not a toilet training problem. It's an orientation and mobility problem. As for toilet training, you guys are going to need it, because you sure are full of it."

Of course I didn't say any of that. I got out of there and let those folks enjoy feeling superior. I was almost in tears, but what else was new?

The words "toilet training" brought back one of my earliest recollections, a memory I've never told anyone. I remember sitting for hours on something hard and cold. Mother called it the "potty chair." As I found out later, the grown-up potty was harder and colder. Whenever Mother got caught up on the housework, she would grab me and put me on the potty chair. "But I don't have to go!" I would wail.

"Go anyway," Mother commanded. "And you're going to sit there until you do."

I sat and sat until I felt as if the potty chair were surgically attached to my rear end. I had marks on my skin made by the chair. If I had an accident Mother would yell and spank me in rhythm. Whack! Whack! Whack! Whack! "What did you do?" I learned quickly.

Years later, when I was a senior in college, I had to go to Kansas City to be interviewed for a Woodrow Wilson fellowship. After my interview, my parents and I were having dinner and cocktails with Dad's friend Bob Howard, the publicity director for an airline, and his wife Margaret. "You must be really proud of Judy," said Mrs. Howard.

"Oh, we are." Mother was effervescent. "Judy is so smart. I didn't have to change a diaper after her first birthday."

Nervous giggles went around the table. I hoped Mother had had too many glasses of chablis. The alternative was unthinkable. This time I did not hold back the snide remark that popped into my mind. "Mother, Mrs. Howard doesn't care when I was toilet trained as a baby. She only cares that I'm toilet trained now." Everybody laughed except Mother, and the moment passed.

The bathroom remains a lifelong problem. Away from home, no matter what I'm doing, in the back of mind lurks the knowledge that I will eventually need to find a bathroom. When I spend the night at someone else's house, I worry that I may not be able to find the bathroom in the middle of the night. The first time I come to visit a new person they usually take me on a tour, placing my hand on nearly everything in the house and then expect me to remember it all with perfect accuracy. They often help by telling me a story of another blind person they know who found their way, not just around the house, but around the city after being told once. This overload of information sends me into a state of brain freeze. The story terrifies and pressures me; the house tour makes my mind swirl as if scrambled by an eggbeater. I quiver with the certainty that my new friend will dump me as soon as they find out I don't have the magic powers of the person in their story. The more awestruck my hosts are by some blind person's accomplishments, the sooner I know I will fall off the inspiration wagon. I have a friend, one of the most accomplished and successful blind persons I know, who confided to me that fear of not being able to find the bathroom in a strange place is so onerous to him that when he spends the night in an unfamiliar place, he takes an empty hot water bottle along in case he has trouble finding the bathroom during the night. When I go out I do my best to observe the three-hour rule. I don't have anything to drink for three hours before leaving home. When I eat out I keep liquids to a minimum. That way I am less likely to need a bathroom.

And finding the bathroom is only half the problem. I have had many experiences in my life, but none to equal feeling around a public restroom. Some are clean, some, the less said, the better. All have the potential for putting my hands in places and on substances where my hands don't want to be. Find the stall. Find the toilet paper, probably the hardest of these tasks. Standardized bathrooms would be at least as much help as braille signs on the doors. Uncle Martin used to tell a joke about a man who couldn't find the toilet paper. He searched his pockets. No tissues. Finally in desperation he tapped on the next stall and said, "Hey, Buddy, do you have change for a twenty-dollar bill?" It can be almost that bad.

Find the flusher. Find the sink. Find the soap. Find the paper towels. Find the trash can. Find the door. You get the idea.

Bathroom technology presents its own set of problems. You never know what gadgets you will encounter. I call it state-of-the-art because figuring it out is more art than science. There are two new kinds of flusher. One is a button to press. The other is weight-sensitive. When you stand up it flushes. These can be frustrating when you are looking for a lever. Most maddening of all is the motion-sensitive sink. The water runs only when the infrared beam sees a hand. The hand almost has to be touching the disgusting inside of the sink. One second you have water, the next your soapy hands are waving in thin air. Apparently there is a light you have to follow because sighted people don't seem to have trouble with this contraption. Then comes the electric hand drier, which may be useful if you drop your cell phone in water. You hold your hands in front of it, hear a noise like a rocket taking off for the moon, then vigorously rub and wave your hands through a weak stream of warm air until the machine turns off, and you wipe your wet hands on your clothes.

I wish I had a friendly medium with me each time I have to explore a new bathroom. I would ask him or her to call up Mother and the two grandmas to help me the way they did at the school for the blind.

Chapter 9

Reading the Bumpy Books (1952-54)

We sat up so straight in the uncomfortable seats in the auditorium of the Wilson School for the Blind that it felt like we had iron rods down our backs. Today was the first day of my second year of school. I quietly thanked God that today I would leave wicked Miss Brookshire for kind Miss Taylor. At least, I had heard she was nice. Miss Taylor was one of very few totally blind teachers in the school. I expected a kind of solidarity with her that I never felt with crabby, sighted Miss Brookshire. Why were sighted people so often crabby? Was it because things came more easily for them and they became impatient with our struggles? In any case, I couldn't wait for first grade and Miss Taylor. I wanted more than anything to learn to read, so that when I got to a good part in a book I wouldn't have to wait for one of my parents or grandmas to read it to me—not that I didn't like being read to; I just didn't want to wait until one of the grown-ups had time.

"Grandma," I had asked Grandma Dent way back last January when I started school, "when I go to school, will I learn to read?"

"Yes, Honey. Reading was more fun for me than anything else I learned in school. Grandpa gave me lots of books. One year for Christmas he gave me the complete works of Milton, which he inscribed, 'To Ida, sweet as apple cider, December 25, 1899. May you love these poems and essays as much as I have.' He gave me the complete works of Shakespeare that said, 'To my lovely lady, now and forever. "Love is not love that alters when it alteration finds."' Those books made me feel like royalty. I don't know if 'Ida, sweet as apple cider' came from the song or he thought of it himself, but it told me he loved me."

I was thrilled with the prospect of discovering all these poems and stories for myself. The big kids had said that first grade was where you learned to read. I never understood, even in the vaguest way, what those blocks with the nails in them had to do with reading. I diligently memorized "A, one, B one-two, C, one-four, D, one-four-five." It pleased Miss Brookshire, so I worked hard at it, but I thought it had something to do with arithmetic, not words. My cousin Janice, three years older than I, was learning her multiplication tables. I thought I was learning something like that. Even when I got up to "Z, one-three-five-six," I never made the connection.

"Now, pupils," Mrs. Hubbert intoned, "We are beginning another year of school. I expect you all to make progress toward our two goals, independence and education. Now it's time to follow your teachers to their classrooms and begin. I'll start with the smallest children first so they don't get restless and disturb the rest of us. We'll start with the kindergartners. When you hear your name, go with Miss Brookshire. I'll announce each class in alphabetical order by last name. Judy Dent, Gary Douglas, Richard Howard, …"

Oh, no! Dear God, please tell me I heard wrong.

"Come on, Judy. The class can't wait all day for you. I see you haven't improved during summer vacation. I won't have to worry about who will take my place when I retire. You'll still be in kindergarten."

"Are you saying I'll be a good teacher, Miss Brookshire?"

"Not if you plan on teaching by example. Now get going or we might as well forget class and go straight to lunch."

The prospect of another of those revolting lunches made me hurry, even if Miss Brookshire's words couldn't. Was this year really going to be just like the last, more of the same blocks, more working with construction paper, more circle games, more being yelled at? There must be some mistake. I resolved to straighten out this misunderstanding right away. I hung back until Miss Brookshire and her herd of infants had left me far behind. I prayed that Richard Howard, he of "son of a bitch" fame, or some new bad person, would distract Miss Brookshire until I could slip away. I listened hard for sounds that would tell me where to go. Bingo! God is good! I heard a typewriter. Where there was typing, the front desk and Mrs. Hubbert's office couldn't be far away. During summer vacation I had gone to a band concert in Kirkwood Park. The band had played a song called "The Typewriter" by Leroy Anderson. Tap tap tap tap tap tap ding! Tap tap tap tap tap tap ding! The same helpful sound was here now, guiding me inexorably into the monster's lair. I was scared silly, but I had to get to the bottom of this problem. Grandma had told me a story about a man named Beowulf who had killed a monster named Grendel. Then he went into an underwater cave and killed Grendel's mother, an even more evil monster than her son. I wondered if Beowulf had felt the way I did right now before entering the cave. The difference was that Beowulf had the strength of thirty men in one hand. I only had the strength of one little kid in my whole body, and here I was about to throw myself on the mercy of the redoubtable Mrs. Hubbert.

Grandpa had told me that Shakespeare had said, "Screw your courage to the sticking place." I wondered where the sticking place was. There was a lump in my chest the size of a basketball. That certainly wasn't it. Shakespeare wasn't here to offer me a wise saying. Grandpa had passed away last summer. I would have to forge ahead without courage.

I crept toward the sound of the typewriter, taking hesitant baby steps the way the teachers and housemothers were always telling us not to walk. This was not the time to fall down any stairs. I had to look brave and confident. I was investigating a story the way Dad had done during a time called "Prohibition," when he had to interview gangsters and bootleggers. He told us many stories about these adventures around the dinner table. Dad said the most important thing to remember was not to look like you were afraid. I didn't know what gangsters and bootleggers were, but they couldn't be any scarier than Mrs. Hubbert.

"Did you need something, Judy?" asked the secretary, whose name I knew then, but can't remember now. "You're supposed to be in class."

"I know, but this is urgent. I need to interview Mrs. Hubbert."

"Well, that's a first. People usually don't work on the school paper until seventh grade. Who sent you?"

I wished I had press credentials like Dad's. Whatever they were, they usually got him into places he wanted to go. I didn't have them, so I would have to talk my way in.

"No one sent me. I'm investigating this story independently." I tried to sound as grown-up as I could, to face down the enemy as fearlessly as Dad did. Maybe when Dad heard I had resolved this trouble all by myself, he would be proud of me and say, "You'd make a terrific reporter," instead of "Goddamn! Such an idiot!" Maybe he would be glad he hadn't put me in an institution. Better yet, maybe I wouldn't have to spend another year in Miss Brookshire's class.

"Mrs. Hubbert is still in assembly," the secretary's voice broke in on my thoughts. "You'll have to sit on one of those chairs in the lobby and wait. After all, you don't have an appointment. Mrs. Hubbert doesn't usually see students without the proper protocol."

What was protocol? How did you spell it? It sounded like it might start with p-r-o-t-o. "Proto" was the beginning or smallest of something. A prototype was the first model of a product. I didn't think that was it, though; the secretary did the typing, not Mrs. Hubbert. Did it have anything to do with protozoa? Thinking about bringing up this topic with Mrs. Hubbert made me feel like the smallest of bugs. There was another hurdle. Where was the lobby the secretary was talking about, and where were the chairs where I was supposed to wait? I wandered aimlessly, all the while feeling less and less convinced that this was a good idea. Soon I bumped into a large, imitation-leather-covered, overstuffed chair, which, instead of impaling me with sharp points like most inanimate objects I encountered, seemed to reach out to welcome me. I sank gratefully into its comforting arms, no longer caring about reporting on this story or interviewing Mrs. Hubbert.

"Well, I see a nap has replaced your urgent need to see me," said that dreaded voice with its distinct overtones of eye of newt and toe of frog. "You can't find anything else, but you managed to locate the best chair in the lobby."

"It was an accident," I barely whispered. "I just bumped into it."

"Well, come into the office and let's hear this big problem—that is, if Your Royal Highness can rise from the grand throne and proceed a few feet down the hall."

I followed Mrs. Hubbert down the hall to her office, bouncing off a few pieces of furniture along the way.

"How can I help you?" asked Mrs. Hubbert. "Better yet, how can I help you to help yourself?"

"I heard my name when you called the kindergarten class. I know all my letters and numbers. I can do two columns of addition and subtraction in my head. Why didn't I pass to first grade? When will I learn to read?"

"Are you ready to learn to read? Do you know your shapes? Can you use a knife, fork and spoon without slopping your food all over the place? Can you dress yourself independently? I don't have to ask you about your mobility. We both know the answer to that."

"Do I have to be an expert in all those things before I can learn to read? What if I never learn them?"

"Then you stay in kindergarten until you're 21 and have to leave school under state law."

My lower lip began to quiver, but I made a mighty effort to maintain composure. I remembered one task Miss Brookshire had given us that had completely stumped me. "Take these two triangles and make a square." Do what? Are you kidding me? I moved the uncooperative pieces of paper around. No matter what I did, triangles they began and triangles they remained—triangles upside down, triangles right side up, triangles on their sides. No matter which way I moved the triangles there were points sticking out. Not a square to be found anywhere. Apparently word traveled fast.

"Why are these skills so much more important than learning to read?"

"You will probably get a job folding dishcloths or making brooms at the Gateway for the Blind. Most blind people end up working at a sheltered shop. If you don't like that option, but you learn your skills, you may be able to come back here and teach."

"But what if I want to teach reading?"

"Then that's all the more incentive to learn your other skills. You can be the most learned person in the world, but if you can't do basic things for yourself, everybody will think you're a stupid blind person. No one will care about your lofty thoughts."

This was early September. I would not be six until mid-October, but already I knew I didn't, and maybe never would, have the skills they valued. If I was to get anywhere in life, I had to get out of this place. I thanked Mrs. Hubbert for seeing me, but couldn't resist a parting shot as I walked out the door. "Now I guess I'll go to Miss Brookshire's class and string those lousy beads."

"That attitude will never get you through kindergarten," Mrs. Hubbert admonished my back as I shuffled off down the hall, feeling for the ever-looming stairs. Eventually I got back to class and eventually that year ended, an exact copy of the first. To my delight, when next September came I was promoted to first grade. I guess St. Jude intervened and Mrs. Hubbert and Miss Brookshire decided I was hopeless—a good decision, as it turned out. I doubt if I would be able to pass kindergarten today. I have accomplished many things in my life, not the least of which I hope will be that this book will help to change the abuses and attitudes that held me back, but if you want to learn to use Tinker Toys or Legos, tie your shoes or zip your jacket, cut your meat or flip a pancake, please ask someone else.

Miss Taylor's class was worth the two-year wait. It was like going from prison to freedom. Mrs. Caine and most of the other unpleasant people were still in my life, but Miss Brookshire and her eagle-claw hands and mynah-bird voice were gone. Miss Taylor was young, not ancient, probably in her late twenties. She had a sweet soprano voice that reminded me of the opera singers Grandpa listened to on his 78 records. Miss Taylor never grabbed us and yanked us into awkward positions. She never made us play games in a circle. We had recess, one of my least favorite parts of the day, and a 45-minute class called "handwork," which I barely managed to pass, but those were the only remnants of kindergarten.

My favorite subject was writing. My older cousin Janice had shown me something she was learning called "Palmer penmanship," in which you took a pencil and drew big circles on a piece of paper. Later, Janice said, she would learn something called "cursive writing," but none of it was anything like what we were learning. Another thing I noticed was that when I practiced the exercises Janice showed me, the paper was completely blank, just like the smooth books I wanted to read. When I felt Janice's paper it was blank, too. I had heard that different schools had different teaching methods; I supposed that the methods used in Janice's and my schools were different and sooner or later we would all be able to read the smooth books. I worked hard, hoping to reach that point any day.

We each had a long board with holes into which we put small nails in assigned positions. The holes in the board were in groups of six, called "cells." Each cell had three holes, called "dots," on the left and three on the right. Actually the dots were the nailheads that stuck up when you put the nails into the holes. Each group of dots represented a written character. Click, went my mind as I slipped a nail into my pegboard. That's what those blocks with nails in them were about. That's why we memorized "A, one; B, one-two; C, one-four." My fingers scrambled to test my new discovery. Janice had learned to write her name years ago, but I still hadn't learned to write mine. I picked up a nail. First dot two, then four, then five—J. One-three-six, U. One-four-five, D. One-three-four-five-six, Y. That was a hard one. Then I went through D E N T in the same way.

"Miss Taylor!" I called out, forgetting the rules about being quiet in class. "I can write my name!"

"That's great, Judy." Miss Taylor came over to my desk and slid her fingers across my pegboard. Miss Taylor read braille with her fingers the way I did. That gave me a warm, close feeling. Sighted people who could read braille—and not many could—did so with their eyes, the way they read print. I've always heard that reading braille visually is bad for your eyes, but I've never met a sighted person yet who could, or would even try, to read braille with fingers. I was eager to know what Miss Taylor thought of my attempt to write my name.

"But you forgot the capital sign before the J and D."

"What's a capital sign?"

"Always put a capital sign before the first letter of a name or sentence," Miss Taylor explained. "Capital letters are different in braille and print. Capital and small letters are shaped differently in print. In braille, there aren't enough dots to make different character combinations for small and capital letters so we make a capital letter by using dot six before the letter. Remember how in kindergarten you learned to spell your name "Capital J u d y capital D e n t?"

"I remember that, Miss Taylor, and I wondered what it meant, but I was afraid to ask."

"No one ever explained to you that there are two reading and writing systems, braille and print? Do you have books at home?"

"Yes."

"Have you touched them?"

"Yes."

"What did they feel like?"

"They felt like blank sheets of paper, but I'll learn to read them soon, won't I? Grandma said I would learn to read at school. That's true, isn't it?"

"We learn to read in a special way," said Miss Taylor.

A finger of apprehension crawled up my back. Every time I heard words like "special" and "exceptional" it was bad news; it meant that the person using those words was going to sugarcoat something bad. "Read in a special way how?" I hoped belatedly that Miss Taylor wouldn't use that fractured sentence as an excuse to change the subject to my faulty grammar.

"Here's a book you can take home over the weekend. See how much of it you can read."

"But Miss Taylor, this book has bumps on it. Grandma Dent's books are smooth."

"We have a special reading system called 'braille.' It's named after the boy in France who invented it. We read with our fingers. What's so wonderful about it is that if it's nighttime or the power goes off we can read just as well in the dark as we can in the light. Touch the book." Miss Taylor gently took my hand and placed it on some bumps on the cover. "These are braille dots, like the ones you make on your peg board, only a little smaller. Try to spell this word and sound it out."

"H-a-p-p-y." I thought about it. "Is it 'happy?'"

"Yes!" Miss Taylor exclaimed in obvious delight. "You've just read your first word. Isn't that a good word to start with? Aren't you happy you can read?"

I assured Miss Taylor I was happy, engaging in considerable sophistry, but not so much to deceive Miss Taylor as to deceive myself. Miss Taylor was so kind, so understanding, that being around her was a delight compared to the past year and a half. I wanted so much to please her that if she had said I could become a Major League baseball player, I would probably have agreed with her. Even with Miss Taylor's endorsement, however, my happiness was seriously watered down. Happy Days didn't feel like any of the books we had at home. It had stiff cardboard covers, rough and scratchy, not smooth and glossy like the Golden Books Mother bought at the grocery store checkout counter. It didn't have blank pages like the books my parents and grandmothers read to me. It was a thin book with dots on the pages. Under the first line of the first page, which said, Happy Days, was a line that said, The Alice and Jerry Series. Grandma Dent had read me two other books with a character named Alice, Alice in Wonderland and Alice through the Looking Glass. I was sure this Alice would be nothing like that Alice. This book was too small to be anything but a short story for babies—and what about those dots? Did they have something to do with the pegboards we used for writing? The dots were much smaller than the heads of the nails we used for the pegboards.

The next day we began reading Happy Days in class. It was so memorable that I can't recall a thing about it, except that it was a much bigger drag than I had expected. Alice was a boring, stupid little girl who always followed her brother's lead and didn't say a single word throughout the whole book. She seemed to take everything at face value, not at all like Alice in Wonderland, who always had questions, or like our neighbor, Alice Lewison, who had a delicious recipe for caramel cake with chocolate frosting, which she had made and brought over for my last birthday. I had one question, though, which the whole book failed to clear up. Alice and Jerry were the same age, just starting first grade. Had one of them flunked kindergarten like me? Were they twins? Was one or both of them adopted? Over the next couple of years we read the whole series, but none of the books ever cleared that up. I preferred the flunking kindergarten hypothesis, as it was more like my experience, but was it Alice or Jerry who flunked? Alice, probably, because she was kind of wimpy and lacked initiative—but I had initiative running out my ears and look where it got me. I supposed you had to have initiative in the right things, like Tinker Toys.

It was with trepidation rather than excitement that I obeyed Miss Taylor and took Happy Days home for the weekend. More than anything I wanted to please my parents and Grandma, to show them that now I could read to them, but I doubted things would go as well as I hoped. What grown-up would listen to a story as boring and stupid as Happy Days? I know I wouldn't have.

After dinner Friday it was time for the great demonstration. My heart pounded. My hands felt clammy. We were all seated around the kitchen table, Mother, Dad and Grandma waiting in suspense for the performance to begin. I opened my book … and couldn't read a word. Finally I remembered to start at the top left corner of the page as Miss Taylor had taught us. "Happy Days," I began. "The Alice and Jerry Series." The next line began with a word I recognized, "By." Then came two words about which I had no idea, which I learned later were the first and last names of the author. But what were these other big words? What were "Volume" and "Copyright"?

"Hurry up, read something," said Dad. "Don't just repeat what you've memorized." He was already getting impatient to retire to the living room with the sports page.

"I don't know these words," I said. "We didn't read them in class." I had completely forgotten that Miss Taylor had told us to skip the pages with letters in the upper right corner and start reading on the page that had nothing in that corner, which would be page 1. After that, the upper right corners would be numbered 3, 5, 7, 9 and 11. I believe that was as far as the book went. In any case, it was really short. I flipped the book over. Maybe I could read it the other way.

"You won't be able to read it that way," said Grandma Loehr. "You have it upside down."

Grandma was right. The book was harder to read upside down than it had been to read right side up. There weren't any words, big or small. It looked like a foreign language. I wondered if it would look like this in Chinese or Japanese.

"Do you know why Judy won't read to us?" Dad demanded in that tone he always used just before yelling at me. "Because she doesn't know how."

My lower lip trembled and I started to cry.

"Oh, cheese and crackers!" exclaimed Mother. "Let's not have a scene! Is the whole weekend going to be like this?"

"It's all right if you can't read tonight." Grandma tried to console me. "You'll do better tomorrow. Come and watch TV with me for a while. Then I'll read you a story before you go to bed."

"But I wanted to read to you."

"We'll be glad to listen when you think you can read to us," Dad said.

The next day was a little better. We sat around the table again while I read the whole book out loud, pausing occasionally to ask about a word. I knew I was reading mechanically, not putting any life into these otherwise lifeless characters. I would quote part of it, but I can't

JUDITH ANNE DENT, PH.D.

remember a word. Anyone of a certain age, who has suffered through beginning readers like Alice and Jerry, Dick and Jane, or Faith and Freedom (the equivalent books for Catholic school students, whose main characters were David and Anne), knows what I'm talking about. I've heard of some unlikely names for towns—Harriet, Arkansas; Fishtail, Montana; Looking Glass, Oregon—but who would live in a town called Friendly Village? It would take several lifetimes to live up to those standards.

"You did fine for the first time," said Grandma, evidently not realizing what a back-handed compliment that was. I felt like I was a balloon and someone had just stuck a fork into me.

"Let's play cards," said Dad.

"Let's have some ice cream," said Mother, both at the same time.

"I want to try another book," I insisted. "I want to try one of the books on my shelf."

"But those are a different kind of books," said Grandma in that sad, holding-the-tears-back voice that had become all too familiar.

"I don't want to read this stupid book!" I exclaimed. "I want to read real books. This one doesn't make any sense. It doesn't even have a good story."

"Everybody has to start with easy books." Grandma was patient and reasonable. "This is only your first one. Mother and Dad had to start with easy books. So did I. Soon you'll be able to read books with better stories when you know more words."

I knew lots of words now. I knew all the words in Heidi, The Wizard of Oz, and even some words from Shakespeare, the Bible, and Greek mythology. I slipped off to my room to perform one last experiment, a final test that would confirm or disprove my suspicion that this wasn't about how many words I knew or how many books I read; this was about what every bad thing in my life, every unworthiness, every inadequacy was always about, sight. I had to be alone to find out for myself. I closed the door and grabbed a book at random off the shelf. How many times, when someone was reading to me, did they have to stop at a breathlessly exciting place! How desperate I had been to read for myself and find out what happened next! Sometimes I would hold the book in my hands, willing myself to know what it said, but the pages were always blank, completely smooth, the way it felt to walk on new snow, when you couldn't tell pavement from grass.

My conversation with Grandma Dent about reading came rushing back to me. It was one of my last talks with her before she passed on. All the time I was slogging through a year and a half of kindergarten, all the time I struggled with blocks and Tinker Toys and triangles that would not make a square, I persevered because someday I would learn to figure out what was on those smooth, blank pages. I would learn to read. Grandma had said so, and Grandma would never lie to me.

I sat in my chair and carefully opened the book. I touched each page, remembering to move from top left to lower right. Nothing. Smoothness. Blankness. I slid the book back on the shelf. I wouldn't be needing it, didn't even know which book it was.

Screams poured out of my body, long, rolling shrieks as if a water main had broken inside me. I lay on the floor and kicked and banged my fists and head. I screamed so loud I scared myself. I felt as if I were floating above myself, watching myself the way we had watched a documentary on television about howler monkeys.

"What on earth is going on here?" Mother's voice was in the doorway.

"I'm never going to learn to read!" I yelled. "Those bumpy books aren't real books!"

"Let's go in the living room." That voice was Dad's. "She'll stop when she gets tired of screaming."

They walked away. Soon I heard the television. I continued to scream. This was the saddest, the most disappointed I had ever been. I would always have to depend on people to read to me. I had to go to that horrible school every day for no reason. I screamed till I got a sore throat. I screamed till I threw up. I screamed till I made myself ill and missed three days of school.

I couldn't read my parents' books; my parents couldn't read my book. Miss Taylor could read the bumpy books, but could she read the smooth ones? It was all too confusing for me.

Gradually I learned to read more words and more books in the bumpy system Miss Taylor had called "braille." The bumps were called "dots", but there was always that nagging awareness that I would never be able to walk into a bookstore or public library and browse like a sighted person. If someone was reading to me and had to stop, I could never pick up that same book myself and continue reading. This knowledge became increasingly important as I grew older.

I hasten to add, however, that I appreciate braille. It took a long time for me to learn the skills to read books that were more fun and challenging than Happy Days, but once I started on library books, I really took off. The library books did not come from the local public library. They came from the library at the Wilson School for the Blind. Later I was able to borrow more advanced books from the Wolfner Library, the Missouri branch of the National Library Service for the Blind and Physically Handicapped, part of the Library of Congress. There are many of these libraries across the country that send books through the mail to anyone who qualifies. There were many more braille books when I started reading than there are now. Now the libraries send out mostly digital audiobooks.

My first braille library book was almost as bad as Happy Days. It was called Surprise for Davy. It was only four double-spaced braille pages. It began, "Davy wasn't three any more. He was four—one, two, three, four." The end was just like the beginning, exactly the same words. Between those sentences his mother throws a party for Davy, including several neighborhood children. The book was too short for conflict. Davy likes all his presents (we never learn what they are). Everyone has cake and ice cream; no one throws a tantrum. The one interesting event in the story is that Davy's mother serves Jell-O in molds shaped like ducks and rabbits. I read the book at home and sent my poor mother on a wild goose chase, looking in every kitchen store in St. Louis for Jell-O molds in the shape of ducks and rabbits. She never found them and I've never seen any in almost sixty years, but Mother did find a cookie cutter shaped like a rabbit, which she used at Easter.

I have read thousands of books since Surprise for Davy, some good, some less so. If I had my choice I'd read everything in braille. Reading braille has made me a good speller; it has helped me understand sentence structure. In fact, I don't know how blind people who use only audio learn to write. I love my husband dearly and he has a brilliant mind in many respects, but he writes like a third grader, and about his spelling, the less said, the better. He learned a modicum of braille in grade school, but never learned to read fluently and did not learn to write at all. He still does not have an efficient way to take down information; he uses audio cassettes, then has a hard time retrieving the information later. He speaks beautifully, but when he has to write, his intellect is trapped inside his head. I know it's fashionable among blindness professionals, and especially blind people who don't know braille, to say it is difficult and unnecessary to teach braille to newly blinded adults; some even say that blind children don't need it, but of all the subjects I was taught in school, braille has helped me the most.

Now with digital books, braille is more accessible than ever. I am writing this book on a digital braille notetaker. I also use it to read books and magazines from WebBraille. I remember the old days when I used a manual typewriter. It gave the phrase "written in stone" a whole new meaning. I had to get everything perfect the first time. Many times I cried in frustration because I made a mistake near the bottom of a page and had to start over. I use braille every day for both reading and writing and can't imagine being without it. Audiobooks are wonderful for study and recreation, and there are many more of them than there are braille books, but, all things being equal, I'd choose braille any time.

During high school I taught my mother to transcribe braille. She worked for hours every day to keep up with me, an impossible task even with the help of audiobooks and a few other braille transcribers. Throughout my high school, college, and graduate school years there were hundreds of nights when I was in my room studying, Dad was at his desk recording a book on tape, and Mother was at the kitchen table thumping away at the trusty old Perkins brailler, a kind of typewriter that produces braille. It has a keyboard with seven keys that represent the six dots of the braille cell and the spacebar. All the characters are made from these seven keys. I am using this kind of keyboard to write this book, although I can also touch type on a qwerty keyboard, the kind sighted people use. My mother had to learn the entire braille system, including many characters in other languages. So does everyone else who transcribes braille.

Literary braille is the most common, but there is a computer braille code, the Nemeth code for mathematics, braille music, arcane symbols for chemistry and physics, and whole separate codes for all major languages. Mother didn't know all these codes and neither do I, but she did a yeoman job, especially considering she had only an eighth grade education. The three of us worked far into the night, sometimes until two or three a.m.

The battle of the books went on for 25 years with hardly any letup. In April we had to start getting ready for September. This struggle still runs in the background of my life, a program that never closes. From time to time my husband Blair has to pop a book in the scanner for me when it isn't available any other way. Blair has been legally blind from birth, so we hope there will be no missing pages or other weirdness when it comes out. So the bumpy books maintain a fragile coexistence with the smooth books (otherwise called "print"), the digital books, the audiobooks, and the occasional help of a live, sighted, human reader. The work of reading never ends, but neither does the joy.

Chapter 10

An Inadequate Language for Swearing (1954-55)

Dalilah and the Cussin' Club

Whack! Whack! Whack! The noise resounded through the dorm, echoing down the long line of beds. Whack! Whack! It had a hollow sound like Uncle Martin's air rifle. I knew as surely as if I could see that Dalilah was lying face down on the bed while Miss MacGrauth beat her with a paddle. I cowered in bed, covers pulled up tight. Thank goodness I hadn't been talking when Miss MacGrauth had sneaked in on night patrol. I wasn't sitting on the bed, eating a candy bar, deep in conversation when the you-know-what hit the fan.

"Dalilah, what are you doing out of bed? It's eleven o'clock at night. And you know you're not supposed to be eating."

"Get lost, you old hag. Leave me alone," said Dalilah around a king-sized mouthful of Milky Way and, from the sound of it, shoving as much more as she could into her mouth before Miss MacGrauth could snatch it away. "Get your own, you lousy thief!"

"What did you just call me?"

"You heard me, you stupid old bag."

Slap! I knew, because the sound was the same as when it happened to me, that Dalilah had just taken a vicious blow to the face and been sent sprawling forward onto the bed. Miss MacGrauth knew exactly what she was doing. Dalilah's small, bony backside was exposed and vulnerable. Whack! Whack! Was the paddle a permanent appendage? Did Miss MacGrauth wear it the way an amputee wore an artificial limb? She wielded it with skill and precision, not like the benign, watered-down evil of Captain Hook's artificial hand. Miss MacGrauth's paddle was the real deal. If you could imagine a Palestrina motet for screaming child and contrapuntal percussion, that was this sound. Whack! Whack! Whack! Whack! "Old Lady MacGrauth can't hurt me! Old Lady MacGrauth can't hurt me!" Dalilah chanted in perfect rhythm with the beating. No cries of pain, no tears, no begging for mercy.

Go, Dalilah! Silently I rooted her on. Stand up to her. Don't let the old bat get you down.

Miss MacGrauth did not get Dalilah down. She beat Dalilah until her arm became exhausted, but Dalilah kept chanting, "Old Lady MacGrauth can't hurt me! Old Lady MacGrauth can't hurt me!" In the end it was Miss MacGrauth who gave up, snarling under her breath as she walked away. Dalilah never mentioned this or any other time when she was beaten or reprimanded. She went on with life, went on taking no guff. If Dalilah had been able to give name, rank and serial number she probably would have used them in her resistance instead of screaming and cursing, but she retaliated in the only way she knew. Dalilah was a smart girl who had learned to fight authority. She did not understand the social conventions that enabled survival in a residential school environment.

Years later when I read Caesar's Gallic Wars in Latin class, I read about Vercingetorix, a brave tribal chieftain who had resisted Caesar right to the end. He was never vanquished, even though paraded through the streets of Rome in chains and later executed. When I read about Vercingetorix, I remembered Dalilah.

There were lots of unusual children in our school, but Dalilah was special even among us "special" children. In those days we were called "exceptional." There was a Council for Exceptional Children whose meetings Mother and most teachers at the school attended. Instead of exceptional children, its members were unexceptional grown-ups who spent their time dithering about how to handle us. Mostly that meant making sure we sat still in class and didn't bother anyone. When I first heard the term "exceptional child" I was thrilled. How cool it was to be an exceptional child—exceptionally brilliant, exceptionally beautiful, exceptionally talented. It was a crushing letdown to learn it didn't mean any of those things. It meant different. It meant the kind of person the "normal" kids—the kids in the neighborhood who went to schools with short, normal names like Tillman, Robinson, St. Peter's and Mary Queen of Peace—wouldn't be caught dead hanging out with. The stuck-up rich kids went to expensive private schools like Priory, Mary Institute, and Principia. But no matter what kind of school they went to, rich or poor, religious or secular, public or private, the other kids had one thing in common: they didn't want a thing to do with us.

Among us exceptional children, Dalilah was the most exceptional of all. If you could have rolled Johnny Cash and Merle Haggard into one defiant female voice, that voice would have been Dalilah's. She was a mythic figure with the stature of Robin Hood, Jesse James or Billy the Kid. As an icon for the blind, Helen Keller was baby-doll passive compared with Dalilah. Dalilah was the model for whom the phrase "wild child" had to be coined. She was in my class and all of us, including the boys, were in awe of her. Authority was always, unequivocally, Dalilah's enemy. No one from Mr. Johnson, the superintendent, right down to the lowliest student held any terror for Dalilah. Respect wasn't given; it had to be earned. As for trust, what was that?

Dalilah's father owned a bar. Her mother was either dead or absent. Dalilah was visually impaired and her legs were deformed. She walked with a kind of roll, hop, bounce. Until she came to the school, Dalilah's father kept her in the bar during business hours. They lived together, alone, and they looked out for each other with animal fierceness. She sat on the bar all evening while the customers came and went. Many of them were men who had progressed well past too much to drink. They poked, prodded, touched and manhandled Dalilah in ways she didn't like. When Dalilah didn't like something people heard about it. She learned to scream, kick, bite and scratch when things didn't go her way, which they often did not. Bullies, drunks, and others who enjoyed power liked to pick on Dalilah. She gave as good as she got, both physically and verbally. She expected attacks from every side, and if you crossed her, you were in trouble. During the year she was in my class I got many bites and scratches, some intentional, most by accident.

Almost everything I ever learned about "bad language" I learned from Dalilah. I was always in trouble for talking, accused of being a smart aleck long before I knew what a smart aleck was. Dalilah was never sarcastic or snide. She never said one thing while intending another. She came right out and said what she had to say. She had an extensive vocabulary of profanity. Dalilah knew every cussword in English and many in foreign languages. There was a rumor that Mr. Johnson had called her into his office to chew her out, and Dalilah had cussed him out for half an hour without repeating a word. When the teachers and housemothers yelled and the rest of us quivered and tried to obey, Dalilah let them have it in language that would have embarrassed my uncles, who were World War II veterans.

Most of Dalilah's words I had never heard before and had no idea what they meant. After one of her frequent run-ins with Mr. Johnson—she was too violent and brash for Mrs. Hubbert, who after all was only the principal—Dalilah sat on one of the hard, wooden chairs in the dorm mumbling to herself, "Mr. Johnson is a cocksucker." She often used that name for anyone who had offended her. I wondered why "cocksucker" was such a bad word. Wasn't a sucker a good thing? Usually it meant lollipop. Uncle Martin had taught me the first joke I had ever learned.

First speaker: "Have you been to the candy parade?"

Second speaker: "No."

First speaker: "I thought there was a sucker missing."

Dad liked W. C. Fields. One of Dad's favorite movies was You Can't Cheat an Honest Man. In it W. C. Fields played a con man named Larson E. Whipsnade who cheated people by convincing them they could get something for nothing. The victims were called suckers. Dad said suckers were stupid people who fell for scams. Maybe Dalilah was saying that the people yelling at us were stupid. I couldn't disagree with that. I usually got along well with Dalilah. We often played together, but I didn't want to ask her a question as sensitive as that. I never knew when she would erupt into an explosion of biting and scratching.

I wondered whom I could ask. The teachers got so upset if you said "darn" or "heck" that they would start screaming louder than Dalilah. Grandma Loehr was practical and down-to-earth, but she never cussed. Dad believed strongly that only men should be able to cuss. He saved most of his cussing for when Uncle Martin and Dad's other male friends came over and Dad got a bad hand at poker. That left Mother. Grandma Dent had read me a story called "The Nun's Priest's Tale" about a rooster who had bad dreams. He was called a cock. Some stores, like Woolworth's and Walgreens, sold big lollipops with pictures on them. They were called "all-day suckers." Maybe a cocksucker was a big lollipop with a picture of a rooster on it, but why was it a bad word? I decided to ask Mother.

Mother was stirring a pot of something on the stove when I came into the kitchen. It didn't smell good, not a good sign. Maybe I would need some candy if this concoction were intended for tonight's supper. "Mother, can I have a cocksucker?"

"What?" The spoon rattled hard against the pot. "What did you just say?"

Something was going wrong again. "Can I have a cocksucker?" I repeated, determined to see this ordeal through to the end.

"Don't you ever, ever use that word in this house again, or anywhere else, for that matter. Who taught you that?"

"Dalilah says it when she's upset with—" I almost said "the cocksuckers" but caught myself just in time. "Dalilah says it when she's upset with people at school. She had another fight with Mr. Johnson today and when she came back to the dorm she called him that."

"Well, maybe Dalilah's family talks like that, but we most certainly do not."

"Then it isn't candy?"

"It definitely is not candy. It's a word you should never use under any circumstances. I should march you right into that bathroom and wash your mouth out with soap."

"What's for supper?" I hoped a change of subject would forestall the plan to wash my mouth out with soap.

"Tomato and rutabaga stew. Go and bother Grandma till I get it ready."

My stomach lurched. The prospect of boiled rutabagas was almost worse than soap.

I didn't find out the meaning of that word until I was researching a paper for abnormal psychology when I was in college. Shortly after that revelation I decided to join our PBS station,

Channel 9. One of the premiums was a pin in the shape of a large 9. They sent me two of them by mistake.

Mother exclaimed in delight, "Oh, that's great! You can wear one of them upside down and it will say 69." That was my graduation year.

"No, Mother, I can't do that." I took a world-weary, rather than outraged stance. I never did have the nerve to explain to Mother what 69 meant.

In my more innocent years on the school playground, Dalilah spoke of other things that Mother might not have understood. Generally I liked the playground. The swings and merry-go-round were my favorite pieces of playground equipment at school. The slides scared me, as did the climbing bars, but on the swings and merry-go-round you moved in a definite pattern. You didn't get hurt unless some bigger, stronger person pushed you off because they wanted your spot. More fun than riding the merry-go-round was pushing it. You could stand in one of the compartments, put your hands on the bar, run as fast as you could without getting lost, and really work up a head of steam—that is, unless there were too many heavy kids on it and they were yelling at you to go faster.

Dalilah liked the merry-go-round, too. She could see a little, but she had a deformed leg, which held her back when competing with others. Her nails and teeth helped her though, as did another strategy she devised for taking control of the merry-go-round. It was the Cussin' Club, of which Dalilah was president, or should I say, absolute monarch. There were no elections. Dalilah got to decide who could be a member and who got kicked out. To stay eligible you had to cuss at recess, cuss in the dorm, and especially cuss in front of the grown-ups. They even had a special song:

Riggedy raggedy russ.
You're not allowed to cuss.
We never discuss or get in a fuss.
Nobody can cuss but us.

If a non-member tried to ride the merry-go-round, they were pushed off and their head rubbed in the gravel.

If you enjoyed the merry-go-round, it behooved you to be a member. Dalilah held auditions in which you had to prove your mettle as a proficient cusser. I wanted to ride the merry-go-round more than anything. It was the only thing besides the swings I liked at recess. The tunnel scared and disoriented me. The slide was dangerous because big boys would get on behind you, whiz down very fast and knock you off. The swings were fun, but everyone fought over them. The merry-go-round was fun and safe, unless of course you got pushed off. So I resolved to earn my way into the Cussin' Club. This would not be as easy as it sounded. We just didn't cuss at our house, except when Mother and Dad's friends came over for card club, when they played five-card draw, seven-card stud, and several exotic poker games, two of which were seven twenty-seven and follow the queen, in which queens were wild and so was the next card after the queen, which stayed wild until the next queen came up. "Damn," said Dad, "a lousy pair of deuces."

"Hell, George, you think that's bad. I haven't had anything above a five all night," Uncle Martin would moan as he threw down his cards in disgust. You can see that Dalilah had them beat by a mile.

In addition to all this, I had the forces of God and my conscience working against me. Dalilah didn't seem to bother with such conflicts. I was brought up to believe that language was important. Your words spoke volumes about you and often determined whether you were hired for a job or chosen for a friend. It felt wrong to use bad words in front of the grown-ups and make them angrier with me than they already were. I attended a class on Sunday mornings after Mass called "instructions." In it a tough, determined nun tried to instill as much Church doctrine as she could into us little public school heathens during her one hour a week. Sister often talked about the "Divine Praises." They were short statements like "Blessed be God" and "Blessed be His Holy Name" which we were supposed to say quietly to ourselves every time we heard someone swear. Swearing, she told us, was an offense against God. The Divine Praises would counteract the bad words. When the uncles came over for card club I felt as if I were in an echo chamber. The vigilance required was exhausting. "Hell, these are the worst cards I've had all night." "Blessed be God." "Shit, George, yours couldn't be any worse than mine. Christ, I've never seen anything like it." "Blessed be God. Blessed be His Holy Name." I couldn't repeat the Divine Praises fast enough. Funny, I never thought about that when I wanted to ride the merry-go-round.

After much deliberation, I came up with what I thought would be an acceptable compromise. I would tell a story. I remembered a story Grandma Loehr liked to tell, which she insisted was true. I practiced for hours like an actress going over her lines. I worked hard to get the timing just right. At last the day came when I would tell Dalilah my story. My social fate would be decided. I would either be a member of the Cussin' Club or I would be a reject.

I took a deep breath and began with my most theatrical delivery. "Grandma Loehr tells the story of a neighbor she used to have who had a dog and a parrot. The dog's name was Nell. Grandma didn't tell us the parrot's name but he was famous for his talking. The woman would say, 'Nell, go in the house. Nell, go in the house.' Soon the parrot learned to say, 'Nell, go in the house.' And here's the cool part: if the parrot told Nell to go in the house, and Nell didn't pay any attention, the parrot would say, 'Nell, go to hell. Nell, go to hell.'" I felt deliciously wicked and devilish. If Sister could only hear me now! I waited breathlessly for Dalilah's judgment. The whole playground seemed suspended, waiting for the big decision. No screaming, no yelling, no creaking of moving parts. Every stand-up comedian has hung frozen in this moment. Was my timing right? Had I spoken clearly enough? Was I funny?

Then Dalilah said, in a voice at once commanding and prissy, like some ancient queen pronouncing sentence on an unruly peasant, "Your grandma must not be very nice."

I could almost hear Dalilah looking down her nose. She was passing judgment, not just on me, but on my smart, practical, resourceful grandma. She was probably jealous that she didn't have a grandma who loved her as much as Grandma Loehr loved me. I held up my head and opened my eyes as wide as I could, trying to look down my nose at Dalilah the way she had at me. No one was fooled. I walked hesitantly back toward the school building, feeling my way as I went. So what if the girls didn't want to play with me? So what if they made fun of my language, my looks, my good grades, my mobility, my clumsiness, the music I liked? Someday I would be rich and famous. I would win the Nobel Prize in Literature and include in my acceptance speech the story of how I was blackballed by the Cussin' Club.

Dalilah lasted only one year at the school. She was too much for them, but they were never too much for her. She was smart and resilient, with a free-spirited, persistent attitude that would have taken her far if someone had helped her channel it. At the Wilson School for the Blind they liked molds. Everyone was expected to fit, down to the smallest detail. I did not fit for reasons that would not be diagnosed for years and are not clearly understood now. Neither Dalilah nor I fit the school's concept of the "good" blind person, but Dalilah had her molds, too. She had her expectations no less than the teachers and housemothers had theirs. I did not fit the mold of people Dalilah wanted for friends. She had an instinctive sense that the Cussin' Club was not where I belonged.

That bid for love and attention did not work for me, but there was another time, about a year later, when I felt more loved than I have before or since, not because I cussed, but because someone else did.

"Du bist eine dummkopt!"

The staff at the school for the blind liked to inflict a painful form of torture called "wrist rotation." It involves grabbing the victim's hand and twisting it backward so the heel of the hand and wrist stick out in front and the fingers dangle uselessly behind. In this position you are supposed to pick up tools and use them. Instructors in the blindness field say that many blind people have trouble with wrist rotation, yet teachers and parents try to force it on us anyway. Why any sane person would want to manipulate objects with their hands twisted backward in such a painful and unnatural way is beyond me, but there are some things about sighted people I will never understand. I have a theory about that, as I do about most things. It is that blind people need their fingers out in front of their hands to "see" what they are doing. It is disorienting to have an object between your fingers and what you are trying to do. Sighted people don't need their fingers as eyes; they can rotate their wrists without getting lost. Why anyone would want to is beyond me, but that's a judgment call. I only know that twisting my wrist in that unnatural way makes fiery pain shoot through my arm, up my shoulder and into my neck. I don't know why anyone would want that.

Dad had to go to New York for a newspaper editors' convention. He took Mother with him. I was supposed to stay at school. That evening at supper we had chili. I was dribbling along in my usual way, forty percent for my mouth, sixty percent for parts unknown. No matter how fast I moved, most of the chili fell off the end of the spoon before it reached my mouth. Miss Melba was off that day, and Miss MacGrauth, who could not hurt Dalilah, was supervising our table. She swooped down on me like a hawk.

"When are you going to learn to work with your wrist, you disgusting little slob?" We all paused, as if we had looked at Medusa and been turned to stone. In Miss MacGrauth's lexicon, "disgusting little slob" could have fit any of us. Only when the hard, viselike hand descended on my shoulder did I realize she meant me. "Put that spoon down. Let me show you for the millionth time how to hold it."

She clutched my wrist and yanked it into the mother of all wrist rotations. "Now put your spoon in that bowl and lift it to your mouth gracefully, without spilling any. I don't want to see one drop of that chili anywhere but in your mouth." I tried to lift a spoonful in that painful position. No matter how much my mind wanted to obey Miss MacGrauth, my hand adamantly refused. My wrist flipped back to normal and the chili went everywhere.

"You did that on purpose, you little devil!" Miss MacGrauth shrieked. "I am going to show you one last time and I don't expect any backtalk, verbal or silent."

Yank went my wrist again. Crack! For a moment I was suspended; my brain pulled back, unable to handle the horror. Then pain, terrible, shooting fire. My hand hung limp and useless. I could almost feel it swelling.

"If you breathe a word about this to anyone, I'll make this seem like a church fish fry. Shut up and don't say a word."

"What should I say happened, Miss MacGrauth?"

"Shut up. Let me do the talking."

Miss MacGrauth called the school nurse, told her an improbable tale about my stumbling and hitting my arm on the sharp corner of the table. I did not contradict her.

I sat in the infirmary for what seemed like hours until the nurse called Grandma Loehr, who was the next person on the list to call in an emergency after my parents. The nurse stomped into the room where I waited. "Your grandmother says she doesn't have a car, and by the time she gets here on buses and streetcars it will be too late for her to take you to the emergency room and back on public transportation, so I'll have to drive you myself. Hurry up. We don't have all day." She grabbed me by the bad arm and I began to scream. "Will you be quiet, you big baby?" She snagged my other arm and began to drag me. I was surprised the other arm didn't break.

On the way I thought about telling the doctor what really happened, but by the wise and cynical age of eight I knew that nobody believes blind people and nobody believes children, so I had a double whammy.

I shut up and let the school nurse do the talking. No one seemed to doubt her. When the doctor set my hand I began screaming again. An annoyed young woman told me to be brave and quiet so the doctor could concentrate. I thought several words that would have made Dalilah proud and made Sister intone a whole string of "Blessed be Gods." I couldn't stop crying and yelling, so a musclebound orderly rolled me over and someone stuck a needle in my butt. After that everything was a blur. I slept in the school infirmary that night and woke up with a heavy cast on my arm.

"Hurry up. Your grandmother is here to pick you up." The nurse saw I was having trouble getting dressed so she yanked and dragged me into my clothes, all the time exhorting me to move faster. Her voice was a ghoulish play-by-play in the background. "For crying out loud, can't you put on your socks with your left hand? Stop making those stupid faces. No need to be a drama queen. This is a school, not a soap opera. Look at your shoes. Your mother has to put elastic in them because you're too dumb to tie your own shoes."

The nurse dragged me to Mrs. Hubbert's office where Grandma Loehr was waiting. "You may take her home now, Mrs. Loehr," said Mrs. Hubbert.

"Just a minute." Grandma wasn't leaving without knowing what had happened. "I want to know exactly what went on."

"I've explained it all to you," said Mrs. Hubbert in a resigned, patient voice, as if explaining something difficult to a recalcitrant child. "Judy slipped in the dining room and hit her arm on the sharp corner of a table. Miss MacGrauth saw it all."

"I want to hear Judy's version. Is that the way it happened, Judy?"

I felt like a person about to jump out of a burning building. To go back was to be barbecued like a slab of ribs. To go forward was to risk a fall that would crush me like a bug. I took a deep breath. This was not the time to be afraid. My voice was so clear and firm that I surprised myself. "No, Grandma, that's not how it happened."

"What!" Mrs. Hubbert's voice cracked more than usual. "Remember, Judy, this is important. It's not one of your stories. You may imagine you're Harriet Beecher Stowe trying to change the world by making up stories about social injustice, but you're just little Judy Dent, so don't try to deceive us with more of your usual falsehoods. I remember when you made up those awful lies about Marjorie Lowell."

"I didn't make up lies then, Mrs. Hubbert, and I'm not making up lies now. I didn't slip in the dining room and I didn't bump my arm on the table. Miss MacGrauth was trying to make me rotate my wrist and she jerked it until it broke."

"What an imagination this child has, always blaming someone else for her own mistakes. Why on earth do you say those terrible things, Judy?"

"Because they're true. She did break my wrist. You never believe me, but I haven't lied about anything. Marjorie and Miss MacGrauth lie to you all the time, but you never question them. How can you believe those awful things, Mrs. Hubbert?"

"What are we going to do with her, Mrs. Loehr?" asked Mrs. Hubbert, trying the conspiratorial approach.

"Don't say any more, Judy," said Grandma in a tone that was unusually gentle and let me know she was not mad at me.

"Mrs. Hubbert, Judy does have a vivid imagination, but she knows the difference between a true event and a story. Her dad is a journalist and he's taught her that. I've never known Judy to lie."

"Well, then you may have a rude awakening."

I was as startled as Mrs. Hubbert when the place exploded. Grandma was proud of being an American citizen. It was important to her to speak English like a native, but she also kept up her German. She spoke both languages without an accent. Only under great stress did Grandma lapse into German. Evidently this was great stress. Grandma Loehr told off Mrs. Hubbert loudly and fluently in German, becoming more expressive and less grammatical as she wound up. "Du bist verricht! Du bist eine dummkopf!" She rolled on, using words she never used at home. I heard several "Gott verdammts" and "Gott in himmels," ending with a resounding "Was ist los mit du?" It should have been "Was ist los with dir," since mit takes the dative case, but Grandma wasn't splitting grammatical hairs. Probably it should also have been the formal "ihnen" instead of the familiar "du," but Grandma was used to yelling, "Was ist los mit du?" at me and sometimes at Mother. It sounded like its English translation, "What's the matter with you?"

"Mrs. Loehr, Mrs. Loehr, please calm down!" Mrs. Hubbert squeaked like a mouse caught in a trap. "There's no reason to be upset."

"Who do you think has a better reason?" Grandma was not finished. "I come here to pick up my granddaughter and find her with a cast on her arm and a story of abuse, and you ask me why I'm upset?"

"Apparently, Mrs. Loehr, Judy learned her disrespectful attitude from you. Never in all my years as an educator has anyone ever sworn at me in a language I don't understand. If you can't express yourself in the language of the country in which you live, you should have brought an interpreter."

"English," replied Grandma in that absolute-power voice she had used on me and no doubt on her four daughters for decades, "is an inadequate language for swearing. It is not sufficiently Teutonic."

I didn't know what "Teutonic" meant, but if it had anything to do with "two ton," Mrs. Hubbert was headed for two tons of trouble.

"Respect has to be earned. Have you people done anything to earn Judy's respect, or mine?"

"Mrs. Loehr, please don't talk to me like that in front of the child." Mrs. Hubbert was not only squeaking, but sulking.

"Her name is Judith Anne Dent, not 'the child.' Is there something you don't want her to hear? Have you done something you are ashamed of? The next time you hear from me it will be through my attorney, who is completely bilingual and does not have to swear to get his point across. He knows the rules of evidence in both English and German, so I would advise you to be careful how you treat these children or you could find yourself in the unemployment line. Let's go home, Judy. This conversation is over."

Grandma took my good hand and we marched out of Mrs. Hubbert's office and out the heavy Spring Avenue door like soldiers after a major victory. It wasn't a decisive or permanent victory. The abuse wound down to a dull rumble for a few weeks, but soon all was back to abnormal. Grandma sometimes played poker with Dad; her threat to sue the school and get Mrs. Hubbert fired was a spectacular bluff. She didn't know a lawyer, bilingual or otherwise. Dad didn't want to go after the school because, as he said, if we lost, the school faculty and staff would abuse me more than ever; if we won and the school was shut down, I wouldn't have a place to go to school. Dad felt trapped. He used all his influence to keep the incident out of the papers.

Even though nothing decisive came of this episode, it made me feel like a triumphant warrior returning from battle. I could slay any monster, solve any problem, overcome any adversity with love and truth on my side. The evening before, I had let Miss MacGrauth get away with lying about how I broke my arm. Today, with Grandma there to give my courage a boost, I had faced down Mrs. Hubbert and told the truth. Grandma had loved me and stood up for me. I would have bet every coin in my piggy bank that no one had ever put Mrs. Hubbert

124

in her place the way Grandma Loehr had. She would probably have been a better principal and a better person if more people had.

We stood at the bus stop and waited. It took two buses and a streetcar to get home from the Wilson School for the Blind. Between buses we stopped at a drugstore to pick up some aspirin for the pain in my arm. To kill time while we waited for the next bus, we sat at the soda fountain and I had a chocolate malt. Most drugstores had old-fashioned soda fountains then. They had high stools that were hard for small children to climb onto, but this challenge was nothing compared with the obstacle Grandma and I had just handled. The malt slid down my throat, cool, sweet, and smooth. Almost sixty years have passed, but every time I hear German spoken I taste cold, liquid chocolate and remember Grandma and how much we loved each other. This was the first and last time I had a chocolate malt for breakfast, and this is the turning point I come back to when things are intolerable: when blindness and autism and being misunderstood have me weak, discouraged, and about to give up in despair, I mentally hold up my head, take Grandma's hand, taste chocolate, smell bus exhaust, hear the ding-ding of the streetcar bell, and begin the long ride home.

Chapter 11

Stories, Pretend and True (1952-58)

Bob and I were alone in the kindergarten room; or, if we weren't alone, it seemed so to us. We sat on the floor in front of a large pile of blocks, seeing who could build the highest stack without the blocks falling. Our minds were uncluttered by visions of houses or towers. Height was our only objective. If some interfering adult had interrupted us to ask what we were doing, one of us would probably have said we were building skyscrapers, in the hope that this answer would get him or her off our backs so we could resume stacking. I started to pick up a block in a round shape I learned later was a cylinder. I thought it would be cool to place it on top as a centerpiece and try to stack smaller blocks around it.

Evidently Bob had his mind on that one too, because he asked, politely and grammatically, "May I have that one?"

I was stunned. Bob didn't just snatch the block out of my hand as any other kid would. He didn't yell, "I want that!" He "asked nicely," as the grown-ups would say.

"Sure," I said, and handed it over.

"Thanks," said Bob.

I knew I wanted him for a friend. Soon I became friends with his friend John and he became friends with my friend Betty. Ellen was friends with all of us. She had a little vision back then, but Ellen liked to play with the totally blind kids, maybe because she understood hard times. I don't ever recall hearing Ellen pick on anyone smaller or fatter or slower than she. Ellen wasn't a wuss, though. She could stand up for herself with a fervor and conviction that put me in awe. Once when we were in Mr. Gilbert's social studies class, he bawled her out for eating peanuts and hiding the shells in her desk. "I didn't do that, Mr. Gilbert," Ellen responded in a calm, clear voice. "This isn't my homeroom, I haven't put anything in this desk, and I never eat in class."

"We know you did it whether you admit it or not," stormed Mr. Gilbert. "We know you did it because we found the evidence."

Ellen didn't back down. "You can't convict someone on circumstantial evidence. I saw that on 'Perry Mason' on TV, and if Raymond Burr says you can't, you can't."

"Stupid way to learn the law. You just sit there for the rest of the period and think about it and maybe you'll change your story."

"You can make me sit here all day and I won't admit to something I didn't do. From now on you better watch who you accuse."

No more was ever said about the incident. Mr. Gilbert didn't apologize and neither did Ellen.

There were few students in our school. My second-year kindergarten class had ten members; first grade had nine. Beginning in second grade the sight savers, who could read large print, were separated from the braille students, although we had some classes together, so some of our classes were smaller than ever. We also had a small faculty and staff. That meant that for some classes and activities—gym, home economics, shop, band, chorus, Scouts—we worked with pupils up to two years ahead and two years behind us.

There were three Bettys in our age group. The oldest was Betty Sanders, sometimes called "Big Betty" because she was two years ahead of my class. She was, and probably still is, one of those "amazing" blind persons. Her mobility was so good she could probably have given homing pigeons lessons in her spare time. I heard she always looked like she came out of a bandbox. I'm not sure what a bandbox is, but if anyone ever looked like he or she came out of one, she did. She could type well over a hundred words a minute without an error. She could make a dress on the sewing machine before the rest of us could even thread the thing. She was such an expert in the kitchen that the teacher let her work independently whenever she wanted. It wouldn't take much suspension of disbelief to imagine that Betty Sanders taught Martha Stewart everything she knows. Betty was tops in academics and braille. After her college graduation she went to Ireland for a year to work on a master's thesis on Yeats. She had a beautiful, soaring, soprano voice that could belt out an aria as clear and strong as Beverly Sills. One Christmas program she sang the solo part in "Jesu Bambino." Her diction was so good you could understand every word in the back of the auditorium, and she didn't have a microphone, just lung power. I was so intimidated by her that I was almost afraid to be in the same room with her. Betty Sanders was nearly perfect; she had so many gifts, but she lacked the gift of compassion. Skills came so easily to her that she was critical and scornful toward dumb-bunnies like me who had trouble with most of what they called the "expanded core curriculum," that is, everything but the academic subjects. It was not until years later that I found out how lonely and isolated she felt.

The next Betty was Betty Smith, a sight saver who, although she was in our grade, did not travel in our social circle. She mostly hung out with the partially sighted girls, of whom there were a relatively large number in our age group, sometimes as many as nine or ten. The term "partially sighted" has fallen into disuse in favor of "legally blind" or "visually impaired." I think "partially sighted" better describes the girls I went to school with. Some of them were almost as sighted as sighted people. They were, as Dad used to say about some of his coworkers, "big frogs in little ponds." They had a brashness about them that most sighted people I've met lack. I didn't notice social segregation among partially sighted and totally blind boys, but the girls had this caste system down to a fine art. We didn't mingle much at recess.

The third Betty was Betty Schuchman, later Schultz, sometimes called "Little Betty" because she was still four in September when she started school and didn't turn five until December. She and I were the only totally blind students in our class, although Betty claimed to have light perception, a status symbol among blind people the way owning a Mercedes-Benz is among some sighted people. I never could tell whether Betty could see light or just imagined she could, but in the end it didn't make any difference to our friendship. Our friendship was sometimes a stormy one, a sad commentary on the brutal competition the school fostered among the students in general, and between Betty and me in particular. Betty could get around and work with her hands a little better than I; I could do academic subjects a little better than she. The school played these small differences to the hilt, blowing them out of all proportion until it was almost impossible for us to be friends, but most of the time we were friends anyway.

The housemothers would say, "Betty can't see a bit, but she can make her bed. It looks beautiful every morning. Judy can't even find her bed, and after she makes it, it looks like dogs and cats have been fighting in it."

Or a teacher would say, "Judy is such a good writer. Betty, why don't you write like that?"

Although Betty might tell you otherwise, I always felt I got the short end of the stick when these comparisons came up. I felt that everyone in school, especially the grown-ups, liked and respected Betty more than me. Shakespeare said, "Comparisons are odious," and they certainly were, and are, odious to me. They never motivated me to work harder. They made me resentful, and brought pain to what should have been a good friendship.

The Wilson School for the Blind is a residential school, based on the philosophy that if students live there all the time they will experience total immersion and eventual mastery of the skills they will need when they leave school. Most students stayed there throughout the year, only going home at Christmas, summer vacation, and sometimes Easter. During the first few years I was there we had school on Thanksgiving Day. Some students who lived within close driving distance of the school went home on weekends. My parents believed five was too young to leave home so I went home every night. For this I was ostracized by the students and ridiculed by the faculty.

Although the social rejection bothered me acutely, I wouldn't have given up my nights at home for anything. I knew my parents and grandmas loved me; that couldn't be said for anyone at school. I don't believe, for reasons that will become clear later, that any number of "skills" would have improved this situation, so I was eager to spend the evenings at home. I'm convinced my parents agreed with me, though they went to their graves without admitting it.

The students slept in long, narrow dormitories with each dorm divided into two rooms with ten or eleven beds to a room. Once when I had to spend the night because my parents had obligations elsewhere, Betty slept in one of the big rooms and I in the other. We had had a minor tiff during the day—at least I thought it was minor (and there were probably other disagreements we had that seemed small to Betty but huge to me). In this case Betty must have felt much more hurt by the problem than I had been.

As I was crawling into the hard, narrow bed for the night, I heard and felt a sound like a barrage of giant hailstones. It was a kind of call and response, a shrill, throbbing noise that combined the intensity of religious ritual with the feral sound of jungle animals destroying their prey. These girls were not speaking in tongues, however. The tongue was English, I could understand every syllable, and the words were just for me.

"Do you think Judy Dent's spoiled?" Betty's voice came clear and loud from the other room, even though there was a long hall between us.

"Yes!" roared the other girls.

"Do you think she helps her parents at home?"

"No!"

"Do you think she makes her bed at home?"

"No!"

"Do you think she changes it?"

"No!"

"Do you think she cuts her own meat?"

"No!"

"Do you think she knows how to sew on a button?"

"No!"

On and on it went, highlighting every task I had failed to master in my entire life. I began to sob, deep and hard, as if a surgeon were using big knives to perform heart surgery inside my chest without anesthetic. "Do you think Betty Schuchman is a vicious little sadist?" I mumbled into my pillow. I was sure the other girls would have said, "No!"

We were supposed to be quiet for the night; when we were having a pleasant conversation about books, music or homework, the housemother was there like a shot to put a stop to it, but no one came to end the attack on me. Why was I not surprised? Years later when I read about communist reeducation camps in China, I recalled that night and felt a small part of the horror and abandonment those "campers" must have experienced.

No housemother came to my aid, but someone did. Another girl sat on my bed and I heard a small, tentative voice.

"Are you alright, Judy? Can I help?"

It was Donna Thompson, a new girl who had not yet learned the political realities of the school.

"Everyone hates me." I was still mumbling into my pillow.

"I don't." Her voice was so calm, so matter-of-fact that I took great consolation from it.

"Have some candy," offered Donna. "It tastes like apples. I bought it at the store."

I thanked her again. I am still thanking her. Every time I smell or taste apples, I remember her kindness. I hope someday I may give someone the comfort Donna gave me.

It is significant and poignant that the best times I had with Betty were when we were away from school. She often came to our house on weekends. On one of those occasions the talking book version of The Lion, the Witch and the Wardrobe, by C. S. Lewis, arrived at my house. After dinner we started listening to it together and spent almost the whole weekend glued to the talking book player until we finished it. I believe we spent several more weekends listening to other books in The Chronicles of Narnia. We read the rest of them independently and were spellbound. WE didn't find the books too didactic, nor Aslan too cloying; as for a lion being a Christ figure, we never gave it a thought. Who wouldn't love to be able, when things were going badly with other kids or your parents, to walk into a musty old wardrobe, into a completely different world, a world of power and adventure? Whenever the big, strong kids pushed me around—which they often did—I longed to be spirited away to Narnia. We liked the stories so much that we acted them out at school at lunch and recess, inserting ourselves into them and speculating about whether, faced with these adventures, we would have been brave and noble like Peter, Susan and Lucy, or whiny and treacherous like Edmund, but at school, even in our stories, we vied with each other to see who could go deepest into the plot, eclipsing the other and sometimes leaving her far behind. We played stories from other books, too—Heidi, Tom Sawyer, Huckleberry Finn, Oliver Twist, Hamlet, Pygmalion—the George Bernard Shaw version, not the classical myth.

We played other, more dramatic stories, too, during morning and afternoon recess, when the girls were not separated from the boys as they were after lunch. During the first few years we were in school there were still dramas on radio. They were perfect for blind kids, because we heard exactly the same things sighted people heard. Unlike with TV shows, you didn't have to nudge a sighted person every time a collective gasp or laugh went up and say, "What's happening?" Usually you would be ignored, and the fun of the program would go down a notch. Our favorite radio show was The Shadow. The thought of being invisible and scaring the heck out of bad guys just by laughing gave me a great thrill. Bob usually played The Shadow. His laugh would have made Orson Welles shake in his boots for fear of losing his job. So what if the laugh came out in a little-kid voice? Bob wasn't Lamont Cranston; he was The Shadow! I usually played Margo Lane, although it galled me that Margo had such a dumb-broad part. "When does Margo get to solve a mystery?" I complained. "She's way smarter than Lamont, feeds him most of the good ideas and information, then he puts her in horrible danger so he can rush in and save her with his laughing. Besides," I was on a roll. "Lamont is such a jerk. He never gives Margo a kiss, never tells her he loves her. He's supposed to be a 'rich young man about town,' but he never buys her an expensive present, especially a diamond ring. If I were Margo, I'd find myself another boyfriend who wouldn't get me killed."

"But Margo can't solve mysteries. She's a girl."

I whacked my dear friend Bob on the arm, wishing I were playing Rocky Marciano.

"Come on, folks, let's not argue." John asserted his authority as Commissioner Weston. "We have to finish the story before the bell rings."

"We weren't arguing. Judy was making a speech," said Betty, coming out of her role as a beautiful German spy who almost gets The Shadow killed. Betty could do female villains better than any of us, particularly exotic, foreign ones. She had a terrific ear for dialect and could use it to chilling or hilarious effect in our stories.

The bell did ring for the end of recess that day, but—our small disagreements notwithstanding—our stories continued most days for as long as we had recess.

One of too many sad incidents that marred the friendship between Betty and me occurred when we were in fifth grade. We were talking about what we were going to do when we grew up. I was too absorbed with my own plans to remember what Betty said, except that she wanted to get married and have children, something in which I was not a bit interested at the time. "I want to learn lots of languages and become an interpreter for the United Nations. I'll be able to work for world peace. Then in my spare time I want to be a famous author, maybe win the Nobel Prize in Literature like Pearl S. Buck."

"Who's that?"

"She wrote lots of good books about China, especially The Good Earth. It's on talking book, read by Ethel Everett. It's wonderful. You have to read it."

"I don't have to read it just because you tell me to."

"Calm down. Don't get all upset. I didn't mean you have to read it. That was a figure of speech. I meant I thought you would enjoy it."

"Will you stop lecturing me! No wonder the other kids call you 'the old prof.' And furthermore, Ella Schumann calls you 'fat, dumb, and goes around in circles.' No one else in this school goes around in circles."

"Oh, forget it! I don't care what you read! You can spend the rest of your life reading The Bobbsey Twins if you want to. They're about on your level."

I stomped off to hide in the library stacks where I could have a good cry. I had shared some really important ideas with Betty and she had turned on me. As for Ella, if she actually had called me those names, she didn't have much room to feel superior. She excelled in the dumb department herself. The bell rang. I did not go to class.

By sheer coincidence, a few days later, Mrs. Raymond, our teacher, went around the room asking each of us what we wanted to do when we grew up. As bad luck would have it, Betty's turn came before mine.

"I'd like to learn lots of languages and be an interpreter for the United Nations, Mrs. Raymond. I'd also like to be a famous author and win the Nobel Prize in Literature like Pearl S. Buck."

"Those are some noteworthy goals, Betty." Mrs. Raymond was obviously impressed. "You really have thought through your plans for the future."

"Thank you, Mrs. Raymond," said Betty. I had recently heard a new word, "simpering." Now I knew what it meant.

"What would you like to do, Judy?"

"'I want to go to heaven when I die, and I hope that will be soon."

No one laughed.

"You always seem so unhappy, Judy. You know that wasn't a responsive answer."

I ignored her, trying hard not to put my head down on the desk and bawl like a baby. How could I be such an idiot? How could I be so lonely, so desperate for a friend that I would tell Betty my innermost secrets? I was so mad my stomach hurt, mad not so much at Betty—she was just working the politics of the place—but at myself running my mouth instead of keeping my ideas to myself. We were friends again the next day; I never did learn my lesson.

There are more good memories of Betty when we were away from school. Her grandmother and uncle loved her very much and they were kind to me because I was her friend. They often invited me to their home, read us stories, and found other activities to entertain us. Sometimes during the week, Uncle—as Betty called him—would come to the school and pick us up, bring us to his home, and serve crispy fried chicken, fried potatoes, and strawberry sundaes for dessert. They liked the breasts and I liked the legs and thighs, so I got to make a pig of myself. Then Betty and I watched TV while Uncle cleaned up the dishes, after which Uncle drove us back to school.

Every year for Betty's birthday, Uncle let her invite a few kids from school and we went to Bevo Mill, a wonderful German restaurant in South St. Louis. Uncle said we could order anything but lobster. "They have a tank here with live lobsters in it," Uncle teased. "You select a lobster by sticking your hand into the tank. Whichever lobster hangs on, that's yours."

None of us tried to test Uncle's theory.

We usually had apple strudel for dessert. It had lots of apples and wasn't loaded with raisins like some apple strudel. The pastry was rich and crumbly with butter. There were roving musicians, a violinist and an accordion player, who wandered leisurely through the restaurant, pausing at each table to take requests. Betty always chose "Estrellita," Spanish for "Little Star." I always chose "Traumerei," German for "Dreams."

(Years later, after Betty had moved away and Uncle had passed on, I still went to Bevo Mill for my birthday. The musicians were there for many years, and I always asked for both "Traumerei" and "Estrellita." Now Bevo Mill is gone, but I was able to track down the musicians and they played for our wedding reception when Blair and I were married. I still have the video. The musicians were aging then, and by now they are probably gone, too.)

Noteworthy in all this was that Betty and I never fought with such fierce intensity when we were away from school. I can only imagine how deep and lasting our friendship would have been if the school hadn't continually pitted us against each other. I hope Betty has someone to play "Estrellita" for her now.

Chapter 12
Mean Girls (1953-61)

Marjorie

"Take her upstairs, Fran." The voice of the grumpy dining room lady crackled like lightning. "She's too dumb to find her way by herself."

Fran was Marjorie Lowell, my nemesis, an almost grown-up fourth grader, while I was still in kindergarten. She was partially sighted, while I am totally blind. My uncles had served in World War II and told hair-raising tales about atrocities committed by Nazis. As a small child, it seemed to me that Marjorie terrorized me in much the same way.

"Hurry up. I don't want to get old and gray waiting for you." She yanked my arm so hard she almost wrenched my shoulder out of its socket.

"You're already old," I said. "I didn't have anything to do with that. God only knows why you're still in fourth grade. As for gray, who cares what color your hair is? I know I don't."

Whack! My neck snapped and my teeth rattled as Marjorie slapped me across the face.

"Shut up! You're supposed to respect your elders."

I bit back the impulse to say, "You're not my elder. You're just older." That was hard. I bit back the impulse to cry. That was harder.

"Good afternoon, Mrs. Caine," said Marjorie in a tone suggesting she hoped to be mistaken for Amy Vanderbilt. She had evidently recognized Mrs. Caine by sight as we walked through the hall.

It was now or never. I wasn't going to take this abuse forever. "Mrs. Caine, Marjorie slapped me."

"I didn't do that, Mrs. Caine. I would never slap a student. Why would Judy tell a vicious lie like that?"

"Not only a stupid little smart aleck, but a liar as well," said Mrs. Caine. "You should be sent to reform school. Apologize to Marjorie."

"I'm sorry Marjorie is a mean, two-faced jerk." I tried to run off down the hall.

"Not so fast." Mrs. Caine grabbed my arm. I knew I would have large bruises to explain to the folks at home. "We're all going to the principal's office to explain this incident to Mrs. Hubbert."

"Why should we do that? Mrs. Hubbert won't believe me any more than you do."

"Stop that back talk right now or I'll slap you myself."

"Yes, Judy," said Marjorie. "How can you be so disrespectful? Mrs. Caine, have you ever seen anything like it?"

"Never in all my years of teaching," Mrs. Caine agreed. "Here we are at Mrs. Hubbert's office. We'll soon find out what she thinks."

"Well, well, if it isn't my old friend back again!" Mrs. Hubbert was clearly delighted to see us. "It took two of you to bring her in this time. What's the trouble now, Lucy?"

"Not only back talk, but lying," Mrs. Caine launched into a version of events heavily weighted to support Marjorie.

"Is that how it happened, Marjorie?"

"Yes, ma'am." Amy Vanderbilt again. "She just made up that vicious lie for no reason. Why would she do that, Mrs. Hubbert?"

"I've been principal of this school for a lot of years." Mrs. Hubbert sighed like Atlas getting tired of holding up the world. "Every time I think I've seen it all, I see one more. What about it, Judy? Is this true?"

"It's true, Mrs. Hubbert, except the part about me lying. Marjorie really did slap me. She made my neck pop and my teeth rattle."

"She slapped you in the face?"

"Yes, ma'am."

"I did not!" Screaming Mimi had replaced Amy Vanderbilt. "I hate her! She's a little—" Marjorie gasped for breath as her limited vocabulary failed to come up with a word sufficiently evil to describe me.

"Now, let's all calm down. Judy, you don't seem to have any bruises."

"But my neck still hurts, Mrs. Hubbert."

"Whining will get you nowhere, Judy. Neither will yelling and calling people names, Marjorie. This seems to be one person's word against another's. We'll never settle this by arguing. Judy, if I see you back here again for lying or back talk or any offense perpetrated by your small mind and big mouth, I'm going to whip you until you cry."

I wanted to short circuit the whipping and start to cry right then, but thought better of it. I didn't know what "offense" and "perpetrate" meant, but this was not the time to ask. The next day Marjorie was again assigned to watch over me after lunch and the bullying was worse than usual. My tattling had caused me nothing but trouble.

Shortly after my unsuccessful tattling experiment, Mother bought me some plastic charms to attach to the handles of zippers on dresses, skirts or jackets. Mother sewed the bottoms of my zippers together to make them easier for me to open and close. I pulled the dress or jacket over my head and then zipped it up. Even with this help my fingers often fumbled with the little handles, usually resulting in the zipper getting stuck. Mother thought the charms would help me pull the zippers up and down. The charms were shaped like little animals. Though tiny, they were three-dimensional and extremely detailed, just the kind of object I liked best. One of them was a collie dog that Mother said looked just like Tuffy. Mother said the charm would serve a dual purpose: it would help me with my zipper, and when I felt lonely or afraid, I could touch it and remember that Tuffy loved me.

The next day I had a bit more confidence, knowing that Little Tuffy was there to remind me that Big Tuffy was at home waiting to welcome me. I did fine until lunchtime, when Marjorie arrived to drag me, mentally kicking and screaming, to the dining room. One point needs clarifying: Marjorie didn't escort me from the dorm to lunch and back because she wanted to; she did it because the housemothers told her to, and to make brownie points with the people in power, and because she needed to feel superior to someone.

As we walked, or rather, Marjorie ran and I stumbled, I kept reaching up with my other hand to touch Little Tuffy. He reassured and comforted me, like the rabbit's foot Uncle Martin had given me a long time ago.

"Can I see that?"

"Sure."

I nearly fainted. Marjorie had spoken to me in a kind voice. She was actually being nice to me. I said a silent thank-you to God.

Yank! I felt a sharp tug on my zipper and heard Marjorie running away. Little Tuffy was gone forever. I retracted my prayer, angry at God, at Marjorie, and most of all at myself. Why had I allowed myself to trust her even for a second? I told Mother about it that night. She said some people were so jealous and afraid that they thought they had to steal.

"Try not to let her bother you," Mother advised. "Someday you'll be a famous author and you can write a story about her. Bad people are always more interesting than good people in a story, although they drive you crazy in real life."

"You mean like the two wicked stepsisters in 'Cinderella' or Satan in Paradise Lost?"

"Exactly."

I went to sleep that night concocting elaborate stories about the grisly death of Marjorie Lowell. Speaking of grizzly, maybe a big bear could rip her to shreds. Maybe she could drown trying to go over Niagara Falls in a rubber barrel. But those deaths were too quick and easy. I wanted something slow and scary that would make her think about how mean she had been. When I got my revenge I wouldn't be indecisive like Hamlet; I would be resolute like Poe's character in "The Cask of Amontillado" or Chillingworth in The Scarlet Letter, and Marjorie would know that stupid little Judy Dent—strong, implacable Judy Dent—had been her undoing.

I felt much better after killing Marjorie at least ten times in my head, but I never again wore one of my zipper charms to school.

The many deaths of Marjorie Lowell soothed me for that one night, but she was back with a vengeance the next day. During the morning it poured rain. The ground was squishy with mud. After lunch every day, rain or shine, the girls were sent out to play on the "girls' cloister." When I first heard of the place, I looked forward to visiting it. The term "cloister" brought to mind church bells, Gregorian chant, and best of all, silence. I thought it would be relaxing to have a short period of quiet meditation before afternoon classes. I didn't relax during siesta, and in all the years I attended the school I never slept. Maybe the cloister would provide spiritual renewal.

Wrong again. The cloister was a small porch, paved with something that felt like cobblestones, where only girls played. There were two small buildings like horse stalls with ladders inside called "ladder boxes" where girls could play. At the end of the cloister, opposite the door to the inside of the school, there were several concrete steps leading down to a small, grassy area with playground equipment. This was called "the ground." Mrs. Caine supervised this early afternoon play period. On this day she made a stern pronouncement regarding what we were allowed to do. "Now, remember, girls, do not go down on the ground. The maintenance people don't want you tracking mud all over their spotless floors. We try to keep a clean school here."

Marjorie dragged me outside. No meditative silence here. The noise cut through my brain. Neurons exploded. Fear of Marjorie and the noise of girls running and screaming rushed violently through me as if someone were putting my brain through a carwash.

"Walk, Judy. Don't just stand there. You look stupid."

Obey Marjorie. Make that voice stop. Fear. Heart palpitations. Adrenaline rush. Disorientation. Whooshing noise in my ears. Will get slapped if I go around in circles. Walk straight ahead. Maybe no one will hit me. Maybe no one will yell. Forward. One foot, the other foot. One foot, the other foot. One foot, the other foot.

Bang! Bang! Falling. Falling. Splash! Squash! Pick myself up. Oh, God, where are the steps to go back up? Turn around. Walk. Walk. Obey Marjorie. Grandma! Mother! Dad! "St. Michael the Archangel, defend us in battle. Be our defense against the wickedness and snares of the devil ... the wickedness and snares of Mrs. Caine and Marjorie Lowell ... everyone at this school."

"Mrs. Caine!" Marjorie's voice whistled shrilly over my head like one of those giant, old-fashioned whistling firecrackers that aren't legal any more, except in public displays.

"I told Judy Dent you said not to go down to the ground, but she went down there anyway, and she's down there tromping around."

"Thank you, Marjorie. Thank you so much for keeping an eye on her."

"I'm happy to help whenever I can."

Where was that grizzly bear when I needed him?

"What's the matter with you? What are you doing down here after I strictly ordered everyone to stay on the cloister?"

I felt yet another iron grip on my arm.

"What a disobedient little troublemaker you are! You should be grateful you have a nice girl like Marjorie to look out for you."

I wanted to say, "Marjorie doesn't look out for me. She bullies me and insults me and hurts me, but what would you care? You're the same kind of person." Of course I kept all this to myself while Mrs. Caine went on berating me.

Soon we were back at the dorm. "My goodness! What happened to you, Judy? You're filthy! What have you been doing, making mudpies?" Miss Temple's voice was added to those of my other tormentors.

I just stood there saying nothing. My parents had always told me to hold my head up, to project an air of confidence. I didn't feel confident. My head hung limply as I withdrew into a deep, safe place where no one could hurt me, where I did not have to respond to the endless barrage of accusations.

"Let's get you cleaned up and back to class. Put those muddy shoes in this bag and take them home for your mother to clean. Then your parents will see how disobedient and disrespectful you are."

I had to wear my gym shoes to class. That night while Mother cleaned my shoes I told her the story.

"Didn't you know where the steps were?" asked Mother in astonishment.

"Marjorie told me to walk, so I walked, and I fell down the stairs."

"Judy, I don't know what to do with you. You have to learn to take better care of yourself."

I slunk away and went to bed early. Apparently only my two grandmas and Tuffy loved me. I held Jacko the monkey as close as I could and cried until, long after midnight, I fell asleep.

One lesson I had learned from this experience was never to tattle. When Marjorie tattled she was praised and rewarded. When I tattled I got in trouble. I never tattled again, not because keeping quiet was part of a lofty honor code, but because I wanted to survive. Marjorie continued to bully me and to get me punished whenever she could, but after years of persecution I found out I wasn't the only one she bullied.

By the time I reached seventh grade and Marjorie the eleventh, she had long since stopped taking an interest in me. Not that she didn't throw a casual insult my way every time she saw me, but she was no longer a constant, terrorizing presence in my life. She had found smaller, younger girls to bully. When Marjorie was exercising her malevolent power over me, I promised myself that when I was older I would stride in like one of Wagner's valkyries and put a stop for all time to Marjorie's abuse of weaker girls. I never did. Every time I came near her, every time I heard that scolding, harpy voice, I quivered like the mercury inside a thermometer. The teachers said that this hazing by the older students built strength and character. It didn't make me strong; it made me a coward. I chose not to help other girls who were being bullied because I was afraid of being bullied myself. Decades later, when I read about Snape and Voldemort, I recognized in them the same evil power I found in Marjorie, but they were fantasy and Marjorie was real. I haven't made many decisions in my life that I believed were morally destructive, but letting fear prevent me from helping the victims of bullying was one of the worst. I hope this book will, in some small way, address this issue.

Brenda Pitre, whom the girls called Pete, was our scout leader, which means she was also Marjorie's scout leader. She liked to combine the middle grade and senior Scout troops and take us on field trips to events both rugged and cultural. The powerful girls liked to sneer at the cultural experiences because they thought contempt was cool. I had decided years ago that I wanted to be a writer and, as Dad never tired of telling me, writers couldn't gather any material if they were constantly running their mouths. That gave me an excuse to stay in the background, be quiet, listen, and hope no one would notice me, so I wouldn't have to engage in any more mindless social interaction than necessary.

One day we visited the original St. Louis Cathedral, one of the first buildings to be built when French missionaries and fur traders founded the city of St. Louis in 1764. A priest gave our group a fascinating talk about the history of the cathedral.

In the middle of his presentation a loud stage whisper reverberated through the building like a demonic toccata and fugue. "Let's get out of here! This joint feels like a tomb!"

It was Marjorie, again trying to prove her coolness, but the cathedral had the last word.

"Like a tomb … like a tomb … like a tomb …" The echo bounced off the walls, went around several more times, then once or twice more for good measure. "Like a tomb …"

I could imagine all the other visitors, those not in our group, maybe some from other countries, craning their necks to see whose blaspheming voice that was. I waited expectantly for God to send lightning through the ceiling and strike Marjorie dead. If there were any justice in the world, Marjorie would soon find out what a tomb was really like.

"Marjorie, for heaven's sake, be quiet," hissed Mother, who had come along to help us on the trip. "You're in God's house!"

139

"This isn't God's house. It's just an old building."

"Marjorie, that will be all." Mother's voice was cold and calm, a tone I knew only too well. Mother had been assistant scout leader for three years and this was the first time she had ever stood up to Marjorie. Maybe it wasn't lightning from heaven, but it was the moral equivalent. When I heard that voice, I obeyed. So did Marjorie.

When we got on the bus to go back to school, Marjorie was on it. Not dead yet. The day was not a total loss, however. I felt closer to God than ever before. I had castigated myself over and over for not confronting Marjorie, but when she had insulted God in His own house, He had backed down. "I know how you feel," I confided to Him that night when I said my prayers. There was Almighty God, but there was almightier Marjorie.

When I was in fifth grade, bullying hit a new low. It started with Mother throwing up all her food. She stayed in the house, lost weight and hardly ever went out. I felt I had to tiptoe around and be quiet all the time. Soon Mother went to the hospital for tests. They found something called "polyps." I didn't know what polyps were, but they sounded like nasty little critters crawling around inside Mother and causing trouble. Dad said Mother would have to go back to the hospital to have half her stomach removed. She would have to be there at least two weeks, then come home for several months' recuperation. Her activities would be extremely limited: no driving, no gardening, no lifting, no activities with the Girl Scouts. The doctors were afraid she might have cancer.

If cancer is a terrifying diagnosis now, it was almost a sure death sentence in 1958. Mother scared me at times; often she even hit me when her illness was upon her. She would fling her arms around and shout irrational warnings about demons and avenging angels coming to get us. She would say my disabilities were a punishment from God for her sins. Dad called it her "rave and wave." Despite all this, I loved Mother and didn't want to lose her. She made all my clothes. She read to me for hours. She taught me all I know about nature, mostly with hands-on experiences. I learned more about science from her than I ever did in school. She wasn't very demonstrative, didn't show as much affection physically or verbally as I wished she would, but I still knew she loved me. The thought of losing her filled me with dread. On top of all this, Dad spent most of his time at work or the hospital, Grandma had never learned to drive, and I had to stay at school. In my desperation I told these troubles to Betty.

The next day it was all over school. "Judy's mom's gonna die! Judy's mom's gonna die!" jeered the girls. The large group of partially sighted girls in my class adopted me as a kind of class action project, vying with one another to see who could abuse me in the cruelest, most ingenious way. The clear winner was Nancy Roberts, who must have spent time in Las Vegas, because she started a betting ring on the exact day and time Mother would die. You could bet any amount from five to 25 cents. She knew how to figure odds; she understood over-unders;

if her customers wanted to, they could bet day, minute, hour and second, but you had to bet at least day, hour and minute. She carefully wrote the bets in a notebook. If nobody won, Nancy got all the money. I didn't understand her figures, and I was pretty good in math. One thing Nancy forgot, though; she neglected to provide for the possibility that Mother would recover. Mother did get well, the polyps were benign, and in addition to the comfort that gave me, I rejoiced in the dejection and confusion Mother's recovery caused those girls. I never did find out what happened to the money, but there was considerable squabbling over it, which I enjoyed with the enthusiastic delight of the most bloodthirsty boxing fan.

Darlene

None of these events changed the bullying tide. In sixth grade a new girl, Darlene Stitt, came to school. Why she was there I'll never know. She could see better than most of the sighted kids I knew. She never got lost. She could recognize people by their faces. She found school colossally boring, and she read trashy paperbacks in class—in tiny, "regular" print, not the large print the other sight savers read.

She must have been picked on in public school, because she quickly zeroed in on me as a way of exacting revenge for anyone who had ever given her a hard time. That's the only theory I can come up with now to explain her, but I wasn't that charitable at the time. She picked on me constantly. Because Darlene was the best at everything but academics, and I was the worst, we were constantly thrown together by the faculty so Darlene could "help" me. She helped in the same way Marjorie had—yanking me around, ridiculing me, and receiving accolades while I received punishment every time I tried to stand up to her.

Physical education, otherwise known as gym, remained, along with its teacher, Mrs. Caine, one of the many banes of my existence. Darlene was the big star in gym class. Two of our activities were swimming and bowling. Swimming was the only sport in gym class at which I excelled. I had learned it from a kind lifeguard in Florida when we were on vacation, long before I started school. I got no satisfaction from swimming class, however; first we had to enter a huge dressing room where we must locate a stool with a pile of towels on it, choose one, then find our bathing suits, which were hanging on assigned hooks. Then we had to find a locker for all this and our clothes. The lockers were not assigned, so we had to find one each time. (We swam once a week.) Then we changed into our suits. Only after performing all these orientation and mobility tasks were we allowed actually to swim. When we had swimming tests I was downgraded every time for being late because it took me so long to do the preliminary tasks. In addition to all this, the only organized team sports at the school when I attended were boys' wrestling and track. There were no sports for girls. That was years before Title IX was a gleam in the NCAA's eye. So instead of enjoying swimming class, I dreaded it.

Then there was bowling, another exercise in orientation frustration. First you had to find a cabinet with bowling shoes, select a pair that fit, then put your regular shoes in a place where you hoped you could find them again after class. Bowling balls were lined up on a rack. You had to select one that fit, then sit on a bench and wait your turn. Only then could you bowl. Being late for this class didn't bother me the way being late for swimming did. I was a terrible bowler. I calculate that my lifetime bowling average is 13. My bowling was like my mind when listening to dirty jokes: always in the gutter. Rumble, rumble, rumble would go my bowling ball, an encouraging, thunderous sound. I almost held my breath as the ball rolled slowly down the alley. "Maybe I will actually knock down some pins this time. Don't roll sideways. Don't roll sideways. Please don't roll sideways." Boom! Bang! Into the gutter.

"There goes Miss Gutterball again," sneered Darlene as her ball on the other alley knocked down all ten pins for a strike.

We had guide rails which were supposed to help us line up to roll the ball down the alley, but they never helped me. The partially sighted girls used alley one and the totally blind girls used alley two. One alley had a bell and the other a buzzer to tell the bowlers that the alley was clear and it was safe to bowl without worrying about hitting the pinsetter. I never knew which was which because Mrs. Caine never let us use the bell and buzzer unless there were visitors touring the school.

I was a bad bowler, but an even worse pinsetter. Guess who they always paired me with? They put the biggest dunce with the biggest star, Darlene Stitt. Darlene set the pins on alley one, I on alley two, the "blind alley," as some wags loved to describe it. Instead of using the bell and buzzer, we were instructed to yell, "One's clear!" and "Two's clear!" when the pins were set and we were out of the way.

The pins had to be configured in a certain way—out in front was one pin by itself called the kingpin. That was the first time I realized that kingpin referred to anything but gangsters and drug dealers, call "pushers" in those days. The rest of the pins are set up in three rows of three, but I'm still not sure how they go. There was a pin setting machine with places for each pin. You pulled a string and the machine automatically set up the pins. Mrs. Caine would shout out the numbers of the pins that had been knocked down.

"Judy, the pins are one, four, and seven."

It was my first day setting pins. I had no idea what Mrs. Caine was talking about. I had not understood it when she had explained it the first time. I felt around on the alley for the three pins. Then I felt around on the machine for three holes to stick them in. I pulled the string. Bang! Crash! Pins scattered all over the place.

"Judy!" Mrs. Caine bellowed. "I said, 'one, four, and seven!'"

"I don't understand where they go, Mrs. Caine. I thought I just had to put them anywhere."

"Listen to her!" Darlene's voice was a derisive falsetto. "She thought she could just put them anywhere."

"Judy, you're hopeless. I don't know what to do with you. Can't you learn anything?"

By that time I had learned that comments like that were rhetorical questions not needing answers. I imagined Mrs. Caine's nail clippings in one of those glass reliquaries I had to kiss at Sainte-Anne-de-Beaupré. Except that Sainte Anne had to perform several miracles in order to be canonized; being the Virgin Mary's mother wasn't enough. Maybe Mrs. Caine's retirement would count as a miracle. That worked for me.

"Judy, sit down on that bench and don't bother anyone. Darlene, can you set both alleys?"

"I'd be happy to, Mrs. Caine," said Darlene, performing her usual imitation of maple syrup drizzling onto pancakes.

"Thank you, Darlene. I wish all the students were like you." Mrs. Caine had a remarkable gift for changing her tone of voice. When she spoke to me, she sounded like the actors who played Nazi Gestapo guards in movies. When she spoke to Darlene, Marjorie, or anyone she liked, Mrs. Caine's voice sounded as gentle as a babbling brook. I wondered why she stayed in her stupid little job with the state instead of taking up acting. Now that almost sixty years have passed, I believe that, as with most sadistic people who work with the disabled, it's about power. They like to feel superior. They like to make people quiver and quake. She and others like her scared the spirit out of me, and made me withdraw into myself at school, but I resolved they were not going to repress all of me. No matter how much they humiliated and frightened me, no matter how much outsiders raved about how wonderful this school was, I would not let them take away my soul.

Such resolutions did not prevent these persecutions from continuing, however. They didn't stop people like Darlene and Marjorie from being rewarded for bullying. The bullies were always the most popular kids in school. That always perplexed me until I got a little older and figured out that the most aggressive bully was always the leader. She has the most power, and the small fry like to hang onto power's coattails, hoping some of it will rub off.

Our school had a store in the recreation room which served two purposes. It provided a place for the students to buy soda and candy in the evenings. It also served as a training ground for students to learn to run a vending stand. After years of lobbying, blind people had won the right to be proprietors of vending stands in state and federal buildings. These small snack bars provided jobs for many blind people. The store offered training and a way to determine which students had an aptitude for this work. As usual when it was my turn to run the store, I was paired with Darlene. I was in charge of dispensing soda, Darlene, candy. The soda came in variously shaped glass bottles. I quickly learned the difference between Coke, Pepsi, Dr. Pepper and Orange Crush. Sodas were a dime, candy and chips a nickel. The first customer came to my counter. I handed over the bottle she requested. She handed me a dime. When she brought the bottle back, I remembered that when my parents returned soda bottles, they received two cents for the deposit on each bottle. I fished around in the change drawer for two cents.

"What are you doing?" Darlene's eagle eyes had me in their sights again.

"Getting the two cents for Carolyn's deposit."

"We don't do that here. Why do I always have to work with the stupidest person in the whole school?"

I had been wondering the same thing. "They pay deposits in other stores."

"This isn't other stores. This is here."

I stopped trying to pay back deposits on soda bottles. The evening dragged endlessly. I was never again asked to mind the store.

Years ground by. I continued to get lost, continued to fall down stairs, continued to be called "stupid" and to say, "I don't know." I felt like two different people, one who raised her hand and knew most of the answers in class, and one who slunk around, intimidated and silent, while Darlene became more and more brazen, more and more popular.

We were in eighth grade on January 20, 1961. Someone had brought a television into our social studies classroom so we could watch John F. Kennedy's inauguration. Into the fanfare came the venerable Robert Frost, ready to recite a poem he had written for the occasion. There was a brisk wind that day. It blew Mr. Frost's notes all around. He hesitated, mumbled, tried several times, then whispered an apology.

"What's wrong with that old fool?" Darlene demanded in a strident voice. "'He shouldn't be here if he can't even read."

I couldn't stand up to Darlene when she ridiculed me, but I couldn't tolerate her disrespect toward Robert Frost.

"Oh, shut up, Darlene. Do you have to be so brazen about demonstrating your abysmal ignorance? A thousand of you wouldn't have the brains of Robert Frost's little toe. He's one of the greatest American poets of all time. What did you ever do besides act like an obnoxious idiot? Talk about two roads diverging! I wish ours had diverged before we met."

"Mr. Gilbert, are you going to allow Judy to talk to me like this? The talking dictionary is on the warpath again. Why can't you make her speak English like a normal person? She thinks she's so much better than the rest of us."

"Lay off, Judy," said Mr. Gilbert. "Darlene hasn't had the advantages you have. She probably doesn't know who Robert Frost is."

"Right," I said under my breath, but evidently not as far under as I intended. "I do have advantages. I'm not a lobotomy case."

"That's enough, Judy. Neurosurgery should not be fodder for vicious jokes."

"But a great poet is?"

"That's it," said Mr. Gilbert. "Come up here to the desk, Judy. I want to show you something. Do you know what this is?" He handed me a thick book.

"It's the first volume of the King James Bible from the Royal National Institute for the Blind in England."

"Look at the first two pages and last two pages, before and after the text. See those owo's?"

I looked again and felt the little ovals: 2-4-6 for ow sign, 1-3-5 for o. No spaces between.

"I want you to get out your slate and stylus and write four pages of those."

"What will you make Darlene do?"

"That's not your concern. Go back to your desk and get started."

I banged the heavy steel slate hard against my desk as I got ready to begin my punishment. That was before slates became aluminum, then plastic, but in those days you could really make a good noise with a steel slate. As I got into the rhythm—owo, owo, no spaces, 14 sets to a line, four lines to a slate, loud bang again, move slate down, or was it paper up?—I went into a Walter Mitty-like trance. Never mind the Boston Tea Party. Never mind "No taxation without representation." Give me liberty—liberty from stupid assignments like this, liberty from being misunderstood, liberty from bullies who were praised for their strength of character. Those tedious, wrist-destroying owo's would be enough to inspire revolution among braille users in the United States and United Kingdom alike.

When the bell rang I had not finished, so I had to come back after classes to complete my punishment. I was no longer thinking about the repetitious design of the owo's. I was thinking about Robert Frost. "Something there is that doesn't love a wall." I wasn't sure I agreed with him. I would have loved a wall to protect me from this school and its military-academy values. People usually said Frost was being ironic when he said, "Good fences make good neighbors." But I was sure a good fence would have made me a better neighbor.

A quotation I liked better was, "The woods are lovely, dark and deep, / But I have promises to keep, / And miles to go before I sleep, / And miles to go before I sleep."

That night I decided to imitate Robert Frost and fight back with poetry.

Before I slept that night, I lay in bed composing the following doggerel:

There's a girl in school whose name is Darlene.

Vicious and evil, vindictive and mean,

Is awful, revolting, misguided Darlene.

Ugliest person you ever have seen,

Just a long, lanky, walking, talking string bean,

Not good for much except venting her spleen,

Is mean Darlene.

Always a critic, never a poet,

If she were a baseball, how I'd love to throw it

Deep down in a river, ocean or stream.

She'd sink to the bottom, nevermore to be seen, would mean Darlene.

From a tenth-story window she should be catapulted,

But she's too stupid to know she's insulted.

A trashy peasant who thinks she's a queen,

Is mean Darlene.

Mercifully, I fell asleep at that point.

I wanted to publish my poem in the school paper and call it "Frost's Revenge." Then everyone would laugh at Darlene for a change. They might even go around chanting, "mean Darlene" for a few days, but knowing how things worked in this school my victory would be a pyrrhic one. The bullies would find a way to make it backfire.

Ella

Ella Schumann, who had declared me "fat, dumb, and goes around in circles," had disappeared from school for several years. That same year of the Robert Frost fiasco, Ella reappeared. I had not been especially solicitous toward her because of that long-ago remark, but when she came back to school I noticed some alarming changes. She was broken and solitary, completely different from the girl I remembered. She kept to herself and paid no attention to her real peers. She traveled in an elaborate circle of imaginary companions. They spoke to her and she answered them, out loud. She had an imaginary cousin named Kathleen who went everywhere with her, protecting and caring for her. She was late for chorus practice one day and the music director, Mr. Chance, was becoming more and more annoyed. I offered to go back to the dorm and look for her.

"Are you sure you can find your way there and bring her back?"

"Yes, Mr. Chance." I restrained the impulse to add that I didn't blame Ella for hiding from his lousy music and snide mouth. When I got to the dorm, sure enough, there was Ella, as deep inside her locker as she could go, talking animatedly to a pile of her clothes, which she had taken down from the rack and fashioned into a wad roughly suggesting a human body. "Hello, Ella," I said, at a complete loss for something appropriate to say.

"Hello," said Ella. "Kathleen says hello, too."

Shades of Mother's episodes. Why was I so often called upon to talk down people undergoing dangerous psychotic breaks?

"Where is Kathleen, Ella?"

Ella seemed not to feel challenged by this question. She knew I was blind and she did not feel attacked by my implying that I couldn't see Kathleen. "She's right here. Kathleen, this is Judy." Ella put my hand on the clothes dummy.

Doctors and psychologists said not to go along with a patient's delusions, to try to get the person back to reality instead of encouraging their fantasies. I had never found this tactic to work with Mother, however. Many times I had to get inside her stories and enlist the aid of her archangels and Indians to put the fire out or the knife away.

"Ella, Mr. Chance is worried. He needs you at chorus practice. Help Kathleen hang up these clothes so you both can get ready and come."

"OK." Ella was surprising compliant. Soon we were back in the auditorium ready to resume chorus practice. Mr. Chance did not thank us. He didn't seem to notice when we came in.

A few days later I was walking down the hall to class when I heard a loud crash. "Oh, dear!" came a small, sad voice. Ella's huge stack of braille books had fallen and scattered all over the hall. Ella was crying. My mind went into quick rewind mode. In a split second I saw two old movies simultaneously. Like a drowning person whose life passes before his or her eyes, I saw over and over the many times I had witnessed Marjorie Lowell bullying other girls and hadn't said or done anything to prevent it. The other old film was a time several months before when I had dropped all my books and papers. They slipped through my fingers as I struggled to pick them up. "Judy, stop being such a baby! You're big enough to carry your own books." It was Miss Diefenbacher, the head housemother. She was always yelling at somebody about something. This time it just happened to be me. I scrambled to pick up my things, finally juggling the bulky stack into place. How I wished someone would brave Miss Diefenbacher's wrath and help me get my things together. No one did.

"Don't cry, Ella. I'll help you pick up your books." I set my own stuff down and began helping Ella get her things organized.

"No, you won't!" came an angry voice. "How will she ever learn to do things for herself if you help her?" It was Mr. Gilbert, who was a brilliant history teacher, but a raving militant when it came to independence.

"No one was there when I needed help." I calmly continued helping Ella with her things. "Here are your books, Ella. They should be all right now."

I picked up my own stack and turned to head on to class.

"Wait just a minute." Mr. Gilbert had to get in the last word. "Are you defying me? I thought I told you to stop helping her."

"You did." I hadn't been defying him before, but now I was.

"And?"

"I helped her anyway."

"Why did you do that when you were specifically instructed not to?"

"Because what you told me to do was wrong, Mr. Gilbert. This cult of absolute self-sufficiency is evil. The atmosphere at this school is like a concentration camp. Somebody has to do something about it."

"And you think you are the great messiah who will be the one to do something about it?"

"I don't know about that, but somebody has to start somewhere."

"What you can start doing right now is walking down to Dr. Easton's office. You can explain your complex to him."

"I'll talk to Dr. Easton if you insist, Mr. Gilbert, but I don't have a complex. This school does. This philosophy of promoting bullying and total independence is destroying people."

"That's enough. Talk to Dr. Easton. Then go back to the library and write four pages of owo's."

"That's another thing. This silly assignment not only doesn't stimulate our brains. It puts them to sleep."

"Go talk to Dr. Easton. I have to get back to class."

Mrs. Hubbert had died two years before. Our new principal was Dr. Wallace Easton. He had a habit of beginning each sentence with "By golly, now." Dr. Easton wasn't as intimidating as Mrs. Hubbert. He quickly acquired the nickname "By Golly Wally", although the students never called him that to his face.

Ella had disappeared. I trudged down to Dr. Easton's office, hiking my books farther up on my shoulder lest Ella's recent predicament become mine.

I did talk to Dr. Easton. He said, "By golly, now, we can't have that," several times in a bemused way, as if what he really wanted to say was, "What in the world is going on here? This is way too deep for me." I don't think Dr. Easton ever had a clue why his school would be compared to a concentration camp. I don't think he had any idea that the school's harsh policies, which were intended to build character, made some people quiver and shake and cry and have flashbacks more than 60 years later.

Everything went back to business as usual. I swallowed my principles one more time and never again helped anyone pick up his or her books.

The Ella incident had one effect for which I was not prepared. One day I got home from school to be told by Mother, "Ella Schumann's mom called me today. She wants you to visit Ella for a weekend. They live in Union (or maybe it was Moberly). You would go with Ella on the train. Ella has told her mom how nice you are."

I nearly fainted. No one had invited me to visit them for a weekend before, except Betty Schuchman a few times and Betty Smith once. Would Kathleen go with us? Would Ella talk to herself on the train? Did she make clothes dummies at home? I felt like a slimy slug for having these thoughts. I knew firsthand how it was to be a weirdo that nobody liked. I had long since decided to forgive Ella for calling me "fat, dumb, and goes around in circles," if indeed she had said it. That report had been secondhand gossip; Ella had never said it to me. But to go home with her for a whole weekend?

"I don't know. We'll have to see," I said without enthusiasm.

Mother must have understood without my saying so how much I did not want to go to Ella's house for the weekend. The subject never came up again.

The virtue of giving up

I often wonder where the morally upright line is between "being nice" to someone and doing something together out of genuine friendship, because you really want to spend time with that person. Years of mumbled excuses, of waiting by the phone for calls that never came, of being treated with condescension by people who hated every minute we spent together, of being some do-gooder's project, have taught my head not to be as angry as my heart about social isolation. I haven't always been the defender of the despised, but neither can I recall a time when I took away someone's dignity and did something with or for someone while grinding my teeth with resentment. I suppose the real moral high ground for me is that if I can do something without resentment, I'm happy to do it. If I can't, I say no. That's the way I would like people to handle me. Marcia Robertson, my best friend in graduate school, was the kind of person who could do that. If I asked her to do something, the answer was always an unequivocal "yes," "no," or "some other time." If Marcia said some other time, she really found time to do it. I haven't seen Marcia in over 20 years, but I shall always love her for her straightforwardness.

One of my favorite shows on National Public Radio is Fresh Air, an interview show with Terry Gross. I usually love her empathy and thoughtfulness, the ways she draws guests out and gives them a chance to freely express their points of view. One of my particular favorites was her interview with Temple Grandin, a well-known university professor with autism. I've heard other interviews with Temple in which she responded with monosyllables. The interviewer was not very helpful, but Terry asked questions that helped Temple to express complex aspects of autism that many of her listeners probably did not understand.

The same technique worked less well for me when I heard Terry interview Ray Charles. He explained eloquently how much he missed his mother when he left home to attend a school for the blind. Then he went on to praise the school because the students and faculty beat and ridiculed that babyishness out of him and extolled the school to the skies because it "built character." I realize that Terry Gross didn't have the same experiences I had with residential schools for the blind, but if I had been interviewing Mr. Charles, I would have asked, "If the school for the blind experience was so good for you, why did you spend so much of your life using illegal drugs?"

I realize that if Terry Gross asked questions like that, her show would be called Slaughterhouse and not Fresh Air, and no one would want to be interviewed by her, but it broke my heart to hear that destructive myth perpetuated on NPR.

I still live in a suburb not far from where I grew up, and from time to time people say, "Oh, isn't that a wonderful school you have down your way?"

I mumble something noncommittal, but I really want to say, "Oh, isn't that a wonderful penitentiary they have down in Leavenworth, Kansas?"

The authorities at that school tried to break up my family. They especially criticized and slandered my mother, who tried to help the kids and stand up for me, even while she fought valiantly every day against recurring episodes of paranoid schizophrenia. I know blind people in their 70's who pine for the school and live near it as if still trying to bask in its glow. I have heard former students of the school wax eloquent about how great the place was and how they wish they could be back there. Not me. Lots of people have suggested that I go back there as a volunteer to teach braille. Not on your life. I took so much abuse from the people at that place that never would be much too soon to go back. I only wish I had been a better friend to others who, like me, were not "good" blind persons, did not fit the profile, had their talents and abilities squelched by people trying to force them into rigid molds. These fruitless struggles made me feel worthless and no-good, made me try for decades to do things I will never be able to do if I live to be a hundred, almost stopped me from believing I could achieve anything. I felt this way for decades, terrified every time I had to meet another blind person, expecting them to keep score on all my inadequacies. When I heard about Tom Sullivan skiing on Good Morning America, I wanted him to fall and break a leg. When people tried to inspire me by telling me Eric Weyhenmeyer was going to climb Mount Everest, I hoped he would take a fatal plunge into a crevasse. I felt as if people were saying, "All these other blind people are doing amazing things. What's wrong with you, you lazy, unmotivated little rat?"

It took a lot of years and a lot of life before I could experience a radical change of perspective, could begin to inch toward happiness. I met a blind person, my future husband Blair, who taught me the virtue of giving up. He lives independently and interdependently, cooks and cleans, pays bills and does laundry. His wisdom astonishes me every day, and that wisdom says that what matters most is not doing, but being.

Chapter 13

Mother: No comment, no cookies (Christmas 1954)

Mother's idea of solving a problem was to identify it, attack it, and apply an obvious and easy solution. She never dithered, discussed, or analyzed. She usually rushed off to Central Hardware or Sew-and-Sew, both of which are gone now; small hardware and fabric stores hardly exist these days, and hardware had a completely different meaning, unrelated to computers. Mother would wander around the store in a kind of trance, then come home with a bag of nondescript items from which she would make or invent something. Much to my delight and frustration, these Rube Goldberg devices nearly always worked. Mother worked out creative ways of labeling long before we ever heard of color tags or Dymo tape. She could do wonders with safety pins, paper clips, and plain old adhesive and Scotch tape. Occasionally she even used letters from alphabet soup. We never used Alphabits cereal, because it had sugar on it and became sticky.

Mother never minded drudgery in a good cause. One Saturday we spent the entire day labeling all my records. Mother read the titles and I laboriously wrote them out on the slate and stylus. We then attached these braille labels to the album covers with rubber cement. Mother found many uses for Elmer's glue, rubber cement and plastic wood; that was before you could buy locator dots, four for ten dollars (the cheap ones did wear off sooner, but the expensive ones do eventually wear off as well). Mother's hands seemed to be in complete coordination with her brain at all times. They actually did what Mother told them. Mine, on the other hand, were almost useless; other than for reading and writing braille, they might come in handy as paperweights.

Mother always said, "The only good Christmas presents are the ones you make yourself." Her family was poor, so they saved and scrimped and made do with whatever they had. Grandpa Loehr built all the furniture. Grandma taught all four girls to make their own clothes. If they wanted a toy or a home accessory they made it themselves from whatever they had around the house or farm.

This philosophy was effective for a rural family growing up during the Depression, but it left Dad and me out in the cold. Dad was a crack editor, but that wasn't the kind of creativity that meant anything to Mother. She had a narrow idea of what "making something" meant. Write a poem? Ho, hum. Make a Santa Claus out of an old Reader's Digest? She practically went into hysterics with pleasure. Dad was almost as inept with his hands as I am, except in electronics. One year he built her a radio with AM, FM, and a weather band. Mother said dismissively, "I don't care about that. I'd rather watch the weather on television. I have to see the jet stream."

The Christmas I was in second grade our Brownie troop made cookie jars from detergent containers, then wrapped them in construction paper and painted abstract designs on the paper. The abstract part saved me. If we had been told to paint something representational, like a Christmas tree or Santa Claus, I would have been in big trouble. I wonder what Jackson Pollack's first art project looked like. It had to be better than my cookie jar—which I'm sure was an aesthetic disaster—but I had made it myself. I could hardly wait for Mother to open it on Christmas morning.

"What is it?" asked Mother with a distinct lack of enthusiasm.

"It's a cookie jar with an abstract painting on it. I made it myself in Brownies."

"Well, it is abstract," said Mother. "Now it's time for Dad to open one of his presents."

That was it. No comment, no cookies. Long after the Christmas festivities were over, I was looking for something in the living room coat closet. There was the cookie jar I had made for Mother, on a high shelf in the back. It had a hat on top, like a sad snowman in solitary confinement. I found Mother sewing in the basement. "Why are you using the cookie jar I made you as a hat rack?"

"It will be more useful there. Nobody in this family needs more cookies."

"But no one will see it in the closet."

"They will if company comes and they hang their coats in the closet."

Years later, when I was in college, I inadvertently returned the favor. Mother gave me a beautiful afghan for Christmas, which she had knitted herself. She said, "Now you won't have to lie down without any cover." She meant it to be a family heirloom I could keep forever. I took the afghan to my room and laid it on the bed, neatly folded as Mother had given it to me. The next time I wanted to rest during the day I unfolded it and covered up. It was warm, soft, and long, even covering my feet; still, I felt a sense of impending dread as I got up. I could not fold it. There it lay, all wadded up, leading Mother to the inevitable conclusion that I did not like it. I did not have the courage to tell Mother I couldn't fold it. The afghan was gone the next time I came into my room. The next day Mother returned it, about half its former length. "I thought you might like it better shorter," she explained.

"I liked it better long. I just couldn't fold it."

Mother did not comment but the next day the afghan was gone. Long or short, I never saw it again. I wish I had it now, but I still can't fold a blanket. We were never able to talk about it. I wish I had that afghan now.

Chapter 14

Touch or Spill? (1955)

The bowl was large and hot and heavy. It trembled in my hands. What was I supposed to do with it?

"For heaven's sake, Judy, serve yourself some corn and pass it on. We don't have all day. Other people want to eat lunch, too." Miss Lily's voice cracked like a bullwhip I had heard in a movie called "Uncle Tom's Cabin," about an evil overseer mistreating slaves before the Civil War. I wish I had a nickel for each time someone tried to rush me by saying we didn't have all day. A word to the wise: that tactic doesn't work on me and it probably doesn't work on most people.

"How can I do that? I need both hands to hold the bowl."

"Set it on the table, pick up the spoon, and put some on your plate. Are you really that dumb or do you just act way to get attention? Look what you've done now. You've spilled it all over the table."

I passed all the bowls on without taking any food and went without lunch. Today was the first day of third grade. Everything felt chaotic and new—new teacher, new subjects, new routine, and now I was expected to serve myself family style, no introduction, no explanation. Mother always fixed my plate at home. She brought it to the table already filled. I never had to handle a large bowl or serving spoon. To make things worse, another authority figure was angry with me. I don't understand to this day how other students at this school learned the skills that pleased those in charge. When you reached a certain age, you were expected magically to develop certain personal care skills. Evidently serving oneself from a bowl was something you were supposed to master by third grade. It seemed to happen to other kids automatically, like turning on a light switch. Yesterday they couldn't do the required task; today they could. This happened over and over, and always ended with me failing to perform in the way the grown-ups expected. This recurring trauma scared and confused me no matter how often it happened. When I asked how other people learned these skills, I was told, "They stay here at night when they have to do things for themselves. Most students don't go running home every night to be spoiled by their parents." This answer was wrong on two counts: first, my parents did not spoil

153

me. No matter what I did it wasn't good enough. They complained about my table manners, about the way I combed my hair, about my inability to tie my shoes. They said I was too quiet and withdrawn. They said I made too much noise. They punished me for talking back and for not answering when spoken to. They became especially incensed because I couldn't remember where all the light switches were in the house. If that was spoiled, what did unspoiled mean? Second, I stayed at school some nights when Mother was ill and there was an evening activity my parents wanted me to attend. No one taught skills at night. The other kids just knew what to do.

I had bread and milk for lunch that day and for many days to come. I did not try, after that disastrous first day, to manipulate the heavy bowls and giant serving spoons. On the second day Miss Lily began yelling at me about it. "Is that really all you want for lunch every day? Don't be a coward, pick up that spoon, and start serving yourself."

"What's in the bowl, Miss Lily?"

"Let the spoon tell you. That's what everyone else does."

"Let the spoon tell you." What kind of cryptic message was that? I wished Uncle Martin were here. He had helped break codes for the Navy during World War II. Maybe he could tell me what "let the spoon tell you" meant. I also wished Miss Lily would quit her job with the state and become a code expert for the CIA. We weren't in a war now, but as Dad liked to say, with President Eisenhower going on about the "military industrial complex," we soon would be. Then our country would need Miss Lily more than our school did. It would also give her something to do other than pick on me. "Let the spoon tell you." I loved fairy tales, especially stories about animals and inanimate objects talking, but this spoon was real. I was not in a story, much to my dismay. "For heaven's sake, Judy! Stop daydreaming. Put some food on your plate and pass it on."

I dug the spoon in tentatively. Something soft and mushy. I lifted the spoon hesitantly. Splash! Mashed potatoes and gravy were all over the table, all over me, and probably on the floor.

"See what you did, you clumsy ox! You don't deserve lunch. Get back to the dorm so Miss Temple can clean you up."

I ran out of the dining room crying, bumping into several tables along the way. Back to the dorm to be yelled at by Miss Temple. Various permutations of this drama took place every day at lunch until Christmas vacation. About half an hour before lunch every day I began to sweat and get stomach cramps. I knew there was no point in going to the nurse. She would just tell me to stop shirking and get back to class.

At Thanksgiving we had a turkey dinner for the first time. At school everyone called it "turkey day," with never a mention of giving thanks for our blessings, not that at the time I thought I had many blessings for which to give thanks, except that Christmas vacation was coming soon and I could get away from the place for a few days. They held the dinner the day before Thanksgiving, as this was the first time the students were allowed to go home for the holiday. Miss Lily for once was gracious enough to fix our plates, but she had only a half portion of the holiday spirit. She loudly and vociferously refused to cut our meat. Touching food with fingers was not allowed. I sat for a minute contemplating what to do. Then I ate the dressing, mashed potatoes, cranberry sauce and green beans, but left the turkey.

On the way home that afternoon Mother asked me what I had for lunch. What was that all about? Mother had never asked me before about lunch. I told her with a growing sense of dread. Something was wrong. I could tell from Mother's voice that she was about to be angry with me, not her usual slow burn, to which I had long since grown accustomed, but on a scale of one to ten, this was going to be an eleven. She was boiling like a teakettle as she said, "You didn't eat the turkey?" She clamped her mouth hard on each word, as if biting the heads off small flying creatures who had the misfortune to stray into her mouth.

"No." I knew right away that this was the wrong answer. I was bewildered and frightened. Why did Mother care whether I had eaten the turkey? Why was she pressing me so hard on a subject we had talked about many times before? Didn't she know that I still couldn't cut my own meat?

"What's wrong with you, you ungrateful little wretch? How do you expect anyone to provide good food for you if you won't eat it? This is a fine way to celebrate Thanksgiving! You should be ashamed of yourself!"

When Dad came home Mother told him I hadn't eaten turkey for lunch and the yelling started all over again. "Dad, what have I done wrong? Why are you and Mother so mad at me?"

"Don't play innocent with us." Dad's voice sounded as angry as I had ever heard it. "You know why we're upset with you. We spent a fortune buying turkey dinners for the whole school and you don't have the decency to eat it."

"Maybe Judy didn't know you bought the turkey, George." Grandma Loehr always seemed to walk in when a crisis was brewing. "Don't jump to conclusions, George. I'm sure Judy wasn't defying you. There must have been something else going on. Judy must have had a reason for not eating the turkey. What was it, Judy?"

"I couldn't cut it."

"Why didn't you just ask Miss Lily to cut it for you?" asked Mother. She seemed to think when you had a problem, all you had to do was ask, and people would be glad to help.

"Miss Lily made a big point of telling us that even though it was a special occasion, she wasn't going to spoil us by cutting our meat. I couldn't ask her after that."

"Let's talk about something more pleasant." Grandma tried to fend off the rising tension. "It's a holiday weekend. Let's stop thinking about problems for a few days. Better yet, Erna, let's go in the kitchen and get supper ready."

"But she has to learn to cut her meat," Mother persisted.

"George Shearing doesn't cut his meat and he's a famous jazz pianist," I said. "James Joyce was a world-renowned writer. His wife cut his meat." I must have had a death wish, because I kept trying to defend myself in the face of all this parental rage.

"They are famous. They've earned the right to have their meat cut."

"If I do something to get famous right away, can I stop worrying about cutting my meat?"

"Wash your hands and get ready to eat. You're not famous yet, especially not in this house."

The food got cold while we practiced and practiced cutting the meat, the long, recalcitrant broccoli spears, the rock-hard baked potato, which I would have loved to pick up and eat like an apple, but the repercussions that would have created were almost beyond imagination.

"Jee-zuss Kee-rist!" Dad had long since lost patience after about an hour of silverware clattering impotently through my fingers, and food landing on the table, the chair, my clothes and the floor—everywhere but in my mouth. "I've always thought that what distinguishes human beings from animals is the use of tools. Do you want to go live at the zoo with the other apes? Hold with the fork. Cut with the knife. For heaven's sake, put some pressure on it. Christ Almighty, look what you did."

The entire piece of roast beef, which was not cut all the way through, flipped onto the floor. It had been hanging by a thread. Tuffy made a lunge for it.

"Now see what you did," Mother screamed. "Can't you learn to do anything for yourself?"

"I don't want anything to eat." I was sobbing into my napkin, but didn't try to leave the table because I hadn't been excused yet.

"No snacks later if you don't eat your supper." Mother was adamant. "And you stay at the table until everyone is finished."

I wondered why Grandma hadn't come to my defense. Was she mad at me too, or had my parents instructed her to stay out of it? "Are you mad at me too, Grandma?"

"Of course I'm not mad at you, Judy, but you have to learn to do these things for yourself."

Was Grandma brainwashed, too? Even Tuffy seemed to have turned against me. I began to scream again, as if a window had opened in my brain and loud, high-pitched waves came rolling out. "I hate this dinner! I hate this family! Home is as bad as school! No wonder Mahatma Gandhi went on a hunger strike. He probably stopped eating meat because he couldn't cut it and people yelled at him. Then he stopped eating altogether because he couldn't cut those stupid broccoli spears. Right now I'm starting a campaign of civil disobedience."

"You're not being very civil now," observed Dad, "but you are being disobedient, so you're halfway there."

"Don't bait her, George," Grandma Loehr said. "She's upset already. I think we may have pushed her too hard."

"I know it's hard, Kate, but she has to learn these things. She could be the most brilliant writer or professor in the world, but nobody will recognize that if she can't cut her meat, butter her bread, or fold her napkin."

I jumped up and ran from the table. In my haste I knocked over my chair. It hit the floor with a clatter.

"You come right back here, young lady." Dad sounded as if he might be screaming soon. "You haven't been excused yet. And pick up that chair. I don't buy nice furniture for this house just so you can break it in a fit of anger."

"I didn't break it, and I'm not coming back to pick it up no matter how mad you get. You can eat this house for all I care, but you have to cut it first." I rushed from the room, screaming louder than ever. Tuffy tried to follow me, but I slammed the door in his face. Traitor.

I lay on my bed and cried myself to exhaustion. What a Thanksgiving this would be! I buried my face in my pillow and pounded my fists on the bed. I fell asleep with my clothes on. The next thing I knew, Grandma's hand was on my shoulder.

"Wake up. It's time to go to bed." That struck me so funny I started laughing hysterically. "Shhh," said Grandma. "Mother and Dad are in bed. You don't want them to get stirred up again."

I got a hilarious picture in my mind of Mother and Dad in a huge pot being stirred by a gigantic spoon. I controlled my giggles and with Grandma's help got quickly into bed. The mental picture of Mother and Dad being stirred up amused and comforted me until I went back to sleep.

The next day, Thanksgiving, wasn't so bad until time for pie at the end of dinner. The entire extended family was there, rendering the ensuing events all the more humiliating.

"We have a special treat for dessert, in addition to the pie."

"Is it ice cream?" asked Janice. "I scream, you scream! We all scream for ice cream!" chanted all three cousins, doing the "I scream" part with unusual gusto, even for them.

"Something much better than ice cream." Mother's enthusiasm convinced no one.

"Judy is going to show us how well she can cut her pie."

"Bo-ring," said Janice.

"Re-mark-able," said Ben in an extended falsetto that sounded like a small, deranged animal dying.

"I want pie!" yelled Bobby, banging his fork on the table. As a boy and the youngest in the family he felt he had the right to demand service, which he always got.

"Hurry up, Judy," said Dad. "We want to get this over and watch football."

Oh, no! I hadn't been told about this in advance. Now I had to demonstrate a skill I didn't have in front of a table full of annoyed people who wanted me to finish quickly so they could eat pie and watch football. I tried to plunge the fork into the slice of pie. This was not one of Mother's baking successes. The crust felt like the Rock of Gibraltar. The fork bounced off. I tried again using all my strength. This time the fork sank in and wouldn't budge. I felt like Arthur trying to pull Excalibur out of the stone, only I was failing the test. Yank! Yank! No fork, no bite of pie. Tears stung the backs of my eyes. Rage and frustration set in. I sawed at the pie. Nothing. I started to shake the plate, not caring whether a bite or an empty fork came up.

"For Christ's sake, Judy," Dad exploded, "don't shake it like a dog! You have the manners of a repulsive animal."

"Then why don't you donate me to the zoo? The animals don't have to cut their food, and the people who gawk at them are strangers, not their own families."

"That's enough backtalk," said Mother. "You sit there and behave and cut that pie."

"I will sit here because you tell me to. Whether I behave is a subjective judgment. I don't want the stupid pie. It has the texture and consistency of asphalt."

"That's enough out of you." Dad's voice rolled over me like the ocean. I was sinking, slipping away, drowning in everyone's scorn and disapproval.

"Judy, if you would stop talking back to your parents and having such a big chip on your shoulder, they wouldn't be so mad at you." Grandma was trying to be reasonable again.

"But they knew I couldn't cut the pie, Grandma. They made a fool of me in front of the whole family. Now everyone thinks I'm stupid."

"You are stupid," said Janice.

"Spoiled, too." Uncle Clive added his two cents' worth, and two cents was just about what it was worth. "I wouldn't put up with that nonsense from Janice. When I tell her to do something, Janice does it."

I could imagine Janice preening. He yelled at her so much, they had so many screaming fights, that she was probably lighting up like a sparkler and getting ready to levitate from the sheer novelty of his praise. I knew she wasn't such a paragon and so did she, but who cared? At last the spotlight was off me. I restrained a sigh of relief. Nobody, not even Bobby, asked for seconds on pie.

The weekend went by with the speed of all weekends. I had time to read only one talking book before it was back to the Wilson School for the Blind and the horrors of lunchtime. Mother had talked to Mrs. Hubbert, and I was transferred from Miss Lily's table to Miss Melba's. She was nicer than Miss Lily: not someone with whom you would expect to go home and live happily ever after, but she did not yell at me about serving myself. There was still the problem of meat cutting, however. Miss Melba handled it with benign neglect. She neither yelled nor helped. You were on your own. You struggled along as best you could. One day I was served a slice of roast beef about the thickness of plastic wrap. No matter what I did with my knife and fork, it folded and crinkled, slithered and slid, wriggled, fought and escaped. I knew the bread plate was near me. Getting what I thought was a brilliant idea, I grabbed two slices, put the offending meat between them and began eating the dry sandwich.

No sooner did I take one good bite than I felt one of those ever-present talons grasping my shoulder. The pain was exquisite, and I quickly put down the sandwich lest I drop it and add to my always-growing list of offenses.

"Haven't I told you a million times that sandwiches are for picnics?" Miss Diefenbacher's voice went with the evil, clutching hand. "No more lunch for you today. Then maybe you'll learn to follow orders and practice your skills."

I could feel the ill wind—clearly blowing no good—of her eager hands snatching my plate away. Had she told me anything about sandwiches? If so, I didn't remember it. I tried to think about Miss Diefenbacher on a picnic. The image wouldn't conjure itself in my mind. What I do remember is that Miss Diefenbacher never spoke to any student except in anger and that she never called anyone by his or her name. It was always "You," "Hey you," or some other impersonal form of address, followed by a pinch, a slap, or some derogatory invective like "dumbbell" or "idiot" that hovered in the air long after polite and just before profane. We were never individual human beings to her, just indistinguishable little savages whom it was her job to whip into shape.

Another day we had spaghetti. I could not get the stuff onto my fork, much less into my mouth. The spaghetti felt like earthworms, and the noodles flopped around like newly caught fish, struggling in their death throes. Some were on the table, some were in my lap, some were on the floor; none was in my mouth. One of the skills they try to teach blind people is to take a piece of bread and use it as a pusher to slide the food onto the fork and thence, one hopes, into the mouth, or so goes the theory. Supposedly you used the bread to touch the food so you wouldn't have to use your fingers, and your hands would stay clean. As the Beatles sang about ten years later, "Yeah, yeah, yeah." Since I am one of those subhumans who can't use tools, the bread got soggy and the food went everywhere but where I wanted it to. Usually I gave up in despair, but this day I was unusually hungry. The smell of the spaghetti was inviting. I listened. No sound but the babble of kids talking and the clink of silverware on plates. The coast seemed to be clear. I surreptitiously slipped my hand into the spaghetti and glided some onto my fork. Then I brought it carefully to my mouth.

"What's going on here? Stop that right now!" The voice startled me and almost made me drop my glass of water. I was in for it now. To my surprise, however, the wrath of Miss Diefenbacher was descending not on me, but on Betty Schuchman, who was sitting next to me.

"What did I do, Miss Diefenbacher?" Betty wailed.

"You know what you did. You're supposed to eat your food with a knife and fork, not put your fingers in it like an animal."

"But I didn't put my fingers in it."

"Don't lie to me. I saw you with my very own eyes."

Betty got a good yelling-at, one of the worst she had received since she had been at the school. Sometimes Betty broke the rules and didn't get caught. Other times she was able to talk her way out of it. This time she hadn't done anything wrong. I was the culprit with the marinara sauce on my fingers, and I let her take the blame without speaking up. I was so afraid of the anger of those people that I made the cowardly choice and did not stand up for what was right.

During the 2008 presidential campaign I tried to read all the books I could about the candidates. One of these, available from the National Library Service talking book program, was Faith of My Fathers by John McCain. In it McCain discusses his experiences as a prisoner of war in Vietnam. He was tortured, but refused to give information or to make propaganda statements for the Vietcong. Because his father was a famous admiral, McCain was offered early release. He steadfastly declined to be freed while his comrades were still being held in captivity. Because he declined to be used as a propaganda tool, McCain was tortured more than ever. When he came home McCain continued to speak against torture, although many in his party favor torture as a way of getting information from terrorists. Many people in power, although they have never been to war, much less been captured and tortured, believe waterboarding and other forms of "enhanced interrogation techniques" are morally acceptable. McCain, although he favors most things military, staunchly denounces all torture at all times. I was struck with admiration as I read these chapters. Here was a man who, under great duress, maintained his convictions. Not that being castigated by Miss Diefenbacher approached the trauma and horror of being tortured by the Vietcong, but I feel a small spark of solidarity with Senator McCain and hope that if a crisis of conviction comes my way, I will have the strength to follow his example. I did not have such an example to follow that day in the dining room. I believe the dessert was canned peaches, but for me it was Jell-O—cold, slimy, quivering inside, paralyzed with fear outside. I sat there and let Betty take the rap for my misdeed. If anyone had asked me straight out, I would probably have owned up, but when I had the chance to save myself by a lie of omission, I did not come forward.

The battle over eating never stops. I interrupted graduate school to attend two rehabilitation centers, both of which offered a class called table etiquette. We sawed at pork chops, tried to slather butter and salt on baked potatoes and corn on the cob, pour cream in our coffee, butter our bread, and worst of all, put butter and syrup on pancakes. Ogden Nash wrote a poem called "Ode to a Glass of Milk" which says in part, "It holds a half a pint when filled, and half a gallon when it's spilled." The same can be said of pancake syrup. It does not make a bit of difference whether I am dealing with pure maple syrup, high fructose corn syrup, or some other sweet, sticky substance, it spreads and goes all over me, all over my clothes, the table, the floor, sometimes even in my hair. Then there are those annoying little packets of jelly, which I am supposed to open and spread daintily on toast. Actually they don't give me much trouble, because in all these years I have never been able to get one of the stubborn things open. So I'm forever condemned to dry toast, dry pancakes and black coffee.

Some blind people do not touch the food, use a piece of bread for a pusher, and leave the table with clean hands, but the food expands to cover the surrounding space for miles around. These are the spillers. Some blind people's hands contain remnants of gravy, sauce or crumbs, but the food stays reasonably confined to the plate. These are the touchers. I am a toucher. You can be sure that most blind people are one or the other. Each method has its proponents, but neither is entirely satisfactory. The establishment—that is, the National Federation of the Blind, the American Council of the Blind, and the rehabilitation community—strongly prefer the spill method, although they would rather die than admit that any blind person who uses a bread pusher ever spills food. One of the drawbacks of the touch method is that if you are eating with sighted people, especially country club types, some officious person—usually a woman but not always—says in a shrill, carrying voice for all to hear, "Oh, you have gravy on your hands. Let me give you a napkin to wipe it off."

Then the person proceeds to wipe your hands and sometimes your mouth.

Next you take another bite. "Oh my! Your hands are messy again." And so on until you finish the meal or give up in despair. Usually you don't eat or do anything socially with that person ever again. Mostly it's a small loss, but it saddens me each time it happens, because my abilities are not good enough and that person's heart is not big enough for us to be friends. Of course the educators and organizations are right. One should, wherever possible, do as much as one can in appearance and accomplishment for oneself, but what happens to the person who can't do the simplest physical things without a big struggle and a bigger mess, and sometimes not at all? How can you earn respect for your mental abilities when people are preoccupied with your physical disabilities? One woman told me recently that I had to learn to be equal friends. I have tried to help her daughter with English. I composed music for her church when I was a member. I always do my best to look neat and clean when I go out. Is that equal? Is that a friend? I still can't drive a car. I still can't eat like Miss Manners. Which will it be, touch or spill?

When I meet a new blind person, especially if he or she has been represented to me as a super-achieving genius whose accomplishments I am supposed to admire and emulate, the anxiety is exceeded only by the schadenfreude. If we are going to eat together and one or both of us has a sighted companion, the tension goes up exponentially. I anticipate with dread what the other person's sighted companion will say about my table manners. I've ordered so much fried shrimp in restaurants (because I don't have to cut it) that I expect any day to turn into a shellfish. But most restaurants don't have fried shrimp and there are fewer sandwich choices. After the event with the other blind person, I can't wait to hear from my sighted friend, in minute detail, which of us was the bigger slob. If he got a spot on his shirt, score one for me. If I spilled gravy on the tablecloth, that's one for him. These comparisons can be so ridiculous and at the same time terrifying that many blind people will not eat with someone they don't already know and trust.

Whether about food etiquette, housekeeping, mobility or any skill, comparisons are always destructive and useless. Usually after establishing a certain level of trust with another blind person, we find out that each of us is reassuringly ordinary, trying to get through life like everyone else. Comparison seems to be a device that educators and families use as a motivational tool, but I say again that it has never worked with me. It only makes me feel afraid and resentful.

Quite a number of years ago—I don't remember the date or the author's name—I read a New Yorker profile of James Joyce. The writer described in vivid detail how Joyce's wife had to cut his meat for him because he was visually impaired. Was that necessary in a literary profile? I wonder if the author was Ved Mehta or some other blind writer. Blind writers, especially if they belonged to the "aggressive independence" school of thought, would be preoccupied with issues like meat-cutting. They might be forgiven their lack of tact. If the writer were sighted, there would be no excuse for it. I can hardly contain my contempt for someone who would publicly humiliate the author of Ulysses and Finnegan's Wake because he couldn't cut his meat. Could the author of that profile write those books? I'd be willing to bet he couldn't.

The compulsion to use proper sighted-person table etiquette is so deeply ingrained that one is almost as afraid to break it as to wet one's pants in public. Once I had to go on a business trip in another city where I stayed in a hotel. I was tired when I arrived, so I decided to use room service for dinner rather than to brave the stress of the dining room. The man at room service read me the menu over the phone. They had many delicious-sounding items, including a big steak. I wanted to order it, sit alone in my room, pick up the steak and gnaw it off the bone like a cave woman. My inhibition was so strong that I ordered—you guessed it—fried shrimp. How brainwashed can you get?

So the touch-or-spill quandary continues, like a monster always hiding under the table. Some blind people who are unusually secure and comfortable with themselves will ask to have their meat cut in the kitchen. I've done this a few times, but I always feel guilty and inadequate when I do.

Then there is the staring issue. Everyone with a disability, no matter how accomplished and well trained, gets stared at when they go out in public. There's nothing to be done about it, so you may as well get used to it. I had a friend who was a middle school teacher. When people stared at us she gave them what she called the "mean teacher look" and they melted away like ice in summer. Mother claimed she had never seen anyone she couldn't stare down. Some people, though, can't stand the staring and they can't stand my table manners. They can't stand the contrast between my well-spoken, well-educated self and the slob who touches the food on her fork and guides it to her mouth. Make no mistake: it would be better neither to touch nor spill. That's why the blindness establishment pushes table etiquette so hard. At one rehabilitation center I attended, there was a girl who put her face down to the plate and lapped like an animal. I'm ashamed to say I found that revolting. Where do you draw the line? How do you teach everyone up to his or her ability without turning the student into a mental case? We need to stop shoving everyone into the same mold, to concentrate on each person's abilities rather than their disabilities.

Then there's the question of parental influence. The residential schools deny that they try to break up families, but they start working hard at it the first day. Miss Brookshire said, "Her mommy was too good to her" before I had my coat off the first morning and from there it was downhill all the way. Everyone at school from the superintendent down to fellow students condemned my parents for over-protecting me. They had no idea how my parents made me practice skills at home for hours each day. They never quite gave up the skills practice, but they eventually switched their emphasis to academic subjects, at which I excelled. Most people confused this resignation with over-protection and complained vociferously about it.

I never did master those skills. I still go through life spilling a little and touching a lot, but it was not because my parents did not make me try.

Chapter 15
The Pillsbury Cookbook (Oct. 1955)

At school the grown-ups, and even the students, talked all the time about independence: find your way around the school independently, make your bed independently, fold your clothes independently, cross the street independently. If you walked down the hall arm in arm with a friend, one of the grown-ups would whack the intertwined arms hard to separate them and say, "Alright, break it up," as if we had been having a head-bashing, nosebleed-inducing fight. Teamwork was unheard of. Everyone's goal was to do everything alone, everything all by yourself. I always seemed to be in a battle, trying to do things for myself while the housemothers and teachers said I did a bad job and Mother told me she could do it better and faster. Fast was a top priority with Mother, better came next, and independence a distant third.

Into this backdrop came my ninth birthday, for which Mother gave me three small braille cookbooks with instructions for preparing some of the most popular products from Pillsbury, Betty Crocker and General Foods. I couldn't wait to read them and make one of the recipes myself. I chose my favorite, a chocolate cake from the Pillsbury cookbook. Right there was where independence hit a snag. I had to ask Mother to pick up the ingredients the next time she shopped. Mother said she would; we would bake the cake on Saturday and surprise Dad when he came home from work. Saturday morning took forever to come, but when it finally did, I jumped out of bed in high excitement, ready to get to work. Grandma Loehr took care of washing the breakfast dishes and I ran to grab my braille book so we could get started. My plan was to get the ingredients together, then read the instructions and follow them one at a time. "You won't need your book," said Mother with that brisk efficiency I always found so intimidating. "I can read you the directions on the box."

"But I thought the whole point was for me to read from my book and follow the recipe."

"This will be faster and easier."

"Easier for whom?" I muttered. Even though Grandma Dent had been gone for almost three years, I was sure her ghost would haunt me if I said "who."

"Don't pout." Mother's patience was wearing thin even though we hadn't started yet. "Get that lower lip in. You've got it sticking out so far that I could store all three of your cookbooks on it and still have room for War and Peace and the King James Bible."

Best to stop talking and get on with it. "Shall I get out the milk?"

"You won't need milk. We'll use water."

"But the recipe calls for milk. It says so right here." I started to open my book.

"Will you put that away? I just told you, you won't need it. The instructions on the box call for water."

"But why are the print instructions different from the braille instructions for the same cake?"

Mother heaved one of her deep sighs, always a danger signal. "Your book has the recipe for Pillsbury chocolate cake. I bought Duncan Hines. It was three cents cheaper. I'm not about to pay top price for a cake mix when I don't have to. Now let's get some water and start mixing this batter. I don't have all day. Some of us have important work to do."

"But I thought I was going to read the directions from my book and we would make the recipe. I can't read this box, and anyway, the cake won't taste as good with water instead of milk." Mother had no idea why I wanted to bake the cake in the first place; I could not make her understand.

"Do you want to bake this cake or not?"

"No!" I stamped my foot and began to scream. "You deceived me. You said you would get Pillsbury so I could read my book and we could make it together." I screamed and cried at the top of my voice. "You lied to me! I don't want to bake that stupid cake with water instead of milk. It won't be any good. You knew I didn't have a Duncan Hines cookbook."

"Someday you're going to have to learn to save your money. You're lucky I agreed you could have a cake at all. Nobody needs cake."

"But I wanted to bake a cake using my braille cookbook!"

"'I want! I want!' That's all I ever hear around this house. You want! Your father wants! Your grandmother wants! When do I get what I want? Well, news flash! That time is now! Come with me, young lady, and I'll get what I want! Then maybe you'll learn to behave!" Mother grabbed my arm, pinching me hard, and frog-marched me into the bedroom I shared with Grandma Loehr. "Lie down on that bed! No, on your stomach!" Mother grabbed my hairbrush off the dresser and began whacking my rear end. As the beating went on, the whacks became harder and harder until after a while they didn't hurt anymore, and I stopped screaming from the sheer horror of it. My mind went away, as I'm sure Dalilah's mind had when Miss MacGrauth beat her. I was not as poetically gifted as Dalilah; I could not think of a chant that had the rhythmic force of "Old lady MacGrauth can't hurt me!" "Mother, you can't hurt me" did not cut it, but inside I felt the same defiant outrage as I imagined Dalilah had.

As my mind drifted, I recalled a story both Mother and Grandma had told, although from different points of view, about another time and another cake. Mother and Dad had just started dating, but Mother was sure this was the man she wanted to marry. It was Mother's birthday and Dad was coming over for dinner. Grandma offered to make the cake. At some point during the preparation, Mother came into the kitchen and saw to her horror that Grandma was baking a chocolate cake. Mother felt about chocolate the way most right-thinking people feel about Brussels sprouts. "Mom, why are you making a chocolate cake?"

"George likes chocolate cake."

"But it's my birthday. I hate chocolate."

"Erna, this is an important time in your life. You have to decide right now: Do you want to eat cake, or do you want to catch a man?" Grandma went right on stirring the batter for the chocolate cake. Mother caught the man, but she never quite forgave him, or me, for our love of chocolate.

Crack! What had I just heard? I had not known there were bones in my bottom that could break the way Old Lady MacGrauth had broken my wrist. Mother kept on hitting me; I felt something sharp. It was the handle of the hairbrush that had broken.

"Now, you stay here until you think you can act like a civilized human being. Mother's voice was a snarl that sounded neither civilized nor human. "And don't get any ideas about a new hairbrush. Maybe if you have to use this one every day it will remind you to behave."

Mother was as good as her word. That hairbrush stayed in its place of honor on the front corner of my dresser for nine years, until I left for college. Every time I brushed my hair I scratched my hand on that broken handle and remembered. We never did bake that cake.

Chapter 16
Mother (1955-56)

"Pay! Attention! To what! You're doing!"

"I'll be here to do it for you" is a common misconception shared by caregivers and loved ones of people with disabilities. They believe it expresses love and loyalty. "Don't be afraid. I'll never leave you." It's almost always faster and easier for the helper to perform the task rather than to go through the often-excruciating process of teaching the person with the disability to do it. My motor skills were so bad and so intermittent that I drove everyone crazy who tried to teach me to do anything, especially my long-suffering, never-too-patient parents. Out of this tension evolved "I'll always be there to do it for you," but they will not always be there for you. Caregivers leave; friends move away; parents die. That just leaves you and your skills, or lack thereof. As a famous comedian once said, "If you need a helping hand, you'll find one at the end of your arm." If you struggle and struggle, persist and persist, but objects still flow through those hands like water, then your mission in life becomes to find another way, today, tomorrow, forever.

The forever continues to this day. Although my parents are gone, most of my instructors are gone, and all the demanding, pushy, never-satisfied people are out of my life, the battle rages every moment: Jonathan Edwards, Cotton Mather, and Elmer Krochett from New Enterprises for the Blind haunt my dreams. On cold, damp, winter days like today, my wrist hurts and I feel the clutch, jerk, crack of Miss MacGrauth breaking my wrist, and I choose a cup of tea over a bowl of chili every time. When I read the story from Genesis about Jacob wrestling with the angel, and the one from Roman Catholic tradition about St. Anthony wrestling with the devil, I could empathize with them, though I wasn't clear about whether I was wrestling with angel or devil. But the wrestling match never ends, unless I'm having a pleasant conversation with friends—and I do mean friends, not mildly hostile persons who require social skills and small talk—writing, or listening to music, sports on radio, or enjoying a braille or audiobook.

The memory of that day and of Mother beating me is never far away, but at least I've thrown out that broken hairbrush.

One of the stereotypes that prevailed when I was growing up was that all blind women can crochet and knit. Mother was outstanding at both. She also did several types of needlepoint, embroidery, and quilting while watching television. I'm not much of a judge, but her crafts felt flawless. Each year she gave beautiful, homemade Christmas gifts to friends and relatives. The bar was high, both at home and school, when the time came for me to learn to knit.

Mother decided to teach me herself, hoping to encourage the novelty of a decent grade in home economics class. A fine distinction was made at our school between "art," which was made from paper and clay, and "home ec," one of the many disciplines of which was "handwork," that is, knitting and crocheting, made with yarn, needles and hooks. It's a mystery to me which is which, except they have different vocabularies. I can't tell by touch whether a garment with those little holes in it are knitted or crocheted. Maybe it's neither, and I've grabbed a moth-eaten sweater or a hunk of Swiss cheese. When I read a knitting or crochet pattern, which I occasionally do just to see if I still don't understand it, it feels encrypted, as if it needs Uncle Martin or a Navajo Windtalker to decipher its arcane secrets.

I did not consciously resist working with yarn. In fact I have always wished for something to do with my hands while listening to audiobooks rather than sticking them into the cookie jar or chip bag. When I was in eighth grade, Mr. Gilbert assigned me a book report on Gone with the Wind. I told him I couldn't possibly do it. The talking book was 72 records on the old 33-rpm disks, which would require many more snacks than I could afford on my meager allowance; besides, the other kids already teased me about being fat. He laughed and said the best solution was exercise, the exercise of discipline. I did the book report using braille books. There was always that void, however. I listened to many things—baseball on radio, music, talking books for school and recreation. I imagined knitting socks and sweaters for the Salvation Army, or for poor children in what was then called the "third world." I could do volunteer work without leaving home. Mother was eager to teach me and I was eager to learn.

"Now, Judy, the first thing you have to do is cast on," said Mother in a brisk, businesslike way, as though presenting the coming year's plan for a Fortune 500 company. My teeth ground. Shoulders tensed. Hands clenched. Mother sounded efficient yet excited. She was probably thrilled that I expressed interest in learning something she enjoyed.

"What does it mean to cast on, Mother?" As usual I was full of questions.

"You have to get the yarn on the needle somehow. Give me your hand. Let me show you."

Wooly caterpillar slipped through my fingers, except no, this was long and skinny like an earthworm, but dry and fuzzy like a caterpillar.

"This is the yarn, Judy. Close your fingers on it. I'm going to show you how to put it on the needle. That's casting on. Then I'll teach you to make the stitches. When you go forward, it's called knit. When you go backward, it's called purl. Each row needs a different combination of knit and purl."

Two years before, when I was seven, I had received an add-a-pearl necklace for my First Communion. It was only an inch of tiny seed pearls, but they felt alive, cool and a little wet. I could almost imagine seawater and the flesh of the oyster. Grandma Loehr had told me that pearls are made when a grain of sand gets into the oyster's shell. It hurts like crazy until the oyster makes a smooth, protective coating around the sand, which then becomes a pearl. I don't know if adversity makes you stronger—most of the time it has made me grumpy—but those pearls, with their load of legend, and smooth, cool texture, transported me to a mystical space where I had a lot more courage and a little more control. But what did knitting backward have to do with pearls? As usual, I was perplexed.

"Pay attention to what you're doing!" Mother's voice was an emphatic drumbeat: One! Two! Three! Four! "Pay! Attention! To what! You're doing!" It reminded me of the rhythm band at school. I played the triangle, which had no force at all compared to the big bass drum.

"Come on, Judy, don't drift off into dreamland. Close your fingers around this yarn so I can show you how to cast on."

Mother grabbed my hand along with the yarn and put me through a kind of finger yoga that felt clumsy and unnatural. The yarn kept falling off the needle. The less success I had, the more my anxiety went up and my enthusiasm went down. Finally in desperation I asked, "Mother, if I don't learn to cast on, will I be cast off?"

"Oh, for crying out loud!" Mother's voice rose. "Can't you ever put your mind on your work? Do you have to turn every job into a silly word game?"

That was the end of knitting instruction for that day. There would have been another screaming match, except we declared a ceasefire before the tension got too overwhelming. Mother quickly lost interest in teaching me to knit. I never did learn to cast on. My grades in home economics are best left to the imagination. Years later when I read my first knitting pattern in braille, I found out that purl has nothing whatsoever to do with pearls. Maybe that's why my inability to knit, purl, and cast on never made me feel noble about adversity.

"Judy's Turn To Cry"

The kitchen was a continuing source of trouble between Mother and me. When I was sad or upset, Grandma Loehr—who did not play a musical instrument the way Grandma Dent did—would comfort me with cookies, candy, and other sweet or salty treats, most of them homemade. I developed a taste for sugar and salt, perfectly acceptable in the '50s, but anathema today. Fat and crunch made me smile—chocolate, ice cream, lots of butter on my bread, Alfredo sauce on my pasta. Almost from the moment I started school, the kids began teasing me about being fat. One of their favorite taunts was:

Fatty, fatty, two by four.

Can't get through the bathroom door.

So she did it on the floor.

I had no idea I was fat. I didn't understand the concept. Mother soon cleared that up for me by reading me a long book called "Reduce and Stay Reduced." It had a calorie chart at the end, from which I learned another new concept. All the foods I liked were high-calorie, fattening, and bad for me. Thus at the age of nine I was put on a strict diet. The first thing Mother did was put me on the scale. "Eighty-six pounds!" From the way Mother said it you would have thought I weighed 86 tons.

Salad and steamed vegetables for me, and sometimes a piece of boiled meat that, had I been sighted, would have required an electron microscope to find. I threw up after almost every dinner. It wasn't bulimia, just ordinary vomit. I felt deprived and wretched, or should I say retched.

One day in the summer of 1963 I had the radio on, and it played "Judy's Turn to Cry" by Leslie Gore. "What are they saying?" demanded Mother. "'Judy's getting fat'? Is it a song about you?" I switched off the radio, ran to my room, as I so often did, and closed the door. It was time to throw another fit; it was Judy's turn to cry.

In high school Mother loved to take me shopping and show me the fashionable clothes in the petite department. "Aren't these clothes beautiful? If you lose weight, you can wear clothes like that."

I have been on Weight Watchers, Atkins, Protein Power, the South Beach Diet, the grapefruit diet, the orange and graham cracker diet—Mother was especially proud of that one because she designed it herself and said it worked for her. I've lost at least a ton in my lifetime, and it has all come back bigger and better than ever.

"Hail, hail, the gang's all here."

Something wet, slick, cold lay in my hand. It felt a little like Tuffy's nose, but much harder, much colder. It felt like the ice cubes Mother put in glasses of iced tea or lemonade, but shapeless. You could call this object "ice," but not "cube." There was a loud sound against the house, the way a car sounds driving over a gravel road, a sound that my friend Lois Brown, years later, would call "Aunt Matilda's shooting gallery."

THE VIRTUE OF GIVING UP

"Look, Judy, this is a hailstone. Hear it hailing outside?"

Mother had just come through the front door in a flurry of wet, cold air. She had gone outside in a storm to bring me a hailstone. Like the glass of milk and the crystal chandelier, the hailstone was hard in a smooth, good way. "Hail." It sounded like "hell," but hell was supposed to be hot. I remembered a New Year's Eve party at our house when we had all sat around the table and sung, "Hail, hail the gang's all here. What the hell do we care?" It was fun to sing "hell" at the top of my voice and not get in trouble for it. It reminded me of last summer when we had gone to the St. Louis Municipal Opera, known as the Muny for short (which still puts on musicals every summer on its huge outdoor stage in Forest Park). That evening they were performing South Pacific. One of the sailors sang, "Bloody Mary is the girl I love, now ain't that too damn bad?" I giggled and yelled at the top of my voice, "Daddy, that man said a bad word!"

"It's just a song, Pieface. Besides, real sailors in the South Pacific probably said a lot worse than that; war would make people cuss."

"How does war make you use bad words, Daddy? If I were in a war, would I cuss?"

"You probably would. Now be quiet and listen to the story."

Meanwhile, the hailstone was changing shape, getting smaller and wetter. Soon there was just a damp spot on my hand. "Hail, hail, the stone's all gone," I sang softly to myself. "What the hail do we care?" I laughed as the hailstone went away and the words "hail" and "hell" danced and swirled.

"Oh, Judy, see what you did! You got your dress all wet. I brought the hailstone in so you could see what it felt like. It was a part of nature, not a toy."

I did not respond. What was there to say? I was baffled. What had I done wrong now?

Both Mother and Dad wanted to educate me, but Mother's efforts tended toward hands-on experiences, while Dad's were usually about words and ideas. I was better with words; when Mother tried to show me something, in nature or in the kitchen, I usually hurt myself or made a mess, either of which got me screamed at by Mother. I always felt so loved at the beginning of one of Mother's experiments, and so rejected at the end, that I never knew whether to be happy or terrified when she paid attention to me.

Mother had trouble thinking ahead to the consequences of her actions and taking responsibility for them afterwards. She wanted to show me a hailstone, but didn't think about what would happen next. She did not take it from me after a reasonable interval or tell me to put it down the sink; Mother waited until it melted and then yelled at me for making a mess. Messes made Mother frantic. A speck of dust sent her into hysterics. A stain ruined her entire day. Spilled milk was a major incident. Aunt Ida used to say that if not for the psychology of it, you could eat off our floor and drink from our toilet. My cousin Ben, Ida's son, heard that story so often that, at five years old when he was visiting us, he washed his hair in the toilet. Mother was not pleased. "What if someone had forgotten to flush?" she demanded. "You would have gotten a surprise you didn't want."

Later when Ben was outside playing, I took Mother aside. "When I do something wrong, you scream and spank me. I've never washed my hair in the toilet. Are you going to spank Ben?"

"Ben is a guest in our house. You don't spank a guest. As to washing your hair in the toilet, you don't wash it anywhere. I still have to wash it for you in the sink and you scream like you're being tortured. You have an extra obstacle to overcome. Because you are blind, people are afraid of you and don't want you around. So you have to be the very best little girl you can be."

"Is it like being afraid of a monster? Am I a monster?"

"No, silly, but people who don't know you think you are. That's why you always have to be extra good."

I walked away baffled by the unfairness of it. Ben could do something wrong and get away with it; I had to be perfect all the time. That dichotomy haunts me to this day. I know it isn't true, but still it lingers. When someone refuses to wait on me in a store or says, "What will she have?" in a restaurant, I feel a resentful tightening in my chest and jaw, an anger so deep and violent I could be the monster they are afraid of. When an unenlightened therapist or well-meaning friend says, "Don't react. You be the bigger person," I feel that same impotent, little-kid helplessness that I felt decades ago when Mother coddled Ben and spanked me.

Chapter 17

Open Spaces, Deep Dark Places

This is a chapter about nothing. It is so intensely about nothing that I feel tempted to leave several blank pages here and move on to something else, but that would be a gimmick and there is nothing gimmicky about this topic. When people first meet me they often ask what I can see. I tell them I see nothing.

"Nothing?" they always respond incredulously. "Do you see black?"

My answer depends on whether I feel like being honest or grumpy. There are several grumpy answers to this question, ranging from "Why do you need to know?" to "For the millionth time, will you stop with the black already? Do you think you're the first person to ask me that? We don't even know one another and you're asking me intimate personal questions. Please stop."

The honest answer requires much more thought and care. The underlying assumption in this question is that the sighted person's world is a universal frame of reference and I should be willing and able to describe my world in terms of theirs, but I don't know their world. I try hard to learn about it every day, but there are still gaps. One of these is color. I'm told that women usually wear black dresses to funerals. If black were what everyone saw, there would be a lot of naked women attending funerals. What about those "basic black" dresses every woman is advised to have in her wardrobe? If they were as basic as what I see, all the fashion designers would go broke. Once and for all: I do not see black; I see nothing. I never could think of a good analogy to explain this until I read a book about Shackleton's exploration of the South Pole. One of the most disorienting phenomena the expedition experienced was whiteout. The sun shining on the snow and ice caused Shackleton and his companions to see nothing but white. No landmarks were visible, just white. Even the Antarctic explorers saw more during whiteouts than I do all the time. They saw white; I see nothing. It's important to add that I do not speak, here or anywhere in this book, for some vague entity called "the blind." These are my experiences, my memories. No one elected me to speak for them. I speak for myself.

Most blind people I have spoken to and read about say they see lights, shadows, specks, floaters, something behind their eyes. Some people retain vivid visual memories of places with which they were familiar when they were sighted. My friend Ken Johnson is like that; when he rides in a car or on a bus he can track exactly where he is by the number and direction of turns. He can give directions not just like a sighted person, but better than most sighted people. Some blind people are so good at finding their way around that they think of it as a sport. They like to be dropped off and not told where they are so they can see how long it takes them to get home. Can I do these things? Can every blind person? You know any more good jokes?

Lost in my own house

Anyone who has experienced the skills of one of these outstanding blind travelers leaps to the conclusion that every blind person can and should go everywhere with that kind of ease and precision. It comes up almost every time I meet a new sighted person. When new visitors come to my home, I go to great lengths to make sure they don't arrive while I'm walking. Any time I'm walking, I'm struggling. I get lost in my own house several times a day. From kindergarten through death, the blindness rehabilitation system attaches enormous importance to mobility because it is probably our most public face. You can flunk every subject in school, you can have the artistic ability of a bright turnip, you can be the most obnoxious jerk known to man, but if you have outstanding mobility, especially if you are one of those migratory intuitives like Ken Johnson, you can go to the head of the caste.

There were 179 pupils in the Wilson School for the Blind when I started. If Ken Johnson was number one in mobility, I was number 179. I couldn't find my way anywhere. People would say, "Picture it in your mind." Just as I saw nothing in the world around me, I also saw nothing in my mind. That stumped and annoyed people. They equated mobility with intelligence. One of Miss Brookshire's favorite sayings was, "You're so smart. You're the only one in kindergarten who can read, but you can't find your way to the dining room or the dorm or back to class. What's wrong with you?"

I wished I had the answer. Miss Brookshire wasn't the only person who wanted to know what was wrong with me. When I cried from frustration, or the scrambled-egg feeling that whirled around in my head and made me feel as if my brain were a shapeless mass of goo, Dad would shout, "Knock it off! What the hell's wrong with you?" When I couldn't tie my shoes or button my coat, Mother would exclaim, "You're so stupid! Why can't you do the simplest things? Try to be more like your cousin Janice. She can at least dress herself."

Writing about these problems decades later, I see that I've mixed up dressing and mobility. They are part of the same thing, part of the same emptiness, the same terrifying disorientation for which I've been trying to find an explanation my whole life. Most maddening is that it's intermittent, like when your car goes kachunk, kachunk, every time you start it, but when you show it to the mechanic it purrs like a contented kitten.

My parents and teachers would say, "You did it yesterday. Why can't you do it today?" That argument was logical and reasonable except for the deep rage in their voices, as if they were barely keeping it together, when what they really wanted to do was bludgeon me to death with a crowbar. The implication was that mobility and manual dexterity were moral virtues, like love and integrity. If I didn't excel at them, I was bad.

If I pointed out that I was good at English and math, they would say, "So what? Those subjects are easy for you. The real achievement is in working hard and doing well at hard things."

That time I fell down the stairs on my first day was not my last fall down the stairs. I couldn't remember where they were. I would approach slowly, thinking "Be careful. Stairs coming up." or down, as the case might be. I would take one baby step after another, then, bang! Down again.

"Good news, Grandma!" I shouted one afternoon as I came in from school.

"What is it, Honey? You sound like you've had an extra special day."

"I have, Grandma. I didn't fall down once today. It's the first time since I started school."

Grandma gave me one of her famous hugs. "So you've fallen down at school every day until today?"

"Yes, Grandma." My good news didn't seem so good anymore. Grandma held me even closer. Something wet touched my face. Grandma was crying real tears.

"I'm sorry, Grandma. Did I do something bad?"

"No, little Sweetmeat, but I think maybe the school did. I'll have to talk to your father."

"Oh, please, Grandma, don't tell Dad. He'll get mad and yell at me. He doesn't like me to be an idiot."

"Dad loves you. He won't get mad because you fell. Dad doesn't mean to call you an idiot. He knows how smart you are. He just gets frustrated when you have trouble learning to do things. He wishes he could be a better teacher. Patience was never one of Dad's strong points. Things came pretty easily to him when he was little. Your Father God loves you, too. Why don't you talk to Him about it tonight before you go to sleep? Ask Him to protect you and give you another good day like today."

"Yes, Grandma." I didn't tell Grandma that I had asked God many times for help with my troubles at school, with no discernible results. Miss Brookshire, Miss Temple, the lunch woman, Mrs. Hubbert, and especially Mrs. Caine still yelled at me. The big kids still pushed me off the merry-go-round at recess; that didn't happen on the first day, but it was a frequent occurrence after that. I still got lost almost every time I tried to go somewhere. Worst of all, God was never there to catch me when I fell down the stairs.

"Draw a picture in your mind"

Every day was a constant struggle to find my way around. We were always ordered to walk on the right side of the hall, the way cars drive on the right side of the road, but we ran into one another anyway. The big kids, most of whom seemed like powerful giants, would slam into me and yell something like, "Out of the way, slowpoke." I memorized how many doors down the hall each room was where I needed to go, restroom five doors on the right, Miss Brookshire's room two doors, gym three doors after you go down the basement steps. A problem came up when I had to find a room that was on the left side of the hall. The teachers told me to walk down the right side, estimate where the room was that I wanted, put my back to the wall that had previously been on my right, and walk straight ahead. Are you kidding me? I could no more do that complicated maneuver than stand on my head and eat a peanut butter and jelly sandwich. In fact, the latter might have been easier. I tried sneaking down the left side of the hall and counting the doors as usual. Unh-uh. Every time I tried that I was both hit and yelled at. One day when this happened, Miss Brookshire shouted, "Judy, they're going to mow you down, and I don't care if they do."

There were many places where I couldn't use the door-counting method. If the location couldn't be memorized with mathematical precision, if there was anything in the least asymmetrical about it, I was lost. Everyone kept saying, "Draw a picture in your mind." Mother even made a map of the school using lines drawn on thick paper with the sewing machine needle. She then made labels on tape, which she stuck to each place I needed to find. This was a great sacrifice for Mother. Drawing tactile diagrams was not good for the sewing machine and Mother was a professional tailor. The music wing, the dining room, and the auditorium were off limits to me unless I could listen to other students' voices and follow them in. Worst of all, I didn't learn to find the library by myself until fourth grade.

If this book is a bestseller, or even a mild success, I live in fear that I may be asked to speak at the Wilson School for the Blind. I get cold shivers and stomach cramps imagining a new incarnation of Miss Brookshire or Mrs. Caine browbeating me, "Put your back to the wall and cross."

When I was in sixth or seventh grade, they built an addition onto the school. We had to walk outside to reach it. There were no walls to bounce echoes off of and I never did learn my way through that empty space. Just as you need pH balance in a garden, you need noise balance for mobility. I seem to need it more than many blind people I know. If there is too much ambient sound, you can't distinguish the sounds that give you information from the extraneous junk. If there is too little, you can't learn anything from surrounding sounds, and you soon find out what they mean by "dead silence."

The Three Busketeers

At the beginning of seventh grade we began to ride back and forth to school on buses provided by the new Special School District for Handicapped children. Suddenly it became less imperative for us to stay all week at the school to "get our skills." That argument had been a joke from the start, since no skills were taught after school anyway, unless you considered the constant barrage of sarcasm and disapproval we experienced every day teaching. Now we had to go home every night because the school was on such a tight budget that, magically, between sixth and seventh grade, they couldn't afford to have us stay there. All the pupils in K through 12 who lived in St. Louis City or County had to go home every night. Never mind the ironclad dictum the school authorities had espoused all those years that pupils who went home every night would have arrested social development and no friends. I still have arrested social development and no friends of the kind they meant, but now I consider this condition a badge of honor rather than a stigma.

The buses picked up the students at their homes, then dropped them off at their respective schools. Which bus you took depended on where you lived in the county. Three of us who rode the bus to the Wilson School for the Blind took the same bus—Jon Miller, Sandra Tillman, and me. We were all in seventh grade. There were other blind students on our bus, too, but they were younger. Our first class was English, held in the new building. The bus dropped us at the Spring Avenue entrance, so we had to traipse through the shorter but more confusing "outside way" from one building to the other. There was also a circuitous "inside way" which led through several basement rooms, but the totally blind students preferred it because there were lots of wonderful walls to keep us oriented. I've been called a "blind bat" by lots of people trying to insult me. Some people shorten this to "blink," acceptable among blind friends, but fighting words if a sighted person says it. I don't know whether bats are really blind and find their way by echolocation, or whether all that is a myth. Besides, it would be much less alliterative or picturesque to say, "blind as a dolphin," or "blind as a hump-backed whale." In any case, I need walls to get around, but the administration in its infinite wisdom preferred us to use the outside way, even in snow, sleet, rain, or hail—fortunately they never made us use it in "gloom of night" because school was not in session; even those inveterate whip-crackers wanted to go home sometime. Some of us couldn't negotiate the outside way, but the powerful people made us use it, all the while insisting that we had to be independent. If we used the inside way, which most of us, even I, could manage alone, they had a fit and we got the usual tongue-lashing.

Sandra was partially sighted, while Jon and I were totally blind. Usually the partially sighted and totally blind students moved in different social circles, but since we rode the same bus and took the same classes we became fast friends, calling ourselves the Three Busketeers.

It was Sandra's custom to grab Jon's hand on one side and mine on the other and navigate the difficult outside way to keep us from being late for class. If there was anything the faculty and staff hated more than dependence, it was tardiness. If you were late, but got there by yourself after a valiant struggle, that earned you no brownie points. They were as rigid about getting everywhere by yourself and on time as Vince Lombardi was about winning football games. Independence and punctuality weren't everything, they were the only things. Is it grammatical to say "only things"? It is in this case. They merged into one big hunk of trouble when violated.

One day we three were called into the principal's office together to see Dr. "By Golly Wally" Easton. Dr. Easton had settings like a portable hair dryer. He had three lecture modes—mild, medium, and stern. Today we got the mild version, the traffic cop letting his subject off with a warning.

"By golly, now," he began. "We've noticed that every morning since school started you folks have been trailing in, hanging onto one another and taking up the whole hall. Our trains have to get out of the way to make room for your train. By golly, now, we can't have that. We just can't have that. You're at this school to learn to be independent. I don't want to see any more hanging on from now on. Sandra is your friend and fellow student, not your guide dog."

"What does 'independent' mean, Dr. Easton?" I couldn't resist asking. "Does it mean 'alone'? Does it mean blind people are not allowed to have friends or family? Does it mean we can't call a plumber when the sink is stopped up or a roofer when the house has hail damage? Both those things happened at our house and my dad called workmen to help him. He's sighted. Isn't he independent, or are there different rules for blind and sighted people?"

"I'm not asking you to fix the roof," said Dr. Easton, either missing the point or ducking it.

"We declared independence from England because we didn't want taxation without representation. We still pay taxes and sometimes it seems like we get very little representation. How far does independence go? Where does it end?"

"I'm not talking about political science. I'm talking about learning to find your way to class by yourself. You can take up these other issues with Mr. Gilbert in social studies class, that is, if you can find your way there."

He was working himself up, right through medium into stern. I thought of several witty ripostes, but decided to surrender the battle in favor of winning the war.

"Wow," said Jon on the bus home. "You're a lot nervier than I am. I wanted to say all that, but I was afraid I'd get killed."

"Oh, well," I gave a theatrical sigh. "Sometimes you have to sacrifice yourself for a worthy cause."

That night the phones were busy at all three of our houses as we prepared to implement plan B. If Dr. Easton wanted a train, he would have one. After all, we had to be obedient as well as independent.

The next morning we came into school holding one another's shoulders, walking single file instead of holding hands and proceeding in a horizontal line. Sandra was the engine, a steam engine so she could puff and hoot. John was in the middle. He was the coal car. Every steam engine needs fuel. Of course we called him John Coal Train. I was the caboose. I'm not sure what a caboose does, but I was there, right behind my friends. "Woo, woo!" we called at the tops of our voices. "Chug, chug, chug! Ding, ding, ding!"

We hit those swinging doors with a satisfying impact that opened them as wide as they would go. We were just about to escape out the other side of the building when we heard, "Stop right there!" Dr. Easton was roaring. In a single night he had morphed from hair dryer into lion. He even forgot to say "By golly."

"That's enough!" Dr. Easton was getting quite good at roaring. Maybe he wasn't the Casper Milquetoast we had all thought him to be.

"I talked to you yesterday, reasonably and logically, about the importance of walking to class independently. You not only defied me, you made an embarrassing spectacle of my efforts to help you. All three of you are smart enough to go to Yale or Vassar. You could make something of yourselves and become a credit to the entire blind community, but instead you are wasting your considerable talents fighting our attempts to educate you. ESPECIALLY you, Judy. I know whose idea this was. You could go to an elite law school and graduate at the top of your class, but then what will you do? If you crash around the courtroom like a stumblebum, you'll look so bad in front of a jury that you'll have two strikes against you before you even open your mouth. And you, John. You can play jazz trumpet and piano as well as anyone recording today. Do you want to use your gifts, or fold dishcloths at the Gateway? And you, Sandra. You love to help people. When you take John and Judy to class, you are not helping them. You're enabling their dependence just as if you were injecting heroin into their arms. If you really want to help them, let them walk to class on their own. Remember what I've said and change your attitudes, or I'll have to get on the phone for some parent-principal conferences."

I went to class feeling subdued and anxious. Vassar? Law school? I didn't know Dr. Easton thought I was that smart. I had always believed every grown-up in the place thought I was the dumbest, laziest kid in the whole school. Did I really have a brilliant career ahead of me? Did it all depend on mobility? I wanted to go somewhere and be sick. Deep down I knew already that I would never be able to count the turns and know where to get off the bus like Ken Johnson, or do my Christmas shopping downtown on my own like Darlene Stitt, or even navigate the dreaded outside way like Sandra. Dr. Easton had given me more compliments than I had ever received in my life, except from my two grandmas, and I felt like someone had just kicked me in the chest.

A Great White Whale

Mobility was a Great White Whale that pursued me everywhere. Years collapsed upon one another and all I could think about was mobility. Call me Judy. Call me lost. Call me terrified. Call me worthless, unlovable—call me any pathetic, contemptuous name you want to call me; I'm still not going to find my way anywhere by myself, still not going to be able to give you directions; I'm still not going to be able to tell you where to go, although heaven knows I'd like to.

Melville has a chapter in Moby Dick called "The Whiteness of the Whale." It's about scary white things: an eerie, hallucinatory chapter where everything is white and featureless. That's the way I feel about mobility. I've heard blind people rave ecstatically about the first day they picked up a white cane, how they felt free, strong and capable, how their self-esteem went soaring through the stratosphere. When I first picked up a cane, fully expecting to feel like that, the surprise almost knocked me out. The cane went tap, tap, tap, but so did hammers and drumsticks and funny noises in cars. I heard these taps and they gave me no information. The only thing I heard was "Taps" playing for the death of my hopes of ever making progress on mobility. The cane got caught in cracks in the sidewalk, caught in bushes, in holes, in barbed wire, in paving tar. My first cane was a strong, straight one, not one of those folding ones in sections. I got it caught in something. It wouldn't budge. I tried to pull it out. Nothing happened. I reached down, attempting to release it with my hands. That didn't work either. Something hard and sharp dug into my hand. Cane stayed stuck, defying me. On top of that, I had no idea where I was. Panic began to set in. It rose in my throat like bile. I gave Cane a ferocious yank. It made a disgusting sucking sound. Up it came, but it was hardly recognizable as the same old Cane. It was bent in a complete semicircle. I was tempted to have it framed and hang it on my bedroom wall. I could show it to visitors like a military medal.

I still can't give directions, even to my own home. Before I left home with anyone but my parents, I sat down with Dad to work out the directions. Dad had an uncanny sense of direction. If he had been blind, he would have been a mobility genius. I believe you could have dropped him in the middle of the Sahara Desert at midnight and told him to meet you at Times Square at 9:00 a.m. and he would have been there at nine sharp. It was a personal affront to him that I couldn't do the same. He could have written out the directions for the person driving, but that wasn't good enough for him. When I suggested it, he growled, "I can't write the directions for you. They'll think you're stupid and don't know where you live."

"Do you think I'm stupid, Dad?"

"I'll think you're less stupid if you pick that lower lip up off the floor and pay attention."

"Can't I just give them the address ahead of time and ask them to look it up on a street map?"

"You don't want to make it hard for people to take you out, do you? If you make work out of it, no one will want to spend time with you."

"Why do I always have to make things easy for everybody else and hard for me?"

"You know why. You have to be twice as good as anyone else to be considered half as good. You have to be twice as brave, twice as smart, twice as self-sufficient, and above all, twice as pleasant and polite."

"But that's not fair, Dad."

"Who said life is fair? I wanted to play football at Notre Dame, but I was too small, didn't get a scholarship, and my parents couldn't afford to send me there. Was that fair?"

It was a good thing that was a rhetorical question, because if he had expected an answer, I would have said, "Not the same thing," which would have had goodness-only-knew what terrible consequences.

We practiced and practiced—directions from home to Baliban's Restaurant, directions from the restaurant to Powell Symphony Hall, directions from the symphony back home. I learned directions the way an opera singer learns to sing phonetically in an unknown language, the difference being that the opera singer has some idea what he or she is singing about. From my earliest childhood right up until today directions are both a verbal and kinetic blur. When I ride in a car I feel vibration and wind and either heat or cold, depending on the temperature. I still don't entirely understand how a right turn swings you to the left and a left turn swings you to the right. Nor have I figured out why you fly west to San Francisco to go east to Hawaii. I keep telling my husband Blair that if he took me to Hawaii for Christmas I might understand it better. So far he has not fallen for that line.

Back to practicing directions with Dad. (As I write this, nearly thirty years after his death, the subject still fills me with so much anxiety that I will use any excuse to digress from it.) He made me recite the meaningless words over and over. "Turn west on Manchester, until you come to Dickson Avenue. Then south eight-tenths of a mile to Cranbrook." I stopped, hearing that sound in my head, like the perk, perk, of a coffee pot or the whooshing of the ocean. I imagined my brain was a mixing bowl with all my thoughts stirring round and round. Sometimes I was an adult when this happened; sometimes I was a child. Time is irrelevant because it has happened hundreds of times between 1949, when I was three, and today.

No matter how much information I memorized, it was never enough. Someone would ask, "Is there a water tower there? Is there a supermarket? Is there a big church with Gothic architecture? Is it before or after you come to the Chrysler dealership? Don't give me 'north, south, east and west.' I only know left and right."

"Incoming!" said my brain, turning into a gelatinous mass under this heavy artillery barrage.

"I don't know landmarks. I only know the directions I memorized in advance."

My inquisitor would then turn the screws a little tighter. "Why don't you know? You must have passed these places hundreds of times. Don't you even know where you live?" Scorn dripped from the voice like molasses falling off a piece of toast. I knew beyond a doubt that this person would never drive me anywhere again, never be my friend again, that the minute I got out of the car they would be out of my life forever. Relief would only come later. My first reaction was always guilt, shame, and fear that I might never get home, that we might wander around for all eternity like the Flying Dutchman.

I always did get home, but I hardly ever heard from that person again. My parents were always waiting at the door to grill me about how the event had gone. Even after hundreds of episodes like this, they would never let me retire to my room in peace. I had to recount every lurid detail. Then it was, "Why didn't you do this? Why didn't you say that? After all the time we spent practicing directions with you, you forgot them again?"

At this point Mother often ran out of the room crying, while Dad would start on his theme and variations. "Damn, such an idiot! Other blind people can give directions. What the hell's wrong with you? You've got more book learning than Milton and Shakespeare put together, but you don't know enough to come in out of a good, hard hailstorm. I wish I had put you in an institution like everyone wanted me to. No wonder no one wants to be your friend. Stop that crying! The neighbors don't want to hear your baby cries."

He would go on and on, ranting and raving, calling me every name imaginable and some that were unimaginable. Even now that we have MapQuest and Google Map, I still hear Dad's voice in my head when anyone asks me for directions.

Therapists and mobility instructors—and believe me, I've had a lot of both—will talk all day about how I have to leave those memories in the past and stop dwelling on them. The problem with that advice is that these are not just memories: trouble with people over directions and mobility and activities of daily living is not just in the past, it is an everyday occurrence. Two incidents that happened recently should serve to illustrate this point.

My husband is visually impaired. With my motor and orientation deficits, along with Asperger's Syndrome—one of my diagnoses, on the autism spectrum, which was not diagnosed until I was almost sixty, and all of which have arguably affected my life more than blindness—it became necessary to hire an employee to help with transportation, reading, and a few personal care activities. We went through several aides before we found one who might be acceptable (although I had my doubts). In her interview, I hammered home my inability to give directions.

I could give her an address and, if we had someone to help us, a Google or MapQuest map. That was it. I asked her if she could find places without help from me. She assured me she could.

I'll call her C. The first time I went out with her, we were looking for a bookstore in a strip mall. Everyone had always told me it had a big sign with its name. She kept asking me for landmarks. "Is there a tire place? Is there a barbershop? Is there a beauty salon?"

She asked about many, many others until my head was reeling.

I requested politely that she stop asking, as I couldn't use landmarks to guide her. "Please park the car and go into one of these businesses and ask."

"I can find it," she insisted.

"But you haven't found it yet." I was trying to be reasonable, but an edge was creeping into my voice. "I have the phone number. Let's call them and get directions." I started to hand her my cell phone.

"I'll use mine. I don't know how to use yours." She wasn't conceding any more ground than was absolutely necessary.

I gave her the number. Long pause.

"Isn't this a bookstore? Sorry, someone gave me the wrong number. You gave me the wrong number." Her voice was accusing now. It had quite a bit more than an edge.

"But I know that's the right number. I've called it many times. Please go in somewhere and ask for help."

This conversation occurred three more times in similar versions. My autism, which I work hard every day to hold in check, began to kick in. My behavior therapist and I have worked out names for three states of mind—"spa," when I'm relaxed and comfortable, "waiting room," when anxiety is heating up, and "control tower," when Katie better bar the door. I was definitely in the control tower now. "If you don't park this car right now and go in and ask for directions, I'm going to scream my special scream, and you're not going to like hearing it. I give banshees lessons in my spare time."

C did not get it. After all my talking and explaining, she didn't have a clue. I had worked hard to head off this perennial bogeyman, but here it was in full force. "From ghoulies and ghosties and all kinds of beasties, and things that go bump in the night, protect us, O Lord." My prayer was atavistic, primal. My chest constricted. I could feel neurons exploding in my brain the way I always can when I'm about to have a falling seizure or an autistic display.

"You said there was an IHOP near the bookstore. I don't see a blue roof. Is the roof some other color?"

I began to scream, long, rolling, shrieks of impotent, little-kid rage that would have made great sound effects for a Halloween party. It was like hitting the reset button while putting my brain through a carwash. The scrubbers worked violently to clean out the accumulated mud and crud so I could behave, hold back, return to politeness, but that time was not yet. A preternatural articulateness set in, the peculiar clarity that always comes to me after the worst of the screaming. "I said 'no landmarks.' I told you over and over I didn't know what other businesses were around the bookstore and you kept asking me anyway. The book is a birthday present for my friend and today is my last chance to pick it up. Park this car right now and ask for directions or I'll scream until the police come. Is that what you want?"

This episode must have cut her to the quick, because she stopped the car and started to jump out, but she couldn't resist a parting shot. "Can you behave here by yourself?"

"Oh, honey," I thought, "will I ever behave! I'll be as quiet as that proverbial mouse." "Yes," I said out loud, meek as the little lamb the screaming had allowed me to be.

Eventually we got the book. We even had it gift-wrapped. Eventually we got home and C left for the day. I felt, in the words of an old novelty song from the late '50's, "like I'd been whupped with the ugly stick." It took two CD's of Vivaldi on the stereo and an hour nap to get me back to normal.

The incident was not resolved, however. Blindness is a deficit of information; autism is an inability to process and communicate information. Together they can make a mess of one's attempt to understand what is happening in the world. My word for this kind of situation is magic. My definition of magic is anything beyond my understanding. The magic in this episode was the telephone. I knew the number I had given C was correct. I had used it many times and always reached the bookstore. C had tried it and got a wrong number. It bothered me like a shoe pinching a sore toe. I told several people about it and nobody could figure out the answer. I told my therapist the next time I saw her.

"What area code was the phone and what area code was the store? I know your phone is 314. Maybe hers was 636."

"Oh, man!" I exclaimed, astonished that I hadn't recognized such a simple fact. There was no magic at all. That didn't absolve C in my mind. I still felt angry, betrayed, and disrespected. The next time C came she was disrespectful in a different, much more serious way which I won't explain here. It does not fall within the scope of this chapter, which is about my ability to find my way around, or the lack thereof. After that next infraction I fired C. I took so much abuse at school, in rehab, and in other random places that I'm not going to take it at home, especially when I'm paying the bill.

The mobility scourge pursues me even in my home, a 1,025 square-foot condo with a small kitchen, two small bedrooms, a fairly large living room, and a bath and a half. Just an hour ago I was walking from the bathroom to the living room. On the way I hit my head on the bathroom door jamb. A few seconds later I was reaching around trying to find the trashcan to throw away an old piece of paper when Pow! My head banged into the side of the pantry, a sharp-edged wooden cabinet with shelves and no door. We didn't have a door put on it so the items on the shelves could be reached easily and so the door couldn't be accidentally left open and one of us would bust their head on it. Being a person of many accomplishments, I found a way to whack my head on it anyway.

This is a good time to talk about the "coffee pot." I didn't have a coffee pot experience just now, but I never know when it's going to happen, so I'm always poised on that famous edge of my seat, waiting, wondering how I'm going to protect myself when it does. It usually happens when I'm tired, under stress, or in pain. It never happens when I'm sitting or lying down, because there's an element of safety that isn't present while standing or walking. I hear and feel a sound in my brain, a whoosh-plop like an old-fashioned percolator. I believe I feel neurons going off the way I do when I'm about to scream, but at a slower, but equally chaotic rate. All thoughts vanish instantly. I have no idea where I am or what's going on. I just fall like a giant redwood crashing to the ground. I often get hurt and sometimes break bones, not from the seizure, but from hitting things when I fall. I was tested by four neurologists between 1962 and 2010 and they all maintain I don't have seizures, but it's not their brain firing off; it's not their body falling. It scares me silly every time it happens. I had an EEG last year that showed that my right and left hemispheres don't communicate properly. The report had a big "abnormal" stamped across the front of it, which my friends who saw it joked that they had known all along.

I get lost everywhere in my house, even when I don't hear the "coffee pot." When I'm home alone, I like to have two radios on, one in each end of the house, tuned to different stations. It's annoying, but it helps me not to get lost.

Tiffany and the landmarks

The other story about directions happened not long ago and was perpetrated by someone with such a good heart, someone so generous and sensitive, that it illustrates how pervasive and unconscious this problem is. Tiffany, my autism therapist, was here for a session. I was reading her this manuscript-in-progress and reached the part where I said my first home was on Sappington Road.

Tiffany had been listening with great interest, but she perked up even more when I mentioned that my first home had been on Sappington Road.

"We used to live on Sappington. What was the number?"

"I don't remember."

"Think a little harder. What was it close to?"

Here came the landmarks again. Even someone I liked and trusted, with whom I had been over this dozens of times, was asking me questions about what was near my house. I have never had a panoramic sense of my surroundings. My whole body began to tighten up. "I was only four when we left there," I hedged, sounding much more defensive than I meant to. "It was near Mary Queen of Peace Church. That's where we went. There was a confectionery named Stecker's. Dad and I used to walk there. They had good, old-fashioned penny candy. You could spend a quarter and come home with a whole bag full of goodies. A little farther away there was a grocery store named Hershbeck's. Or maybe that was near the house on Cranbrook. I'm getting confused trying to remember."

"But Mary Queen of Peace church was on Barry Road. Are you sure you didn't live on Barry?"

"God damn! Such an idiot!" came Dad's voice from 27 years beyond the grave.

"I distinctly remember I lived on Sappington Road. I also remember we went to Mary Queen of Peace, but we didn't walk there. We went in the car."

I was revving up for a major anxiety attack. By not remembering my Sappington Road address, which my parents had drilled me on countless times, I was letting them down. I was letting Tiffany down. If my future editor wanted to know it, I would be letting him or her down.

"I don't remember, but I know for sure it was Sappington Road. I used to know. My parents made sure I knew my address and telephone number by the time I was two. I just can't recall it now."

I was mumbling. My voice had that monotonous, barely audible quality it always gets when I feel worthless and inadequate.

Tiffany works all day with clients who have autism. Most are children and teenagers and some are barely verbal. It is her job to keep gently pressing, to help the clients to put ideas together and express them. The object is to get the clients to talk; maybe she should have a reverse technique to get me to shut up.

Tiffany is also a body language expert. She knows when I duck my head and start grinding my hands together that a change of subject is called for. She managed it so seamlessly that I don't remember what we talked about next. Most people would continue pressing until I had a meltdown. I've never had a long meltdown with Tiffany. There have been one or two occasions when I started to scream, but Tiffany could always say something to bring me back. Some people can stop me by using threats and intimidation, but Tiffany never does.

The horseshoe runs north and south

My next home after Sappington Road was at 700 Cranbrook Drive as described previously. Mobility instructors will tell you it's a rectangular world with sidewalks and neat, square intersections. They talk about parallel and perpendicular as if they are concepts that have real meaning. Wait when the traffic is perpendicular. Cross when it's parallel. Maybe that's true if you live on a checkerboard, but the people who make these rules don't live in Kirkwood, Missouri. They don't live in suburban anywhere. When I first tried to learn the area around home, Dad walked me up and down Cranbrook.

"Which way does the street run, Dad?"

"It runs north and south here. A little farther down it runs east and west."

Whoa! Another school rule bites the dust! "But how can a street run both ways?"

"The street is shaped like a horseshoe. Remember when the McConnells and the Lewis's came over and we played horseshoes in the backyard? Or the U in your alphabet blocks? That's what Cranbrook is shaped like. Sometimes the horseshoe runs north and south, sometimes it runs east and west."

"But it always feels to me like we're walking straight. How will I know when it turns?"

"If you pay attention you should be able to feel it."

When we went inside, Dad got the U from the alphabet blocks, took my finger and showed me the location of every house on Cranbrook. "This is the Lewis' house, this is the McConnells', this is our house, this is the Jones' house." On and on he went, through 36 house locations. The concept of a circular drive was less confusing with the alphabet block than the street, but I never learned to walk up and down Cranbrook by myself without getting lost. Large shapes are still a complete muddle to me. It is this amorphous world that I face every day.

Chapter 18

A Serious Conversation (1959)

One day when I was twelve Grandma Loehr sat me down for a serious conversation, something she rarely did. We were home alone, a good time to speak freely.

"Judy, you're getting old enough to hear this now, and there are some things you should understand."

Oh, no, I thought, not the birds and the bees. I went to the Wilson School for the Blind; I had learned about that from the grapevine years ago.

"You know that your mother gets upset more than most mothers do. I hear her yelling at you that things were fine in her life before you came, that stuff that happens around here is your fault. You must know by now that her mind is sick."

"I know." It wasn't the birds and the bees. Was I about to be chewed out for something that set Mother off?

Grandma paused to get her thoughts together. "No matter what happens, it's important for you to know that your mother's illness is not your fault. She was that way long before you were born. In fact, she ruled our house with an iron hand. We all had to be careful every minute not to set her off. She was like living with an atom bomb."

"Did she always have Chief White Eagle, Azrael the Archangel, and all those others characters?"

"She always had imaginary friends, but I tried to keep her too busy to think about them. Your grandpa thought the way to cure it was to beat it out of her. He used his razor strop on her almost more than he used it on his razor. It got so bad that Erna screamed every time Herman was getting ready to shave. The sad thing was that I believe Erna was his favorite. He often got her up in the middle of the night to look at the stars. If she'd had the education, Erna might have become an astronomer."

"Is that why Mother gets so upset because I can't see the stars?"

"Probably. But that doesn't make it your fault that you can't see. It's nobody's fault. You have to remember that, no matter what happens."

In the same conversation Grandma tried to explain another of Mother's difficult-to-understand behaviors: her compulsive lying.

"It's like a game to Erna," Grandma explained. "If she can tell you a whopper and convince you, score a point for her. If you catch her, score one for you."

I was upset, though not surprised, to learn from her own mother that my mother considered lying a competitive game. Mother's lying had bothered me since I was around five years old. She had categories of lies that ranged from black to white and through the whole spectrum in between. I never found out what an indigo lie was, but every time Mother told a lie, she was able to concoct an elaborate rationalization to justify it. I realized early that Dad, the grandparents, and I had a higher ethical standard than Mother. If she received too much change in a store or restaurant, she kept quiet and boasted about it afterward. If someone asked her to do something she did not want to do, she would always say, "I have to do something for Judy." Most of her family and acquaintances resented me and I got the reputation for being spoiled and overprotected. Mother could never simply say, "No, I don't want to do that."

I knew that Mother hardly ever lived in the present. She feared the future and glorified the past—the past before I was born. She talked with nostalgia about the War, by which she meant World War II, as if it had been a nationwide block party at which all Americans on the home front had a carefree blast as they traded ration coupons and worked in victory gardens. She reminisced about the Depression as a fun time when people shared, saved and helped one another. She had worked as a child laborer in a shirt factory when she was twelve and believed the experience had strengthened her character.

This kind of talk, describing bad experiences as if they were good, was my introduction to the self-deception of positive thinking. I knew from personal experience—because I had tried so many times without success—that I would never be able to pick up a print book and read it, no matter how hard I concentrated or how positively I thought. I would never be able to see the stars, no matter how many times Mother dragged me outside and prayed and chanted over me. My unwillingness to believe that thinking could bring about what Mother wanted—I did not know what I wanted—was more frustrating to Mother than to me. She would scream and cry and hit me until I would scream and cry and run to my room. Sometimes Mother would follow me and give me a spanking, the way she had done with the hairbrush; more often she would produce that saintly sigh that said, "How imposed upon I am!" and walk away. Soon I would hear her slamming things around in the kitchen.

Grandma Loehr's revelations both sobered and relieved me. I was relieved to discover that Mother's illness, the screaming and yelling, the delusions, the incessant praying, and the conversations with imaginary characters were not my fault. They had begun before anyone had ever heard of me. This conversation with Grandma Loehr gave me solace for years, but even now when I feel discouraged with my lack of achievement, when I fail to meet my own standards, I think about the people I imagine I have disappointed, depression takes over, and I feel as if my mind were slipping away. Grandma Loehr's words always bring me back, but some of these episodes take longer to abate than others.

Chapter 19

Growing Up With Mother

Every Moment of Our Lives

Mother's mental illness informed every moment of our lives. She had what doctors today would call "ambulatory schizophrenia." She hardly needed us, because she had a whole cadre of imaginary characters with whom she conversed—sometimes in her head, sometimes out loud, whispering, screaming, crying. She often took me aside and tried to get me to hear her voices. She said that someday the Virgin Mary would appear to me. She hasn't yet, but if she does, I don't believe Mary will have roses on her feet the way Ste. Bernadette claimed. She will probably be holding a mop or a scrub brush and instruct me to tell everyone to get to work and straighten out the world. But I'm not staying up all night waiting for a holy vision. I think that was just Mother's way of justifying my existence.

Mother was fascinated by anything that used to be called "Indian," especially the Maya. She paid attention to their calendar and predicted the end of the world several times. I never believed these forecasts, but with the vicissitudes of home and school, I was always a little disappointed that the world didn't end.

Mother had an Indian chief named White Eagle who was the most frightening of her hallucinations. He told her that she had to learn some hidden mysteries, teach them to me, then I would write a book about them and win the Nobel Prize and change the world. We would make lots of money and be financially safe forever.

Even as a child I understood the desperate fear and sadness of this hallucination. Who would take care of me when my parents were gone? The common narrative among the blindness community was that if blind people applied themselves and pursued the proper training they would be able to live independently, have gainful employment, and be able to handle everything themselves. You didn't take a cab to work; you didn't ride with a friend, coworker or family member; you took the bus all by yourself. If the toilet was stopped up or needed a new flapper, you didn't call a plumber; you fixed it yourself. If you didn't excel at every skill in the expanded core curriculum, that was too bad for you. My parents were not evil people, despite all the trouble we gave one another. They tried to help me become independent, but at the same time tried to earn and invest so I would have enough money to care for myself after they were gone—just in case I never got one of the fabulous jobs the counselors and teachers were always talking about. They yelled at me, yelled at each other, and forced me to practice for hours to achieve a degree of independence and excellence, both academic and physical, that would have made Albert Einstein, Charles Atlas and Martha Stewart cry for mercy. What nobody knew—and it wasn't diagnosed until I was almost sixty years old and Mother was long gone, although I tried to tell them that something else besides blindness was wrong with me—was that I am on the autism spectrum. I'm on the borderline between high-functioning autism and Asperger's syndrome.

I never knew, when I walked into a room, which Mother I would find there. Would it be the loving, resourceful Mother who learned braille to help me in school, read to me for hours, and showed me hailstones and butterflies? Or would it be the terrifying alien who flailed her arms around and screamed about Indians and archangels? The uncertainty made me tense and fearful all the time Mother and I were home together, and since I was tense and fearful every moment I was at school, that didn't leave much time to be relaxed and confident. I loved Mass because I could rest in the anonymous Latin mumble and the caress of white noise, and I could imagine that God was giving me a message.

More than the regular Mass, I looked forward to Midnight Mass and Easter Vigil. They are long, full of ritual and mysticism. I felt close to God at these services. Maybe at these times, more than at regular Masses, God would make me the kind of child my parents wanted. I did not quite understand what sight might do for me, but if it would help my parents stop being so sad, if it would make Mother well, and especially if sight would get me out of that horrible school, I wanted it more than anything, and apparently it was something only God could give.

I was ten. It was the first part of the Easter Vigil, the Saturday before Easter. The priest dunked the Easter candle in holy water, raised it, and sang, "Lumen Christi." "The light of Christ." "Deo gratias," sang the choir, "Thanks be to God." Father did this three times, while each member of the congregation held a small, lighted candle. Suddenly I felt a warm, prickly sensation in my eyes. Was I seeing light? Had there been a miracle?

As soon as the candlelit portion of the service was finished my vision, or lack thereof, returned to normal, but I still told my parents about the experience as soon as we got home. Mother got so excited that she called Monday morning and made an emergency appointment for me with the ophthalmologist. He assured her that I could not see light, adding an admonition that Mother should "stop being silly, take this child home, and get on with life."

Mother was crushed. I was disappointed, not because I could not see, but because I had stirred my parents up for nothing, blown it again.

This apparent end of her long quest to give me sight sent Mother deeper into her delusions and withdrawal. She set up a card table in the living room and arranged a chair so its back faced the rest of us. She sat there in the evenings, reading and scribbling, telegraphing to us her unwillingness to participate in whatever we were doing. Occasionally she would flail her arms and shout at her voices, or she would rave and yell at us to instruct us in whatever breakthrough she was working on. "The Hunza, who live high up in the mountains, live to be 150 years old. They eat nothing but barley and millet, and they are always healthy. Have you ever heard of a blind Hunza?"

"I never heard of any kind of Hunza." Dad tried to keep his voice dry and mild.

"You can laugh all you want, but if we lived and ate like the Hunza, we might be healthier and live to be 150."

"They didn't live to be 150. Their work was so back-breaking and their food was so lousy it probably just felt like 150. I'll bet they actually lived to be 35." Dad was getting impatient already. Grandma Loehr and I stayed as quiet as we could, hoping not to be drawn into the fray.

"Oh, I wish I was as smart as you guys! Every time I get an idea, you just sneer and act superior."

"We wish you were as smart as we are, too. Then you wouldn't fall for all this silly bullshit about Hunzas."

Mother would slam down her book and run out of the room crying. And so it went, on and on, night after night.

Azrael the Archangel and Rose Lady

Whatever the opposite of serendipity is, that's how Mother's illness became augmented by her belief in astrology. Ever since Grandpa Loehr had taken her outside in the middle of the night to show her the stars, Mother had been fascinated by astronomy. She had taken some courses in it at St. Louis University. They were adult education classes, which were just becoming fashionable then, so Mother didn't need a high school diploma to enroll. We were delighted that Mother was taking an interest in something "non-crazy," as Grandma put it, but when Mother went to the library in search of further reading, her peculiar genius for twisting everything to fit her schizophrenic pattern quashed our optimism. Poring over the catalog, looking for books on astronomy, Mother flipped too many cards and found Astrology by Evangeline Adams. The book was written in accessible language, not the impenetrable jargon astrologers usually use when talking to one another. Here was the explanation. Here was the "why" she had been seeking for years. Maybe she had read God wrong on that dark night in Quebec. Maybe God hadn't meant for her to convert to Catholicism; maybe God had meant her to dig deeply into astrology and Eastern mysticism to learn why her life, and particularly her only child, were such a mess.

Now, in addition to Chief White Eagle, there was Azrael the Archangel who spoke to her sternly about her bad karma, and once in awhile, though not often, there was a benign presence named Rose Lady, probably a confused representation of the Virgin Mary. She was kind to Mother and tried to mitigate her angry, hopeless feelings about herself and about me, but she was not much in evidence compared to the mean, scary voices.

I called Wolfner Library (which still sends me talking books) and asked for a braille book on psychology. They were surprised and more than a little disconcerted to receive such a request from a child and sent me Your Child from Six to Twelve, not much help when what I needed was something like When Your Mom Is Mentally Ill. Dad sometimes described her as "crazier than a loon," but I didn't think there would be a book with that title. The doctor called it "ambulatory schizophrenia" and gave her a prescription for Haldol, which Dad and Grandma tried to get Mother to take either by persuasion or by slipping it into her coffee. Neither of these methods worked for long. Mother did not like the way the medicine made her feel. It made her feel dopey and half dead; besides, it gave her what Mother called the twitches and what I later learned the doctors called "tardive dyskinesia." Mother maintained that when her face jerked and spasmed, even her friends stared at her as if she were some kind of monster.

Mother would search the house until she found the Haldol and throw it down the sink and then the cycle would start all over again. Back to the doctor or into the hospital, home with more Haldol, more coffee subterfuges, searching the house, pills down the drain, more hallucinations, more screaming, more hitting. These behaviors escalated until they happened in public, except for the hitting, which Mother had sufficient grasp of reality to avoid when anyone but family was around. She confined her hitting to me, as if, confused as she was, she knew it would be crossing the line to hit Dad or Grandma. Both of them tried to stop it with no luck.

Mother wanted so much for me to believe in her "scientific discoveries," to be as enthusiastic about them as she was, but she tried to attract my interest in precisely the wrong way. Sometimes I would have liked to know in advance how things would turn out, or why some awfulness had occurred, like why I fell so often, or was so clumsy with my hands, let alone why I could not do some tasks that other blind people seemed to do with ease. Sometimes Mother would say "Well, you must have done something very bad in a past life." I thought about Oedipus and Samson, about Gloucester, who had his eyes poked out in King Lear. Was I the person who had said "Out, vile jelly"? My stomach lurched. Maybe I had been one of Milton's daughters and had refused to read to him. That would make the punishment fit the crime.

Then there was progressive astrology in which thoughts and events were influenced by the movements of the planets relative to their positions when you were born. The ways the planets related to one another were called aspects. The ones Mother talked about most were squares, sextiles, and trines. Trines were good, sextiles were medium, and squares were bad. According to Mother I had lots of squares, especially involving Saturn. Mother called Saturn the great teacher. I could relate to that. I had known lots of teachers who, with mild provocation, could have eaten their own children, not to mention their students. There were twelve houses, which governed different areas of life, and lots of other terms that I've long since forgotten. Mother added all this to her tortured worldview, and she insisted that I adopt and understand it all. Every evening after school she had piles of stuff to read me, none of which had anything to do with what I was studying. Mother would say, "Let me read you this. It will only take a minute." The minute would extend to five, ten, an hour. She would never stop until I interrupted. "Mother, I don't have time for this. I have homework. Besides, you said it would only take a minute and it's been over an hour."

"This is more important than your homework. This could save the world. You could be famous forever."

"Right now I have to do math and social studies." I got up and started walking out of the room.

"You come back here this minute!"

"Maybe in an hour," I mumbled. I was increasing the trouble exponentially, but I couldn't resist.

Mother grabbed me and whacked me hard. "You come back here and sit down. I'm not finished yet."

I began to cry.

"Erna, for heaven's sake, leave Judy alone. You did say a minute, and it's been over an hour."

By that time I was out of the room, but I had been through this enough times to know that Grandma's advice would be ignored.

The children she really wanted (1960-61)

Being unable to change me led Mother to seek out people she did not have to change, the kind of children she really wanted. Every month our church bulletin printed a list of babysitters with their names, rates and phone numbers. Mother added her name, explaining, "I just want to help mothers." She had a bank in the shape of a car battery where she kept her babysitting money. Most of it was in change; at fifty cents an hour, Mother did not have to worry about paper money or checks. She explained that she was saving the money to take me to Lourdes, where she was confident that Ste. Bernadette would grant me a miracle. I would be sighted; and most important, I would be normal instead of nerdy. No more reading in bed until 3 a.m.

No more listening to the Spelling Bee on Saturday mornings or the College Bowl on Sunday afternoons. No more dragging a bulky braille book everywhere we went. Best of all, I would be accepted by the family, especially by my cousins. Mother also said her ego was out of control, and she babysat to learn humility.

I suffered often from comparisons with the little brats she babysat for. "Bella is only four and she can tie her shoes. You're thirteen and you still can't do it."

I didn't ask if Bella could see; I knew the answer. Mother talked about the crafts she made with the children and the games they played together. She brought her own lunch, which always included cookies to share. Mother never raided the employer's refrigerator. She drove herself to work and drove herself home. The games and puzzles with which she entertained the children belonged to me. Sometimes they broke them or lost some of the pieces. I was an only child and on the autism spectrum, so this destructiveness gave me fits. Why couldn't the little brats wreck their own stuff? I love the word "brat." It reminds me of brat, the sausage, which is spelled the same way. I wanted to put one of Mother's babysitting clients, especially Bella, on the barbecue grill, burn her to a crisp, slather her with sauce, wrap her in a giant bun and take a huge bite, the way you would decapitate a chocolate bunny. I doubted she would taste like chocolate, but that was the price you had to pay.

Despite all these extras, there was a vociferous and unanimous meltdown among the church mothers when my mother tried to raise her rate to seventy-five cents. She lost most of her business and had to go back to fifty cents—this at a time when college students charged two dollars, expected a meal and two-way transportation, and did homework or watched television instead of paying attention to the children.

"People will think I can't provide for you," Dad complained.

Stony silence.

"Those women are using you. They treat you like a servant."

"I have to learn humility. Jesus washed the disciples' feet."

"You're not Jesus and neither am I. All I know is, I want this nonsense to stop."

It never did, however. Mother was not kidding about foot-washing being essential in learning humility. Every night before Mother went to bed, she washed her feet in the toilet.

"For heaven's sake, Erna, don't do that," said Grandma Loehr. "What if someone forgets to flush?"

"Then I'll learn even more humility, like St. Francis of Assisi."

I'm sure Grandma rolled her eyes and shook her head.

The nadir, the absolute rock bottom of this babysitting ordeal, came when I was in eighth grade and home sick with strep throat. Mother went off to babysit. Grandma was staying with Aunt Beverly in Arkansas. Even Grandma needed an occasional break from Mother's delusions.

I lay in bed, home alone, resentful and sorry for myself. We were studying the Civil War in Mr. Gilbert's social studies class. I had been assigned to write that book report on Gone with the Wind. The bulky books lay heavy on my stomach, but I slogged through all thirteen braille volumes, hating Scarlett O'Hara with the same venomous passion I had toward Bella. Scarlett was an amoral little twerp; the kids Mother babysat for were probably just like her, only younger. I was convinced Mother wanted to babysit because she needed to be around regular children, the kind of children she wished she had had instead of me. I wrote a scathingly pro-Union report, for which I earned a C-plus, and wallowed in loneliness and anger until it was time to go back to school.

I don't know what Mother learned from babysitting, but it did not cure her. She became more and more delusional.

Soldiering On

If there was physical work to do, especially if the work was something to mitigate the everyday stresses of blindness, Mother was eager to help. She made all my clothes; I still have a coat and jacket she made more than thirty years ago. My clothes did not look as if they came from high fashion houses in Paris or New York, but someday archaeologists will find them and marvel at the excellent, durable workmanship these ancient Americans put into their garments.

Mother learned braille when I was in high school, and for 22 years, until I finished my doctorate, she churned out volume after volume of braille textbooks. She reached the point where she could transcribe a page of braille in six minutes with hardly any errors. About most tasks we tried to do together we fought like gladiators, but, although I was her braille teacher, we never fought over the rules of braille, even though they sometimes seemed arbitrary to Mother.

Many of the books Mother transcribed were not simple literary braille. There were math books and foreign language books. I studied Latin, Spanish, French and German, not to mention, in graduate school, Old English, several dialects in Middle English, and as if that were not enough, a smattering of Old Norse, Gothic, Icelandic and Middle High German. Throughout all this, Mother soldiered on, copying words letter by letter, with no idea what she was transcribing. If we needed a symbol Mother didn't know, she consulted the Library of Congress Braille Handbook. If the handbook didn't have the symbol we needed, we made one up. Besides all this, there were German and Spanish contracted braille symbols to learn, both for Mother and for me. Then there was the occasional Greek letter or scientific symbol. Over the years there were hundreds of nights when I would be studying in my room, Mother was cranking out braille at the kitchen table, and Dad was recording an audiobook on tape in the bedroom, all at two in the morning. We worked hard; we did what we had to do; we got me through school.

By a Post-Dispatch Photographer

Reward for Thought

Earl Humphrey, St. Charles chief of police and president of the Missouri Police Chiefs Association, presenting Miss Judy Dent the first-place award for her essay in a contest sponsored by the association. Looking on are Sister Angeline of St. Elizabeth Academy; Lt. Larry Rickmann, representing the St. Louis Police Department, and her parents, Mr. and Mrs. George Dent.

ing standpoint, we have had our engineering department survey-ing streets that have priority in having sidewalks installed."

The city's sidewalk committee has pledged that 100 blocks of sidewalks will be completed dur-ing the city's centennial year in 1965, Reim said. Sidewalk con-struction has been designated Project No. 1 in Kirkwood's Project 100 program.

A four-point program to im-prove safety and get sidewalks for streets heavily used by chil-dren traveling to and from schools has been implemented by the city under Reim's direc-tion.

Parent - Teacher associations have been urged to discuss pe-destrian and bicycle safety with their children, and Kirkwood schools have a continuing pro-gram of safety education, Reim

Student Wins State Contest With Essay Written in Braille

Miss Judy Dent, 17-year-old Dent is a senior, daughter of Mr. and Mrs. George Earl Humphrey, St. Charles R. Dent of 703 Cranbrook drive, chief of police and president of Kirkwood, has been awarded a the Missouri Police Chiefs As-$75 scholarship as winner of sociation, made the presentation the Missouri Police Chiefs As- at the academy.
sociation essay contest. The third-place winner, also

The topic, "The Prevention of from this area, was Joseph Pol-Juvenile Delinquency," was in- lard Jr., son of Mr. and Mrs. tended to stimulate the thinking Joseph J. Pollard of 1434 Gra-of high school-level teenagers on ham street. He is a student at ways of avoiding and combating St. Louis University High School. juvenile delinquency. He won $25.

Miss Dent, a former student Included on the panel judging at the Missouri School for the the 2100 entries were United Blind, wrote her 1000-word es- States Senators Edward V. Long say in braille. It was transcribed and Stuart Symington, State At-and typewritten by a nun at St. torney General Thomas F. Eagle-Elizabeth Academy, where Miss ton and Lt. Gov. Hilary A. Bush.

Student Wins State Contest With Essay Written in Braille

Miss Judy Dent, 17-year-old daughter of Mr. and Mrs. George R. Dent of 700 Cranbrook drive, Kirkwood, has been awarded a $75 scholarship as winner of the Missouri Police Chiefs Association essay contest.

The topic, "The Prevention of Juvenile Delinquency," was intended to stimulate the thinking of high school-level teenagers on ways of avoiding and combating juvenile delinquency.

Miss Dent, a former student at the Missouri School for the Blind, wrote her 1000-word essay in braille. It was transcribed and typewritten by a nun at St. Elizabeth Academy, where Miss Dent is a senior.

Earl Humphrey, St. Charles chief of police and president of the Missouri Police Chiefs Association, made the presentations at the academy.

The third-place winner, also from this area, was Joseph Pollard Jr., son of Mr. and Mrs. Joseph J. Pollard of 1454 Graham street. He is a student at St. Louis University High School. He won $25.

Included on the panel judging the 2100 entries were United States Senators Edward V. Long and Stuart Symington, State Attorney General Thomas F. Eagleton and Lt. Gov. Hilary A. Bush.

By a Post-Dispatch Photographer

Reward for Thought

Earl Humphrey, St. Charles chief of police and president of the Missouri Police Chiefs Association, presenting Miss Judy Dent the first-place award for her essay in a contest sponsored by the association. Looking on are Sister Angeline of St. Elizabeth Academy; Lt. Larry Rickmann, representing the St. Louis Police Department, and her parents, Mr. and Mrs. George Dent.

Judith Anne Dent
1965

Editor: In her introduction to this book, Judy wrote about her freshman English class at Fontbonne College. In the fall of 1965, after Judy graduated from St. Elizabeth Academy in St. Louis, she walked into that freshman English class where she would write the essay she described as "glib, maudlin nonsense" on "The Day My Childhood Ended."

Blind Fontbonne Student Wins New Recognition as a Writer

"I pick up images and colors from listening to people' and from reading," said Judy Dent, a 20-year-old s o p h o m o r e at Fontbonne C o l l e g e who has been blind since birth. "I don't attempt to emphasize scenery in my stories, of course, I try to put an emphasis on sound and characterization."

Miss Dent wants to be a novelist and short-story writer. Her facility with words already has achieved recognition.

When she was 17, she won first prize in a state essay contest on "The Prevention of Juvenile Delinquincy" s p o n - sored by the Missouri Police Chiefs Association. Tomorrow night she will be honored by Lions International. Her entry in the Lions'-sponsored "Peace is Attainable" essay c o n t e s t was judged best in the district.

Judy Dent

on the dean's list at Fontbonne,

was judged best in the district.

Miss Dent will read her essay at tomorrow night's "Lion Appreciation Night" at Missouri School for the Blind. Her essay will be entered in state competition. The winner of the state competition will be entered in international competition this summer.

To win the district contest Miss Dent's essay, sponsored by the Webster Groves Lions Club, was judged along with entries from 24 other area Lions Clubs.

The judges — County Supervisor Lawrence K. Roos; Aloys P. Kaufmann, president of the St. Louis Chamber of Commerce, and Richard H. Amberg, publisher of The Globe-Democrat — saw only numbered entries and were unaware of Miss Dent's handicap when her essay was selected.

Miss Dent, daughter of Mr. and Mrs. George Dent, 700 Cranbrook drive, Kirkwood, is on the dean's list at Fontbonne, where she is majoring in English and Spanish.

She attended the Missouri School for the Blind and St. Elizabeth Academy before enrolling at Fontbonne. She plans to go attend graduate school.

"I went with her before she started at Fontbonne," Mrs. Dent said. "Just to show her around the campus. Now she makes her way by herself. She llives on campus in Medaille Hall."

"I like to write about people," Miss Dent said. "I skip this deep allegorical stuff. I simply write about experiences and how one feels about them.

"Research is a little difficult, but I have had the assistance of a lot of people who read to me.

"I stressed communication in my peace essay. We have to learn to communicate, to talk to one another. Armaments and foreign aid can only put off war. But that isn't real peace."

Gives Up Visit With Nixon to Be With Class

Miss Judith Anne Dent decided that she would rather "graduate with her class than have 10 minutes with the President," her father, George R. Dent,

said. Miss Dent, who graduates from Fontbonne College in ceremonies at Kiel Auditorium today, was one of three blind students selected for a national

award to be presented in Washington by President Richard M. Nixon.

Miss Dent had purchased her airplane ticket to fly to the capital for the presentation Thursday, but all presidential appointments were canceled after the President's Vietnam speech Wednesday night. The presentation of the Scholastic Achievement Awards from Recording for the Blind, Inc., was rescheduled for today.

Miss Dent will r e c e i v e her certificate and check for $500, along with an impressive list of other academic achievements. She is graduating cum laude, is a member of Delta Epsilon and Kappa Gamma Pi, C a t h o l i c women's scholastic honoraries, and has been awarded Woodrow Wilson a n d Danforth Foundation fellowships.

She will leave her home at 700 Cranbrook Drive, Kirkwood, next fall to study medieval English at Notre Dame University. Miss Dent plans to teach c o l l e g e English a f t e r completing graduate studies. She is 22 years old. She has been blind since birth.

Schedule of Satellite Passes

The following schedule for the Pageos — A and Echo II satellites over Missouri has been furnished by Dr. J. H. Senne of the University of Missouri-Rolla. The schedule for Pageos is: today, 11:17 p.m., r i s e s SW, passes med. WNW, sets N; tomorrow, 11:14 p.m., rises SW, p a s s e s med. WNW, sets N; Tuesday, 11:13 p.m., rises SW, passes med. WNW sets N, Wednesday, 11:11 p.m., r i s e s SW, passes med. WNW, sets N. Thursday, 11:10 p.m., r i s e s SW, passes med. WNW, sets N; Friday, 11:09 p.m., rises SW, passes med. WNW, sets N; Sat- u r d a y, 11:07 p.m., rises SW, passes med. WNW, sets N; Sunday, 11:05 p.m., r i s e s SW, passes med. WNW, sets N.

The schedule for the Echo II satellite is: today, 8:44 p.m., rises SE, passes low E, sets NE, 10:21 p.m., rises SW, p a s s e s med. WNW, set N; tomorrow,

9:21 p.m., rises S, passes high SE, sets NNE; Tuesday, 9:47 p.m., rises SSW, passes med. W, sets N; Wednesday 8:36 p.m., rises SSE, passes med. ENE, sets NNE, 10:12 p.m., rises SW p a s s e s low N, sets NNW ;Thursday, 9:01 pm, rises S, passes overhead, sets N; Friday, 9:25 p.m., rises SSW, passes med. WSW sets N; Saturday, 9:46 p.m., rises SW passes med. W, sets NNW; Sunday, 8:31 p.m., rises S, passes med. ENE, s e t s NNE, 10:08 p.m., rises WSW, p a s s e s low WNW, sets NNW.

First Contract

TUPELO, Miss. (UPI) — The f i r s t electrical contract by a city for power furnished by the Tennessee Valley Authority was signed here in 1933. The contract went into effect the following year.

St. Louis Post-Dispatch, 18 May 1969, p.152

Editor: Judy graduated from Fontbonne College with a double major in English and Spanish in 1969. Grandma Loehr—whose practicality, firmness, patience, and ability to understand and manage Judy's behavior had kept the family together—died the next year.

Chapter 20

The surgery that broke her heart

Time passed, and Grandma got a little older, a little more frail. She hardly ever went outside to sit on the patio anymore. The arthritis became so painful that she had to sit at the kitchen table to whip up her famous sugar cookies. Then it wasn't long before she stopped baking them altogether. She stopped playing cards because she could no longer read them. She stopped watching her soap operas on television because she could neither see nor hear them; her refusal to wear a hearing aid was just as adamant as her rejection of talking books. Eventually the doctors found colon cancer. She had surgery, including a colostomy. Kate Wertman Loehr had endured poverty, hard times, an abusive husband—I'm sure I don't know the half of it—but the surgery that fixed her colon broke her heart.

Soon the room we shared smelled like disinfectant and bodily wastes and depression. Until this time I never remembered Grandma Loehr complaining about her sight, her hearing, her arthritis, or any other problem. Not once in my hearing did she blame my blindness for our troubles, and she would not let me do so, either. When I felt too sorry for myself, Grandma would sing,

Nobody loves me.
Everybody hates me.
I'm gonna eat worms so I die.
Big fat juicy ones, little slimmy slimy ones,
Icky-bicky, icky-bicky worms.
It had a second verse that began:
First one's easy,
Second one's greasy,
Third sticks in my throat.

Mercifully I have forgotten the rest, but it had several more verses, equally edifying.

One evening when Mother was ill and I had had a bad bout of self-pity, Grandma fixed spaghetti for dinner. I don't know if Grandma remembered the song and my recent crying jag, and made spaghetti as a reminder to me, but as those wormlike strands slid down my alimentary canal I wondered if I really would die. From then on complaints and criticisms stuck in my throat just like that third worm.

Between arthritis and visual impairment, Grandma became unable to take care of her colostomy. The job fell to Mother, who did it with roughness and resentment. I knew about roughness: the times when I was a small child and Mother gave me a bath and pulled and pinched me and the shampoos when she pulled my hair until I cried are still vivid memories. One of the problems of autism, at least in my case, is that memories can stay alive forever; when reminded of old traumas, I live them again with the same intensity I experienced when they first took place. When I hear about bullying on the news, I feel the taunts and physical abuse of Darlene and Marjorie all over again. When I heard Grandma say, "Don't yank me around so, Erna. If I could irrigate this thing myself you know I would," I recoiled from both the pain and the resentment as if they were happening to me. From time to time Grandma would give Mother a break with brief visits to one of the aunts. Soon they were all on the phone with Mother holding forth about how outrageously Grandma imposed on them. Ida, who was to resentment what Mozart was to classical music, complained loudest and longest. Soon all four sisters were lobbying for Grandma to go to a nursing home. Dad and I were the only family members who were opposed, but we couldn't say much because neither of us was irrigating the colostomy.

During the summer of 1970, the last summer of Grandma Loehr's life, the last summer before I went away to graduate school in Indiana, I came home one day and walked into the bedroom I shared with Grandma. It felt like a re-creation of the Amazon rain forest and smelled like death, like intimations of mortality, disinfectant, urine, and feces. I was more taken aback by the sound of the room than the smell. Grandma sat on the edge of her bed crying. That was a first. In all her years of challenge in what must have been endless frustration with her husband's alcoholism, Mother's illness, my disabilities, with my mental brilliance and physical ineptitude, I never knew that Grandma Loehr cried.

"What's wrong, Grandma?" I was about ready to cry myself. "Is there anything I can do to help you?"

"Nobody can help me." For the first time I heard despair in her voice. "I can't do anything for myself anymore. Nobody loves me. I smell like Lysol and shit. All four of my daughters want to put me away. You probably want to put me away, too, so you can have a room to yourself."

"I don't need a room to myself, Grandma. Dad and I don't want to put you away. We love you."

"But my daughters are the ones who have to take care of me. You and George don't."

"Dad and I will do all we can to keep you from going away. It doesn't smell that bad in here. The room is just a little stuffy and hot with the window shut." I walked over to the window and started to open it.

"Don't do that. The wind is wet and clammy and stinky."

I stood irresolute, not knowing how to handle this major turning point. My intellect had expected Grandma's decline for a long time, but my heart screamed in rebellion. I felt like Scarlett O'Hara: "I'll think about that tomorrow." I prayed about this the way St. Augustine had prayed about chastity. "Lord, give me strength, patience, and poise when Grandma gets old, but not yet." I wanted more time to think, more time to plan, more time to prepare myself for the inevitable future when I wouldn't have Grandma to lean on and look to for encouragement.

This conversation had produced two more firsts. I had lied to Grandma, something I had never done. The place wasn't just stuffy, it reeked, and speaking of reek, the most poignant first of all was I had heard Grandma Loehr say "shit." She didn't say it when things went wrong at home, she didn't say it when Mother tried to burn herself, she didn't say it when she told off Mrs. Hubbert in the "sufficiently Teutonic" German. She had always been practical, while remaining cool and refined. Grandma Loehr could be firm, and the firmness projected a ring of truth that all Mother's violent rages never could. Now here she was, falling apart like a discarded doll, breaking down like an abused jalopy, oozing bodily fluids from every orifice, including her eyes. Her mind was as clear as it had ever been; she watched all this with revulsion and horror, and the worst horror of all was that she believed no one loved her, that, now that she could no longer serve them, her family wanted to throw her out with the trash. "I still love you, Grandma." I approached her slowly, clumsily—physical grace was never one of my skill sets—and kissed her forehead. "Things will get better. As long as I'm here you'll have someone who loves you." I did not say, "They can't get any worse," because they could and they did.

I walked into the bathroom and turned on the water loud and sobbed until I could get control of myself. It was time to start thinking and speaking for myself. It was time to assume responsibility. It was time to grow up.

Grandma did go to a home. Ida took charge of it and Grandma went to a place in Waterloo, Illinois, near Ida, but far away from the rest of us. I went off to graduate school at Notre Dame—yes, the football university—and never saw her again. When I came home for Thanksgiving, Grandma had been dead for a month. No one had told me. The official word was that Grandma had an abdominal aortic aneurysm that burst. Unofficially I believe she died because she had decided no one loved her. I had been made to touch all those dead bodies when I was too young to be anything but scared; now at twenty-three I was kept away. I wish I had been able to tell her good-bye. It has been over forty years, and I miss her still.

Editor: Following her time at Fontbonne College (1965-69), Judy went on to graduate studies in philosophy at the University of Notre Dame in Indiana.

Judy with Abbey, the first of her four guide dogs

Editor: In August 1984, when Judy was 37 years old, her father George Dent died from diabetes and kidney failure. Judy had been teaching at Washington University, but when her dad became ill, she lost her means of transportation and his support and had to give up her work. Her mother Erna cared for both her husband and Judy. The next summer, at the Christian Science church in Kirkwood, Missouri, Judy met a man named Blair Gleisberg. On April 25, 1987, in Elliot Chapel in Kirkwood, Missouri, Judy married Blair, keeping her last name. Shortly after the wedding, she completed her dissertation, whose full title was Sickness and the "Siker Wey": Themes of Illness and Health in Chaucer, in the Department of English at Washington University in St. Louis. She was awarded a "Philosophiae Doctoris" (doctoral degree) in 1987.

TABLE OF CONTENTS

Dissertation Table of Content

Judy's baby picture as displayed on her wedding day.

Judy and Blair at their wedding reception, April 25, 1987

Chapter 21

My Husband Blair

I remember a phrase I learned in my first college course in introductory psychology. The instructor said that heredity and environment were "reciprocal and interdependent." What an accurate way to describe all of us! I believe we are all here to sustain and care for one another, not to exert power for its own sake, or to show off how much more self-sufficient we are than someone else. I feel somewhat uncomfortable saying this because it sounds so self-serving, considering all the help I need just to get through daily life. My husband—who, according to the usual stereotypes should be relaxing as I write this chapter on this Saturday evening, watching the NFL playoffs and waiting for dinner, which can be served only when the game is over—is rattling around in the kitchen putting away groceries, which were delivered a short time ago by the person we pay to do our shopping, while I work on this book. We are reciprocal and interdependent.

The noise is getting louder and louder. Bang. Crash. Thud. Something fell out of the refrigerator. I hear Blair wiping something off the floor. I would go and help him, but I have learned from long experience that I am more of a hindrance than help, just as I was when I lived with my parents. The noise goes on and on. Blair is looking for something. Since he's mostly blind, looking for something means he is looking with his hands. More crashing and banging. I have a throbbing headache. A few years ago Blair got me some expensive noise-canceling headphones. They produce great sound, but don't cancel much noise. They are difficult to use and need extra batteries for the part that's supposed to cancel the noise. My neurologist recommended earplugs at night to help me sleep. Nothing doing. Elizabeth Oleson, a close friend, put a sound machine in my office that makes a noise like the ocean. No help. Then she installed wind chimes and a fan to make them play. They are pleasant, but don't shut out noise. Between the crashing, head-splitting impact on my senses and the fear generated by not knowing what is happening, I'm about to go crazy; I can't stand it any more. I raise my voice and yell, "Blair, what's happening? When is that noise going to stop?"

"I can't help it," he says, as he always does. "I have to fix dinner."

"I'm sorry. I know you can't help it," I mumble. I don't know if he heard me. On top of sensory overload, now I feel guilty. I know he does his best. I am also convinced that no other man in the universe would put up with me the way Blair does. He isn't suppressing a resigned sigh or a passionate oath. That's just the way Blair is.

He lives constantly with my sensory issues—no loud, cacophonous music; not much tolerance for walking in traffic, because the sounds seem to come from all directions at once; nothing sharp or scratchy; no food with too much acid, too much fiber, or any beta carotene. Despite these and many other challenges, he keeps right on loving me, and the more I learn about him, and the more I understand him, the more I appreciate and love him.

Blair R. Gleisberg, "My Story," 1936-1987:

I was born in Middletown, Connecticut in 1936. Unfortunately, my mother died five days after I was born, due to complications. Her name was Mildred A. Gleisberg. Meanwhile, they didn't think I was going to make it either, so I stayed in the hospital. I was born with congenital cataracts and was eventually declared legally blind. It took years to get them removed, because it took injections over four or five years. My father was Richard Paul Gleisberg; he was an only child, as was I.

Dad had a pasteurizing business and had to go to work. My mom's sister Evelyn and her husband Alfred Dean didn't have children of their own and stepped in to take care of me. They were known as Ev and Al, but I called them Ma and Dad, or eventually, as I grew older, Mom and Pop.

I don't have a lot of early memories. I was too busy trying to get along in life. Being blind, going to school, falling down a lot, several broken bones—a leg and a shoulder that I remember.

We lived on Vine Street in a two-family house. My aunt and uncle, Marge and Lee Elliot, lived upstairs. They didn't have children either. We had one dog for about a month and then it died. Mom didn't want the first one, so we never got the second one.

With Pop's help, I learned to ride a bike when I was around four or five years old, and that was a long process. I had to not only learn to ride a bike, but also how the pedals worked. I couldn't see the pedals or understand how to use them, but we were patient and we got there. He was a good teacher with that. What he couldn't handle was when I got older and couldn't do things with my hands like other people could. I had a quite a job learning how to tie shoes. Anything to do with my hands was a challenge. I couldn't see what other people were doing with their hands; I could just see motions. I told people for years, "I can see hands flying, but that's it". That annoyed them to no end, but that was the truth.

I walked to Middletown Elementary for first grade. I was partially sighted, and I had a few falls along the way, but I got there and back.

When I started second grade, Mom took me to Hartford, Connecticut every day for sight conservation class. They didn't make you use your eyes too much on the work, so you could save your vision. I went there second grade through eighth grade. That's where I met Miss Edith Hennessy, who was the sight conservation teacher. She did her best, and I liked her, but she was helping eight grades. She had a big impact on me. She always encouraged me and told me I could do it, and not in a mean way.

I never went to camp. My folks wanted me to, but I wouldn't. I knew I'd be competing with people with vision, and that wouldn't work. School was like that, and life was like that, and I didn't want more. I listened to books all summer to review the books for the coming school year. But there was the occasional break for vacation.

We went to the shore several years for vacation and rented a cottage, usually at Plum Bank on Long Island Sound, and once on Cape Cod. Sometimes aunts and uncles came, too: Mable and Larry had a daughter Pat who was about my age, and Ruth and Ray had two younger sons, Brian and Rick. The cottage was on the waterfront, and we could walk right down to the water's edge and swim. My favorite part was getting away from books and not having to study.

I was always uptight about everything. People don't realize that when you have a disability, you spend your time trying just to get by. There wasn't time to worry about socializing. But I enjoyed picnics we had as a family. We had a nice backyard at the time. Pop made some swings and I played on those; we had a slide. Mom wasn't much for having people my age over, or anyone, for that matter. She was sort of a loner, even up till the end. We would have Ray and Ruth over sometimes, and I enjoyed them. We played games like croquet, and that was fun. Ruth was a school teacher, and Ray worked for the state.

Ev, my Ma, worked for Raymond Engineering as a secretary for quite a few years while I was in school. Al, my Pop, worked as a tool and die maker at Lyman Gun Sight Company. They made sights and scopes for guns. We had one .22 caliber rifle, and I did target practice at the range now and then when I was 10 or 12. Between my glasses and the sights, it was magnified enough for me to see. Pop went to the range regularly as part of his job, but he hated guns. He didn't like the idea of guns, and he didn't like the idea of practicing after he had worked all day.

My grandparents, Fred and Freida Anderson, were around till I was in my teens. These were Ev's parents, and also the parents of Ray, Marge, Mable, and Mildred, my birth mother. We visited, and mostly it was adult talk. I didn't feel very close to them, but not too distant either. We just didn't talk about much; a lot of families were like that when it came to difficulties.

After years at the sight conservation class, I went to Middletown High for regular high school. The transition was what I had expected. The difficulty at this point was that I was thrown in with all sighted people, and of course I didn't fit in at all. Mom read to me a lot; I got talking books when I could. We did it, but it wasn't easy.

In high school, I didn't take gym, but focused on academics. I liked music. We had music studies that focused on classical music and opera. I enjoyed singing, but mostly on my own, for the joy of it. Another class I enjoyed was typing. I memorized the keyboard, A-S-D-F on the left hand and :-L-K-J on the right hand, and then you learned to reach over with one finger from each hand to get the G and the H, and then you had the whole first row! Years later, I ended up making my living that way. Math was difficult, due to the rows and columns. It required writing one number under another, and I couldn't see the one over it while I was writing under it—the numbers ended up all over the place. No one could understand that. It was frustrating that I couldn't do it, but maybe more frustrating that people just didn't understand.

I graduated with my class in 1954. Then I worked at a vending stand as a state employee, a typical job for blind people. We sold coffee, cigarettes, candy, etc. One stand was in the Department of Labor. I only gave change on the dollar, not fives or tens: I could tell how to make change with the coins. A lot of blind people never get beyond jobs like that. The jobs for someone blind are very limited.

Then in 1956, I started x-ray processing at Middlesex Memorial Hospital and did that for about 15 years. I lived with Mom and Pop. The job didn't pay much, so there was no way I could live independently. I started at $1.25 an hour, which even back then wasn't much money. I worked and came home and life was pretty much the same—we spent time with Ray and Ruth and went to the shore for vacations. I cooked here and there—usually when I was home by myself, since my parents wanted to do it all for me and have it done a certain way, meaning Ma did most of the cooking. On the one hand, people want you to do things on your own. On the other hand, they end up doing it for you.

I began attending Christian Science Sunday School in the first grade. I started trying to read the six-part Bible Lesson, meant to be studied daily for a week. At that time, I saw very little and knew even less. After many years of trial and study, I could read the Golden Text, which is a one-verse introduction to the lesson. I studied those few lines all week. Then I graduated to both the Golden Text and the Responsive Reading, adding a few more lines. Then, in time, I got up to the Golden Text, the Responsive Reading, the first section of Bible verses, and the correlative passages from Mary Baker Eddy's Science and Health with Key to the Scriptures. Then, finally! the whole lesson with all six sections. It might have taken me all week to get through the whole lesson, but I did it.

I really began to appreciate Christian Science more in my 20's, as I realized that people didn't respect me because of my limitations. I prayed, and I began to understand more of what Christian Science had to offer. For example, the idea of the "Divine Comforter" refers to the

Holy Ghost—the direct experience of Christ coming into our personal lives. I was saved from many mental breakdowns by my faith, by studying the Bible and Science and Health, and by talking to some consulting practitioners and Christian Science friends. I had a lot of church friends once I got into adulthood. In 1967, I applied for Christian Science Class Instruction, which involves a two-week course of study into Mary Baker Eddy's teachings on Christian Science. This was held in Boston and was called Association. It was there that I met Karen, and we became friends. One day a year thereafter, there would be an Association meeting—a sort of reunion with on-going study—with our class members from all over the country. Karen gave me a ride some years, because my house was on her way. She lived in Milford, and I lived in Middletown.

After a few years, Karen became divorced and was living in Boston and working at the Mother Church of Christ Scientist. I went up to visit her a couple times on the bus, and eventually we became romantically interested in each other. I was about 33 years old and this was my first time to be in a relationship.

We married the following year, 1970, in Delaware, where Karen's parents lived. We bought a home in Middletown with my parents' help. This was my first time to live away from my parents. Karen was maybe 28 and had a daughter, Patty, who was about six at this time. It was a challenge. Patty had trouble accepting me because of my partial blindness and her sadness over her mom's divorce. My wife had trouble because my job had no prestige, and maybe she had some expectations I didn't understand or live up to. I could've told her that my prospects were limited, but when you're young, you don't always realize what to say or even what the expectations are.

We moved to St. Louis to have Patty educated at the private Christian Science school, Principia. Starting over as a blind person, it took me years to get a job. At first, we bought a house and opened a bookstore, which flopped. Then we moved into apartments, and Karen went to Webster University to get a degree, and she began teaching music.

The job I eventually got was in Dictaphone transcription for the State of Missouri Department of Children and Family Services. I took city buses to work, which took about two hours each way. It was the job I enjoyed the most in my life. Even with the difficult subject matter regarding child abuse, there wasn't the lack of workplace harmony there was like when I had worked at the hospital. Also, some of the cases were interesting. Some stories were shocking and, over the 20 years on the job, I learned that the world needed a lot of compassion, which it did not have.

We had some family vacations, such as to visit my in-laws at Rehoboth Beach, Delaware in the summer or Hockessin, Delaware for the holidays. Meanwhile, my folks got a place in

St. Petersburg, Florida, and we would visit them and swim off of the Gulf Coast. Patty always enjoyed their bicycle built for two.

Eventually it became clear that the marriage wasn't working, and my wife asked for a divorce. This was in 1978. This was a low point for me. I had no family in the area and went from having a wife and daughter in the home, to coming home to an empty house. I was still taking the bus to work in all kinds of weather, and this involved many falls, especially on the steep slope coming from the condo where I now lived. My parents encouraged me to buy a place nearer my work, located in Kirkwood, Missouri. I did so, and this became my home for the next 30-plus years.

During the years that I lived on my own as a single man, life was humdrum. Go to work, come home. Go to work, come home. To break that up, one year I took a bus tour to Florida on my own. It was a chance to relax. Another year I took a trip out west. At that time I could see enough that I enjoyed taking photographs.

In the 80s, I began attending the church near my home, which is where I first met Judy, in the summer of 1985. I called her one day to come over to listen to the audio of a slideshow I had of a trip I took. We started spending time together. Judy's mom would bring her to my place, and I went over there sometimes. Judy had her guide dog with her at that time. We talked about everything under the sun and hit it off right away because our outlook on life was the same. Everybody said, "Don't get married, 'cause you have too many problems already." But no one could tell us what to do. We were in love, and our relationship wasn't the problem. The problem was other people looking only at our physical limitations and not our potentials. After our wedding in 1987, Judy moved into the condo with me.

Editor: Early in his marriage to Judy, Blair's step-daughter Patty came to visit.

Patty:

The first time I met Judy was in the spring of 1988. She had just married my stepfather, Blair Gleisberg. Blair and my mother had divorced during my teen years. After several years of not being in contact with him, I sought him out to reunite. I was now about 23 years old, preparing to get married and move to Florida for graduate studies.

When I called and found out that Blair was newly remarried, I wondered how his new wife would feel about a stepdaughter from a previous marriage showing up, along with her fiancé.

As it turned out, Judy was very warm and welcoming. My first impression of her was that she was full of joy and was visibly radiant. She had the softest, clearest, and palest skin I had ever seen, and it seemed to be translucent. It was as if the light from within extended out through her skin into an energy field surrounding her. Her hair had the same soft quality, and she smelled wonderful. She did everything possible to make me feel comfortable and asked lots of questions. It was obvious from that first visit that she had a strong intent to love, and a strong drive to learn and to understand. I was impressed with her educational background, her commentary on current events, her wit, and her obvious love for Blair.

Blair R. Gleisberg, "My Story," continued:

In 1994 Judy's mom, Erna Loehr Dent, died. For the last few years of Erna's life, her relationship with Judy had improved a lot. I continued to work until my retirement in 1996. Judy taught school from time to time, but then her health would take a dive or the transportation situation would peter out. She wrote songs and poetry. She began writing the text for this book before we were married and continued off and on as her health allowed.

We went to visit my folks now and then in Florida. Other than that, we didn't travel much. We would go out to eat by walking or taking the bus. We both had the white canes, and sometimes all went well. I would listen for traffic so we could cross the street. Other times, it was terrible, as one of us would fall.

I loved Judy's sense of humor. She could always come up with a joke or a funny story. Without the humor, we never would have made it. I loved that we could talk together and didn't just sit and argue over everything. Judy needed a lot of help, and I did what I could to make life better for her. This was good for me, too, and gave me more of a sense of purpose. We enjoyed sharing Christian Science ideas and studies, even though she wasn't too orthodox about it. We spent hours each week and sometimes each day listening to audio books, news stories, and music, or working with braille reading or writing, and trying to learn the latest technology that would help us interface with the world.

Challenges—sometimes I couldn't understand where she was coming from. She would get upset and scream, and I'd have no idea why. I knew it wasn't my fault, and we didn't go around blaming each other, but these things still happened, and I didn't know how to stop them. We didn't know about the autism at the time.

When Judy got informed about autism, the information was no magic bullet. But at least we knew the cause of the discord in her life. It made it easier just knowing why she couldn't get along with people, had trouble making decisions, and was so sensitive. She always wanted to take responsibility for her behaviors, but she never knew how. Now she was able to educate some of the people around her, so that everyone could help avoid things that triggered her over-reactive behavior. This also let people know in advance not to take it personally if she started to escalate. Knowing the cause of her brain functioning made it easier to be patient. It still wasn't easy, but it was easier.

But long before that, Judy had sought many remedies to get relief. There were psychotherapists, psychiatrists, neurologists, nephrologists, Reiki masters, massage therapists, private yoga instructors, physical and occupational therapists, ENTs, gastro doctors and many more for her many symptoms. Again and again, she turned back to her Christian Science studies to see how the mind and spiritual life played a part in her symptoms. It was obvious from her doctoral dissertation that she understood these connections, and we will experience this in her own words. Her doctoral work focused on Geoffrey Chaucer, known as the Father of English literature and widely considered the greatest English poet of the Middle Ages, as well as a philosopher, astronomer, civil servant and diplomat. He is best known in our times for *The Canterbury Tales*. From her Dissertation, Medical Themes in Chaucer, Judy writes about God and science:

...Chaucer was deeply devoted to and interested in the "One Physician", and [his] works convey an intense interest in the way man's medicine contributes to or conflicts with God's. This contrast between and convergence of human and divine medicine raised profound theological and philosophical issues for Charter. How can mankind best work with the One Physician? What is the boundary between religion and magic, legitimate science and charlatanism or legerdemain? How far can mankind trust his own intellect, his own experiential knowledge, his own technology?

Chaucer was so fascinated by medicine, its ideas and application, that he created a series of characters and situations which involved the healing art. Chaucer placed a physician among his Canterbury pilgrims, a practitioner so imperfect, so suave and pseudo-elegant that he became the target for some of Chaucer's highest satire. He is apparently a man of great knowledge but few principles, a deadly combination for one who tries to heal others. "The Physician's Tale" is an exercise in horrifying extremes. He portrays a situation in which virginity becomes even more important than life, a shocking reversal of the kind of values a physician, in Chaucer's time, or anytime, should have. Judith Anne Dent, PhD

Judy could empathize with being a patient without much self-determination, with others more powerful getting the call the shots about what kind of treatment was needed. I can imagine her delighting in the satirical aspect of the great poet's writing. From the Conclusion section of her doctoral work:

Thus I have tried to show in a modest way how far Chaucer was out of his time, possibly even of ours, and the questions he asked about and the skepticism he felt towards science and technology. Yet at the same time Chaucer was rooted deeply in the 14ᵗʰ century. His speculations about science led him not farther away from medieval mysticism, but deeper into it. His object, like that of Gower, Langland and others among his contemporaries, led him toward union with God brought about by profound declaration of faith. It is this circuitous route by which he arrived at this faith that I have examined. Judith Anne Dent, PhD

Judy certainly knew a thing or two about a circuitous route to faith! Those who knew her best saw how her doubts and speculations about both modern medicine and religion brought her to a deeper faith. She combined her studies of religion with her love of language, and wrote many poems. She set some of them to music. I enjoyed hearing her sing these again and again, and I know singing them brought her comfort. I've included two of these songs at the end of this chapter.

It was especially useful for Judy to turn to metaphysical religious healing when the doctors couldn't agree on the causes of all of her physical and mental conditions. So at times, she went off all medications and tried to approach things solely through prayer and mental attitude. She consulted with Christian Science practitioners, some of whom seemed to help for a time. She was often in so much suffering, with pain in several areas of her body, mental anguish, and lack of sleep, that she was back on the medicines in a week. One area where Christian Science did help her intermittently, along with counsel from those few who understood her autism, was to work on the issue of self-contempt. She practiced the Christian Science teaching of "knowing the truth", the Divine truth that she was a child of God and that her human conditions did not define her worth or her true being. Those who sympathized with her autism, with all its brilliance and peculiarities, helped her remember from time to time that she was not a bad person. Rather, her mind was not neurotypical and needed some special understanding, both from herself and others.

On a good day, she could explain clearly what might set her off and how to work around that. Sometimes just explaining this to others seemed to calm her. We knew we were all on the same team managing the autism, rather than on a different team against Judy.

On a bad day, she was awake almost around the clock and could not figure out what to eat, what she wanted, how to calm the thoughts and anxiety, or how to manage the pain, numbness, or other bodily distractions. And on a bad day, she forgot that her mind worked a certain way, and she blamed those around her, which sometimes alienated others. Some days were a mix of good and bad. Through all the other people coming and going, I was the one who was there constantly, and she was the one who was there for me. Judy would note from time to time that she stopped making serious suicide attempts after we got together. She still struggled with those thoughts for the first couple of years and had some short hospitalizations, but no actual attempts. Without the love we shared, we never would have made it in our marriage, and I don't know how either of us would've made it, period. Our love helped me because I knew I was helping her, if that makes sense. Just my being able to help her made my life better.

We went for many years with just the two of us managing independently. I did the cooking. I had enough vision to ride the bicycle to go grocery shopping. I labeled some things around the house. I made audiotape recordings to keep in touch with friends and family afar to keep those relationships going. Judy did her part by managing many tasks mentally. She kept track of what we needed at the grocery store, when and where appointments were, and those kinds of responsibilities. She made the plans for what books or shows we would listen to on tape. She memorized phone numbers, birthdates, and addresses routinely until the last year of her life.

Diabetes was another hurdle for her, because she had to take insulin. I think she had this the last ten years of her life. She gave herself the injections several times a day, but she couldn't check her own blood sugar and neither could I, so it wasn't clear when an injection was needed. Blood sugar levels affect mood and mental functioning as well. They had all kinds of gadgets designed for the blind to check their own blood sugar, but none of them were truly practical. They involved the use of sight at some point along the way. Bottom line—if a sighted person were present, it could be used, if not, it was useless. This is a real problem for blind people, as many of them have diabetes. They have trouble getting enough exercise, and with fewer outside activities and senses, they have to do something, so they eat, probably the wrong things. Then the treatment is difficult to do because the right equipment is not available. I know of one blind person who committed suicide, more or less because he just let his diabetes go, due to the difficulty of trying to manage the illness.

So eventually, we needed more help around the house. Things became more difficult after Judy's knee surgery, which affected her mobility. We needed aides to help with medication, check blood sugar, work on Judy's feet and nails, and clean the house some. I was still doing the laundry and taking out the garbage and cooking. We needed help to go out to eat, not just for transportation, but also to stay with us and manage getting us to our table, finding the food when it arrived, etc. Getting and keeping caregivers was a challenge.

At times we went out to The Muny (the municipal opera in St. Louis was an outdoor musical theatre) or other concerts or community events. We especially did this when Judy's mom was still living and would take us. What we enjoyed most together was reading books and just spending time in our living room chairs in conversation. We would reach out as we sat side by side and pat the arm of the other if we needed reassurance, or calming, or just to say, "Hi, I'm here." Or "I love you". We sometimes slept in those chairs due to aches and pains or insomnia that got one or both of us out of bed during the night, but when the physical allowed, we enjoyed sleeping in bed together. Putting our arms around each other was the most important way we showed our affection. Hearing her sing some of the songs she wrote was a great source of pleasure for me. Here are a few examples:

"Absalom, Absalom"
by Judy Dent

Cushi came and my heart just broke.
He said, "Absalom's head is stuck in an oak."
Vengeance is mine says a wrathful Lord,
But I know revenge isn't part of God's word.
Absalom, Absalom, my son, my son,
Why are you so angry?
What have I done?
How can I help you?
What can I do
To show that my love is always with you?
The armies they fight,
They clash and make noise.
Hate ruins the lives of men, women, girls and boys.
What can I do to replace war with love?
The answer came peacefully down from above.
David, O David, my son, my son,
Absalom's safe and the victory's won.
He's learning and growing and so are you.
My love for you both is strong, faithful and true.
We fight over politics, law and opinion,
When all that we need is a sense of dominion.
Divine Love alone governs all that we do.
God is All-in-All and His love sees us through.
All of my children, my daughters and sons,
Life isn't a struggle,
It's joy and it's fun.
Sing praise to the Lord and things turn out all right.
It works in the daytime and also at night.
It works in the daytime and also at night.

"You Shall Never Die"
by Judy Dent

Abraham came from the land of Ur.
His life as a shepherd was hard and unsure.
His future was doubtful, dark and dim,
When the Lord appeared and said unto him,
"Thy name is no longer Abram,
But Abraham shalt thou be.
I will make you a great nation for all the world to see.
Your children cannot be counted.
They are more than the stars in the sky.
My promise is always with you,
And you shall never die."
Abraham always did God's will.
When challenges came he obeyed God still.
He lived in a country new and strange,
But he knew God would help him through every change.
Thy name is no longer Abram,
But Abraham shalt thou be.
I will make you a great nation for all the world to see.
Your children cannot be counted.
They are more than the stars in the sky.
My promise is always with you,
And you shall never die.
The promise I made to Abraham
Is the same one I make to you.
I am forever faithful,
Strong, loving, kind and true.
You don't have to ask me questions,
No how, what, when, where or why.
My promise is Life eternal,
And you shall never die.
For I am Life eternal,
And you shall never die.

Patty:

Over the years, I visited Blair and Judy many times. Judy and I enjoyed singing together, and sometimes I would play the flute. Blair and Judy and I knew many of the Christian Science hymns by heart. Judy often had a problem with her throat and would tire easily of singing or even speaking, so she would come in and out of the songs, lightly soaring over the top in a delicate soprano. I was fortunate to hear her sing solo on a few occasions. Judy had written over a dozen songs with Bible story themes, such as the ones above. Some were complex, both in lyrics and musical composition, and most were in the style of ballads. Her voice was a wonderful combination of poetic adult sophistication and childlike delight in tone, interspersed with clearly changing emotions that hinted at danger and mischief, but always ended in hope and harmony. My favorite was her version of The Prodigal Son, and I wish we still had a copy. This one had special meaning for me as a daughter who had been away from all of her parent figures for some time. I imagine Judy's interpretation was closer to the Biblical intention, a metaphor for her prior rejection of God and her efforts to return to grace. Judy composed an especially catchy melody about the story of Jesus and Zacchaeus, the tax collector, as told in Luke 19:1-9. In each of Judy's songs, it was easy to hear her own themes of having been judged, feeling isolated and in despair, yet holding the promise of having one's eyes opened and being delivered into faith and love. Acceptance of those who were outcast was woven throughout.

When I visited, I usually stayed with them in their condo. Sometimes my husband Johnny and our young son Shad came along. Shad called them Grandpa Blair and Judy. I appreciated the opportunity for Shad to see the challenges and resourcefulness of people living with handicaps, as well as for him to develop empathy for life experiences so vastly different from his own. We were on a tight budget, so we usually would sleep on air mattresses on the floor in the small condo. This was quite a change in the routine for Blair and Judy, and we would need to be very careful not to leave anything in the pathway where they might trip and fall. When staying in the condo, any small noise that any of us made needed to be explained. "What's that?" Judy would query, whenever someone moved something or shifted in their seat. Her need to feel in control bordered on hyper-vigilance, which was very understandable, given her early abuse and difficulty navigating her environment. In addition, our sleeping in the living room cramped their style, because both Blair and Judy had insomnia often, especially Judy. With no light coming into her awareness, there was no sense of day or night, other than the mental construct of clock time. She frequently got out of bed during the night and came into the living room to read or doze back off in the recliner. Eventually, I learned it was wise to find other accommodations, but I am grateful for the years that they graciously housed us.

At first, our visits were mostly pleasant but had some tension involved as well. This was partly due my tendency to be more spontaneous, whereas Judy needed to know the plan well ahead of time. If I had any nonchalance about a plan, this was upsetting to her. We also had a habit of trying to pack way too much into a visit. Judy and I would talk ahead of time on the phone, and she and Blair would be so excited that I would be coming with a car to get around in. We would cook up all kinds of wonderful things to do together, and there was an idealism that she and I shared. This would often backfire, though, because it was realistic to do one activity a day that was outside of their routine, and we would plan three or four! Blair finally helped us figure that one out, and in recent years, we learned to keep it more simple.

Besides idealism, I think there was a deep grief we shared: on my part, because I thought I should somehow fix their lives, and on her part, because she hoped I would be some kind of solution, if only for a few days. Each time I fell short—for example, if the restaurant we went to had a small flaw, or there was some other disappointment in the plan—her emotions ran high. What would be a minor irritation to most people, such as the temperature in a theatre being too chilly, would be a personal affront to her, supporting the idea that her best efforts would always be foiled and somehow she would fail. So a plan for the evening could go from high hopes to dashed hopes in an instant. There were many times she quelled the fires of despair and went on with the outing, with minor tension felt by all, but sometimes it was more than she could tolerate. We might have to wait for her verbal thunderclouds to pass, or we might have to abandon the plan altogether. After leaving an event that didn't go well, Judy would apologize and then replay the event—out loud—again and again, alternating between blaming herself and blaming others. Processing a disappointment could take the rest of the evening, or sometimes the rest of the visit.

It was a challenge for Judy to define her relationship with me, and vice versa. She had had many mental health case managers and therapists and was well aware that I was a practicing psychotherapist. While she would get her hopes up that I could be therapeutic with her in some way, at the same time, she had her guard up against anything I might say that seemed like an intervention. My desire to be helpful to someone who obviously had great needs—and whom I loved—sometimes came across as if I had my social worker hat on, especially in my younger years. I would fall into a trap of offering advice. Eventually I learned to be less in the mode of "fixing" and just tried to set boundaries. Sometimes I wanted simply to be on vacation with family and not have to think about professional boundaries and managing transference (a clinical term for others' projections onto therapists, which lead them to see us in black or white terms, as savior or persecutor). The truth was that Judy's blend of autism and mental health issues made it difficult—though she had the desire—to see others as separate from herself. As a result, she took most things personally, and I really did need to manage the relationship using my professional skills. This put us both in a difficult position. I eventually helped Blair and Judy find a professional elder care manager, and I could let this woman do her job while I tried to be more of a visiting family member (knowing the visit would still mostly revolve around Judy's needs). Fortunately, Blair was supportive of Judy as his wife and of me as his daughter, and he tended to smooth everything over.

Judy and I didn't think of our relationship as mother-daughter. Due to my biological parents' remarriages, I already had a stepmother and a stepfather and, besides, Judy and I hadn't met until adulthood. Also, she didn't have children of her own and couldn't begin to relate to being a mom or step-mom. Adding to that, each of us—Blair, Judy, Johnny, Patty, and Shad—was an only child! So even relating in a family unit as siblings was foreign. But we longed for a sense of family and tried to forge connections.

The ambiguity about whether I was friend or family or helper was difficult for her, because she wanted things to fit neatly into categories. She would ask on almost every visit—nicely and curiously, even tentatively—"Why do you call Blair 'Dad'? You already have a dad." So I told Judy about the years of my mom's marriage to Blair, when I was ages six to fourteen. My last name was changed to his when I was in first grade. I sang to Judy a song that my mom made up to help me remember the spelling of our new last name, Gleisberg, which, I learned, rhymed with "iceberg." The melody climbed in a stair-step manner for three sections and then culminated in a quickly paced surprise ending: "G, L, … E, I, … S, B, …..…. E, R, G!"

I had no pictures of my first dad. We didn't speak on the phone or have visits, just exchanged the occasional letter. Although secretly I pined for him and was mad that my biological parents were not still married—as most children would be—Mom told me that Blair was my daddy now. This was sometimes hard to accept. He had nervous habits, and only in adulthood did I understand they were common traits of people with blindness: constant finger-tapping, leg-bouncing, and fidgeting with his clothes. He would also stare off into space in a strange way; I found all of this unsettling and annoying.

I had a love-hate relationship with my new daddy's corny sense of humor; now I enjoy it and find that I love this trait in my own husband. The good news was that Daddy was not mean and could be fun. We went swimming together many days each summer, played cards with extra-large playing cards with large print that he held close to his face, went to church together every Sunday and Wednesday, ate meals together, including lots of ice cream, and looked forward to summer vacations in Connecticut or Florida with his parents, whom I called Grandma and Grandpa.

Blair was also "there." He was stable and present (whether I liked it or not at the time), and in hindsight I have appreciated his steadying force. This was especially important because we had no other family in Missouri or, actually, within a twenty-hour drive. When Mom traveled for graduate school, Dad was the one home with a young teen, trying to keep track of me and provide fair standards and discipline. He tried to teach me about the difference between the "short-run" and the "long-run," lessons that have come back to me as an adult.

Given all this, when we reunited, I had asked Blair if he would like me to still call him "Dad." I had never called him Blair. He had said yes, he was comfortable with it. I reminded Judy of this. She seemed satisfied until the next visit, when she would at some point bring it up again, circling the idea in her mind, trying to get it to fit. She didn't seem to have a reference for these kinds of connections, other than perhaps mistrust due to past betrayals. Her only relatives lived far away, and Judy shared no connection with them. Many people had tried to help her, but ultimately most of them had judged her or in some other way fallen short in her eyes. These failed connections were especially painful for Judy, because she placed these would-be friends and helpers on so high a pedestal in the first place, and because she had very real needs for interdependent relationships. So trust was an issue, but she was good about admitting that and taking responsibility for it, especially in later years. She worked very hard on self-awareness.

Overall, Judy and I looked forward to the visits, each an opportunity for growth. I must admit that I shared an arrogance with most of the sighted world: I would sometimes pity Judy as a blind person and look for ways to fix her. To be fair, she was also actively seeking ways to reduce suffering in her physical and emotional life and was asking desperately for help, so my motivation wasn't completely from my own overactive desire to fix. In addition to wanting to be of some assistance—limited by distance and finances as that assistance had to be—I also sought to learn from Blair and Judy. I realized the wealth of information, humor, perspective, and life lessons they both had to share. As I matured and learned to recognize more of my biases that led to arrogance, I learned to listen more and offer solutions less. I became more grateful for what I received. Blair offered a window into my unresolved childhood issues that I didn't share with other relatives. He understood how I valued my adult relationship with my other dad—whom I'd always missed during childhood—and he never begrudged it or tried to compete. His was a welcome perspective on the past and its ongoing patterns that rippled into my present. He would reflect without judging or blaming anyone—"just the facts," so to speak—and offered some wonderful insights. Judy was supportive of this process and, since she was psychologically-minded, we had many interesting hours discussing the family dynamics of various branches of all of our families. This led to healing for each of us. Judy always got a kick out of Johnny's family stories, which were more bawdy and outrageous than those of her prim upbringing.

Part of planning a visit was finding the right gift for Judy. This was an adventure, and I hate to admit that eventually I gave up. She appreciated perfume from New Orleans, if it had a story to go with it, giving it authenticity: she wanted to know where the shop was and who owned it and how the scent got its name. She had a sizable collection of lotions and perfumes already. She was physically sensitive in many ways, so scented soaps might not work. Candles were nice aromatically, if the scent was natural and not chemical, but the hazard of fire made them impractical. Food was an obvious choice, but turned out to be a great challenge due to diabetes, dieting, digestion issues, allergies, and preferences that could change from visit to visit. Once I brought along an expensive protein powder that I was sure would be a help to stabilize the erratic blood sugar levels that were affecting her digestion and her psychological problems. She loved the taste of it and drank the whole 16-ounce shake, only to vomit for the rest of the afternoon. I thought I felt as awful as she did, but I doubt it. This was on the same day that a caregiver cooked a sweet potato for herself in Judy's oven, which made Judy sick just thinking about it; she was horribly allergic to sweet potatoes and was appalled that the caregiver would cook one in her home. The caregiver hadn't realized how strong the smell would be and how personally Judy would take this affront. I don't think she would have done it if Judy and Blair were sighted, but that's an example of the attitude that people have—they won't know because they can't see. I was never sure if it was the protein shake or the odor of the potatoes that made her sick, but that gift was a miserable failure.

Johnny suggested specialty popcorn in a variety of flavors—mostly savory to avoid the sugar issue—and this was a treat that was a hit for the last few years of Judy's life. Blair liked it too. It could be delivered by mail as well, and since we were in Louisiana, there were unique local flavors to send: Crawfish Boil Popcorn (too spicy), Jambalaya (a hit), and King Cake (with artificial sweetener). We labeled each flavor in baggies with different numbers of dots for them to feel (our version of Braille), and Judy memorized what number of dots went with what flavors when we talked over the phone. We also sent talking and singing greeting cards, which generally went over well. Blair's favorite was a singing oldie, "I love you a bushel and a peck, a bushel and a peck and a hug around the neck!"

Johnny and I tried to bring gifts that would be stimulating in non-visual ways and avoid adding calories. This led to an eventual collection of percussive instruments that we would play with while visiting: drums, maracas, egg-shaped and lemon-shaped rattles, bells, and a tambourine. The layers of tones, the pulse of various rhythms, and the wealth of tactile sensations were a great combination, with no visual requirements. I had a fantasy of Blair and Judy participating in local drum circles, but the barrier of how others might view them and treat them was ever-present, and lack of transportation to such events was given as a reason not to find such a group. But we had our own drum circle on several visits, which was a wonderful metaphor for listening to each other, expressing our truth in the moment, and cooperating, even as each moved to the beat of a different drum. Judy eventually gifted Blair with his own electronic drum set, which had an honored spot next to his recliner.

Judy's relationship with God, spirituality, and various religions was quite layered and fraught with difficulty. The fact that she had faith at all is a testament to her desire and dedication to choose truth and love. The idea, instilled in childhood, that God would heal her of blindness— built on her mother's paranoia and florid fantasy life, and entwined with the abuse she had suffered at the hands of so many authority figures—seemed to mean that either God was mean like the others who had power over her and chose to punish her, or that she was a bad girl not worthy of healing. Or, perhaps worse, He was inept and powerless to help. She spent countless hours in prayer and spiritual consultation trying to overcome these early specters of God, wrestling with angels and demons, and forging her own relationship with the Divine. What began as a fleeting belief in the goodness of the universal truth—and by reflection the redemption of her own nature—over time grew into a more stable faith in God and in the good in herself and others.

Having tried many medical interventions for various physical and mental symptoms, Judy became frustrated with doctors and turned to Christian Science. This, as previously mentioned, is how she met Blair at the Kirkwood church. Although she was not able to turn away from medicine for any length of time as the religion suggests—most practicing Christian Scientists believe that sickness is an illusion that can be corrected by prayer alone—she used the teachings of the religion's founder, Mary Baker Eddy, to uplift her thought and to transcend hatred, false beliefs about herself, and the brooding focus on pain, shame and fear, which at times threatened to consume her. The basic text and the scriptures, the periodicals, and the hymns both challenged and comforted her in a way that helped her grow. But sometimes, before the growth, the teachings made her "madder than a wet hen," as Judy would sometimes say. She seemed to relate to passages that addressed issues of worth and value in God's eyes, as well as metaphors about blindness and coming into sight. Although there were many days when nothing would bring relief, her connection to the teachings of Christian Science and the way that she and Blair shared this path of faith was often a salve and, on a good day, a source of joy and understanding. On the down side, there were high expectations in that faith that rang with echoes of her childhood: just believe enough and deny enough, and you will be fine. The Christian Science emphasis on positive thinking did not offer enough empathy for her pain. Perhaps more than a sighted person, she needed her reality mirrored before it could be transformed into a new perspective. This lack of acknowledgment of suffering was a constant struggle for her and kept her from embracing the religion fully.

Even though she couldn't practice Christian Science completely, I believe Judy had an advanced theoretical approach to holistic health. She was one of those rare individuals who moved toward a balance between theories of depth psychology and new thought religions. She couldn't be convinced—to her credit, in my opinion—that human emotions should be whitewashed altogether, as some people of faith prompted her to do. She was equally infuriated by the pop psychology of purely "positive thinking," and she used the energy of that anger to validate her own difficult experiences. Only then could she calm the inner storms and use the positive teachings of religion and psychology. She and I agreed that with as many challenges as she was given at birth, trying to deny them all away with a smile and an affirmation took as much energy as trying to hold a hundred basketballs underwater all at once!

The research Judy did for her doctoral degree revealed themes that aligned with her belief that neither mind, emotion, nor faith could be ignored when dealing with illness. She focuses here on his stories that relate to medicine and healing.

Chaucer was deeply interested in medicine, both its theory and practice. He was both distressed and intrigued by the vast discrepancies between the progress of diagnosis and that of treatment. His works promote the holistic relationship between health of mind, health of body, and health of soul. Chaucer's works contain many references to medicine, not just incidental references, but a deliberate study of what it means to be sick and what it means to be well, as reflected in his knowledge of the intellectual and historical background of medicine.

In this holistic approach, sickness was regarded as fragmentation, and wellness was described as being "whole". All elements of self are connected. This resonated with Judy, who studied and strived throughout her life to find the ways that spirit could heal emotion and history and body. She sought to find ways that a deeper psychology could bring understanding and relief through grieving and allowing for new ways of thought to emerge, which in turn eased physical claims of illness. But simply denying physical pain and emotional angst from the outset didn't work for her. Finding emotional depth and validating suffering could not be divided from raising thought to higher realms and transcending illness. Although various authors, healers, practitioners, and physicians focused on one aspect of self at the exclusion of the others, Judy was determined to bring them together in a way that gave authenticity to her unique day-to-day experiences and wove all aspects together into wholeness. At times she seemed to be torn into pieces by the various disciplines trying to pull her into their camp. Those who worked best with Judy were those with the ability to listen and to make space for the wide range of her unusual experiences, rather than overlaying their viewpoint onto her life. That was one reason, I'm sure, that Blair was such a healing power in her life. He had a vast capacity to listen to her and to avoid boxing her into a certain viewpoint. Though not her scholarly equal, he's no slouch in his knowledge of religion, philosophy, and human behavior, especially where the rubber meets the road! He did his best to understand, to reflect, to allow for her interpretations, to mirror, to be patient—in other words, to deeply listen.

My husband Johnny is often that kind of a listener, too. That may be why Judy took to him so well. Over the last few years of her life, as Johnny and I studied mindfulness meditation with Zen master Thich Nhat Hanh, Judy was very receptive to Johnny sharing guided meditations with her. One example: "Breathing in, I am aware of my thoughts and feelings. Breathing out, I smile to my thoughts and feelings." This kind of smiling wasn't an attempt to deny thoughts and feelings, but aimed to change the relationship to those thoughts and feelings by being with them, as if with an old friend. Not to cheer up, but to be with, in solidarity. The meditations also involved her sitting with her thoughts and feelings calmly, not trying to will them away or act them out. Her perceptions were too intense to overlook or will away—and sometimes too intense not to act out. She knew that Johnny's thoughts and feelings had been intense too, and that he had used these meditation practices to recover from severe PTSD from the Viet Nam war, or as our Vietnamese friends call it, the American War in Viet Nam. Johnny's progress was a litmus test of authenticity for her. A couple of times she called on the phone and asked if Johnny could lead her in guided meditation.

Judy was not seeking to be a Buddhist, but in her holistic quest, she used tools from wherever she could find them. She recognized that Buddhist psychology blended an embracing of suffering with finding a way out of that suffering. The "embracing" part had been missing in her life, with her parents and so many teachers and helpers unable to validate her suffering or be with her there in the midst of it, or to help her grieve her intense pain. They just pushed her to move beyond it or to act as if it wasn't happening. Of course, there were therapists and healers along the way who did walk right alongside her and planted seeds that helped Judy make the progress she made over time. Some of those people may never know that they made a difference and that Judy did find some relief in the long run.

Judy found some relief when she "discovered" her autism. Although labeling a person can be harmful, Judy found it empowering to name the autism and have conversations about its effects. She found the Autism Society of America in St. Louis to be a great resource, and she was soothed knowing that others shared this way of thinking and reacting. By learning about the condition, she could get perspective on her issues. This allowed her to separate her over-emotional behavior from Judy as a person. So once she was able to "claim it and name it"—as the saying goes—she was able to tame it, at least some of the time. It helped those around her to react less and to understand how to avoid some of the triggers for her distress. One of the triggers was when others would mention a possible plan and then want to adapt it. Judy had a trait of taking things very literally, despite her advanced intellectual ability to think abstractly and in metaphor. If something was said to Judy that was meant as a possibility or a generalization about a plan, and then someone tried to rethink or change it, that was very stressful for her. The way she quickly memorized things, all timeframes were instantly in place, and she had the plan mapped out as if it were set in stone. Now, someone wanted to change it ... not just the plan, but her reality. In addition to challenging the autistic trait of literal or rigid thinking, this was also a re-do of her childhood, where her reality was constantly denied or re-worked by sighted people who were trying to pull her into their reality. Add to that a mother with paranoid delusions whose reality often didn't match the other adults around, and figuring out what reality was for Judy could start to feel very intense. Falling down the stairs, or getting a beating, or being shamed and blamed for something horrible (real or imagined, in her mother's case) could all be the consequences if she didn't understand someone else's version of reality. So the idea of it shifting and changing plans at someone else's whim was, to her, not an inconvenience, but a renewed trauma.

This need for things to be what someone said they were, exactly and literally, the first time and every time, was a theme that intensely affected Judy's daily life. For example, Elizabeth Olesen, Dad and I will never forget a fateful trip to the St. Louis Zoo. I knew it could be challenging, taking two blind people—with one of them in a wheelchair—and dealing with crowds and heat, bringing or scouting out the right snacks, and finding ways to "see", aka experience, the animals. But I'm an adventurous type, and Blair and Judy had been on successful outings to the zoo before. Besides, Elizabeth was coming with us. Though she spent less time with them than she used to, Elizabeth was a very trusted professional caregiver whom Blair and Judy considered a friend, even a daughter. She knew how to keep things calm and explain things well, and this was a great opportunity with an extra car for people and wheelchair and even an extra person to help. What could go wrong? The short version is this: we didn't get past the gift shop near the gates to the zoo.

Part of the issue was expectations. The bigger they are, the harder they fall: the zoo trip was going to be fantastic, and we were all geared up for it. As I recall, Judy's mood had started to turn before we arrived. Maybe some food had been less than satisfying, or maybe she began to sense that reality might not match up to the fantasy that had been building in her mind for this outing. Maybe it was that I parked my car in the other lot and not by the curb like Elizabeth, and Blair had to walk with me to meet the two of them. That concerned her, although no harm was done. It was only a few yards away, but from her perspective, why didn't I know to park in the correct place? For whatever reason, she was less than jovial as we entered the zoo.

Like any zoo worth its salt, the St. Louis Zoo is designed so that patrons are funneled through the gift shop on the way into the park and then again on the way out, with no detour allowed. I hoped to pass through the gift shop and onto the main event, having been shopping with Judy before, but no such luck. Judy was on a mission to find a realistic stuffed monkey. The gift shop was full and sounded chaotic. There were plenty of monkeys that I handed to her and that employees found for her. No, not this one; no, not that one. This one's fur was not soft enough. This one had a round belly like a teddy bear, and she wanted to know why people have to anthropomorphize animals and give them big bellies. It's okay for a teddy bear to not look real, she said, because it was supposed to be stylized, because it's supposed to be Theodore Roosevelt and not a real bear, but this is a zoo. They should have realistic animals to be educational. Another one looked very realistic to me, with movable arms and legs and proper body proportions, but she didn't like the eyes. The eyes are made of buttons. Buttons are hard, and the eyes of a real monkey would not be hard like buttons. This was beginning to look like a no-win situation.

Judy was on the verge of tears, almost wailing. She seemed grief-stricken, and I strongly suspected that it wasn't really about the shortcomings of a stuffed monkey. My therapist mind was working overtime. What was this really about? Here we were at a zoo and Judy knows she wouldn't be able to experience the animals like other people. She would be once again dependent on others to describe what was happening. If a mutual understanding of what kind of stuffed animal she wanted couldn't be reached with anyone here in the gift shop, how could anyone adequately communicate with her about the infinitely more complex real, live animals?

Looking back, knowing more about her autism, I understand that Judy had a craving for things to be authentic and exact. I think the grief that no one could give her an exact experience of a real animal was at the heart of it. She bemoaned that she had gone to a taxidermist to get a real stuffed animal, but complained they did "a terrible job," because the animal felt hard and stiff. From a sighted person's perspective, the "hard and stiff" animal may look perfect, but she wasn't going for looks. She was going for authenticity, and taxidermy isn't designed to be touch-friendly. With her hands, she could tell that it wasn't realistic. She wanted to experience a real animal, but most real live animals wouldn't allow her to hold them, so the only options available to her were through smelling and hearing and second-hand stories. She wanted a perfect replica, but I don't know that any replica could ever have been good enough, because ultimately it wasn't the real thing.

But at the zoo that day, I didn't know how to help Judy process her grief, and I didn't know how to get her unstuck from the idea of the perfect stuffed animal, and I couldn't even get her out of the gift shop! So Elizabeth and I and the sales associates kept coming up with new animals to explore. Blair got quieter and quieter, apparently unsure how to respond. Judy was becoming more like a child in her demands and black-and-white thinking, but we obviously couldn't treat her like a child, so the ordeal continued for at least 45 minutes. Her intense upset was causing everyone a great deal of suffering, including some embarrassment for Elizabeth and me—we could see aggravation, intolerance, and rejection on the staring faces around us. Children who were shopping nearby and expressing their own wants began to get louder, which incensed Judy. She in turn got louder, which drew comments from around us, and things continued to escalate. I honestly don't remember how we got out of there, but I believe Elizabeth was instrumental in helping with the realization that we were all too worked up to enjoy the zoo.

On another shopping assignment, Judy wanted me to help her find a new insulated cup. This sounded quite doable. I gathered the description of the desirable traits, looked at what wasn't working about the models she already owned, and Blair and I went on the shopping mission. Before I go further, let me say that I may have missed, at first, the incredible significance of a proper drinking cup for Judy. She has written earlier in this book about her struggles with "touch or spill." Food was of high importance to her and fraught with difficulty due to physical manipulation and to her struggles with weight, diabetes, and digestive intolerances, along with her own particular preferences. Sometimes it seemed there was little she could eat without discomfort, guilt, or both. Going out to eat was a big venture, and sometimes just getting up to go to her own dining table was painful and anxiety-provoking, since she did not have a sense of where she was in space. Eating in her recliner left at least crumbs or a bigger mess to deal with, and she didn't tolerate sticky or crumby sensations well. So eating was both a major focus and an ordeal—an emotional and physical rollercoaster full of anticipated thrills and that stomach-dropping feeling.

Drinks, on the other hand, were predictable and comforting, easily contained in the right kind of cup, where they could be kept warm or cold, and could be safely enjoyed in the ease of the recliner—no utensils required. I believe Judy appreciated the symbolism of cups for all human beings—nurture, succor, even love. There were daily rituals in her marriage to Blair, which involved a daily round of drinks (non-alcoholic, I should mention, and usually sugar-free). There was a drink for each time of the day, in a rhythm that they knew as a couple. I'm not sure if water came first, but I know she tried to drink her recommended amount each day. There was milk with breakfast. There was coffee after breakfast that Blair would have ready without her having to ask. There was some kind of drink after lunch. In the late afternoon, Judy would call out in a particularly friendly voice, "Honey?" and Blair would answer, "Is it time for your 7UP?" "Yes, please," she would answer, and even if she had been furious or exasperated moments before, she would be conciliatory in tone, with a tiny voice that was tired, but still grateful. Blair providing Judy with her ongoing series of drinks was something they both knew he could do for her that she would enjoy, something she could count on. Along with this emotional attachment to her drinks, the autism afforded her an incredible physical sensitivity to the cup itself. Her fingers and lips found each tiny variation of a cup's seams, edges, rim, handle, and other details. With the wrong cup, details would be magnified, becoming glaring flaws.

I was not thinking of all this when we brought home the first cup and it was rejected. Or when we brought home the second, the third, and the fourth. I started bringing cups in twos and threes, knowing I could return them as needed. Judy compared each candidate to the cup she had owned for some time, which was good but no longer usable, and no longer, apparently, manufactured. The first one compared was too heavy, the second not weighted in the right place for balance. One had an uncomfortable lip, another had a sliding mechanism to let the drink out that was too hard to understand without vision, and the next could easily pinch fingers. Another had a tiny sharp point that showed sighted people which side opened, but the point could hurt to touch. The next one seemed right and felt good to her hands and lips, but when the drink came out, it was too fast. At first I thought she was making this up, that the speed of the drink was in her control, but then I saw that the lip was taller, farther than others from the hole where the drink came out. Before the liquid could be felt, more than a sip had poured out, no matter how slowly the cup was tipped. After all our efforts, we were no closer to finding what I now understood must be the perfect insulated cup.

So Judy decided to go to the store with us, even though she was not feeling particularly well. We went to the department store with the largest selection in town, hoping that all the right variables would converge. Unfortunately, as she looked at more and more choices, her feelings of disappointment and frustration became more intense, and she began to take the whole thing personally. These manufacturers didn't think of her needs! Her original cup was nowhere to be found; we went home empty handed. (Eventually, one of her caregivers was able to order a cup online that was just right.)

This difficulty finding the correct item was a strain on Judy's relationship with caregivers and family. One example is when I had the notion that a Nativity Scene would make a wonderful gift for a blind person. (Apparently I was not the first to have this idea. She had gone through several nativity scenes that were not realistic enough or had sharp edges.) I sent a crocheted finger puppet version, which had clearly distinguishable characters. Joseph's shepherd staff was easy to feel, the donkey had big ears, the angel had wings, Mary was holding a little bundle that was baby Jesus, and the wise man had a crown and a boxed gift in his hand. They were pretty well made. But I wasn't thinking about how the blindness and autism had conspired to make it nearly impossible for Judy to manipulate detailed objects with her hands. She tried to appreciate them, but they ended up in a tin on a top shelf. The nativity scene that did work well for her turned out to be a woodcarving. It was all of one piece, which was counterintuitive to me but just right for her.

Unfortunately, the stakes were often higher than finding the right item for enjoyment. Judy had diabetic neuropathy, and this caused pain, numbness, and pins and needles in her feet and ankles. She had tried many remedies, but to no avail. Finally, she and Blair discovered that there were warming fuzzy boots with a built-in electric heater. They had settings to vibrate and massage. So, on one of my visits, Blair and I made the trip to buy them from an upscale mall store. I read the box to Dad, and he agreed they were the ones that promised to give her relief. We came home with the prize, hoping it would make a difference in Judy's life.

Judy asked to hear everything that was advertised on the box. I read it all. She agreed that these were the chosen ones and worth opening, and she and Blair talked about how this would finally give her some respite from the constant discomfort and the spikes of all-too-real pain. Maybe it would increase her circulation, since she couldn't exercise, and this would improve her health overall, or at least decrease her symptoms, even when she wasn't wearing the boots.

She put them on, and they were fine at first. They were the right size, but as we went through the settings, the smile left her face. I think she probably couldn't feel the comforting warmth or soothing massage that were advertised on the box because of the progression of her disease, but to her, it was the boots that weren't working.

This would have been a bump in the road if that were the end of the story. A bump of disappointment and a return trip to the store. But as soon as we all determined to take them back and get a refund, she wanted the boots on again. As intelligent as she was, she seemed unable to wrap her mind around the reality of the boots when they were off. She went back to living in the promises recited from the box. She spent an agonizing hour or more asking me to take them off—in disdain of the wretched things—and then to put them back on again, because maybe this time they would fulfill their promise and allow her to feet to feel normal again. Off again, on again. Hopeful, agitated, despairing, raging, pleading … hopeful, agitated, despairing, raging, pleading.

At one point, in thinly veiled exasperation, I said, "Judy, I can only do about 15 more minutes of this, then I need to take a walk or something." She replied, "Don't pull that behavioral modification shit on me!" Thus we had made that progression, or regression in this case, from me being family member to caregiver to therapist. I searched inside and determined that I was not trying to use therapy on her; I was honestly communicating my need for a break. The grief of her physical ailments, combined with her grief that things are not literally what they promise to be, was too much for me to witness any longer. I can only imagine what it was like for her to live inside of that grief.

I came in and out of Judy's life, caregivers came and went (some also unable to tolerate more than another 15 minutes of witnessing Judy's reality), but one person had more patience than all of us put together. That was her life partner, Blair.

Chapter 22

Reflections

Elizabeth Oleson, "Lessons to Learn":

In September 2005 I was working for a nursing facility. I came on duty at 6:45 a.m. and was handed the care plans for my patients that day. One of my patients was a new patient. I had seen Judy before in church, but never had the opportunity to meet her. She stood out a little bit sitting in the back of the church with her husband. My care plan told me not to move anything in her room, so with that in mind, I knew I was going to have to be very careful. I came into her room with the water pitcher, and when I opened the door. I ran right into a heavy-duty trash can with my shin, but I didn't move it. She was sitting up in her chair, and I introduced myself. She could not explain why the trash can was right behind the door, but she often teased me about this moment over the next five years. (It turned out, it had been used to prop the door open, and when the supervisor wanted to close the door because of the noise of her radio, she just shoved the trash can into the room and shut the door.)

I had never worked with a blind person before, but I was told that she would dress herself. After breakfast I'd gotten busy in another room, when I got the message that Judy was lost in her room. She did not know where the call button was, but she kept her cell phone with her all the time and had called the front desk. The nursing supervisor relayed the message to me. I found Judy in front of the closet, but she didn't know how to get back to her chair. The most surprising sight was her outfit. She was now wearing a double polyester outfit in bright orange, and the pants were too tight and too short. I found out later that her mother had made all her clothes for her and sewed in some Braille tags so she could always match her clothes. I also found out that her mother passed away some 15 years earlier. Later, when I became her personal assistant, one of my first duties was to take her clothes shopping—but I am getting ahead of myself.

Judy had come to the facility because she had fallen, but she was mobile. I found out later that her office at home was undergoing a remodeling, which had been causing her some stress during the process, and much anguish afterward. She'd had many stacks of stuff on the floor, and the remodeling included a complicated system of cubbyholes—too complicated. If they had really listened to her, then the design would have been completely different. After she had told them what she needed, she told me, they went to the Society for the Blind to get their own ideas. She said many people assured her it would be beautiful, but only one person asked her if it would be safe. That is what mattered to her.

I'm not sure how long she stayed at the facility, but when it was time for her to go home, I came to say good-bye. She had collected some of our phone numbers in her Braille computer, but when I came by she had already turned it off and put it away. Still, she insisted that she wanted to keep in touch with me. She gave me her phone number and made me promise I would call her. In late October I had plans to make cookies for a Halloween party the next day, but decided I would take care of this phone call I had put off for a few weeks. I called. She was very upset and unloaded a lot on me. All I could say was, "Do you need me to come over?" I didn't go over then, but no cookies were made that night. I just spent time listening to her woes on the phone.

I did visit her home a few days later, and this was the start of a friendship. She needed an assistant and I was hired, the next in a line of many assistants Judy had over the years. Judy and Blair really tried to make me feel welcome. They wanted to get food I liked. I mentioned that I liked to drink soymilk, and the next time I came, they had soymilk, but I unthinkingly said I only drink unsweetened. Later I found out that Blair had walked to the grocery store to buy some for me at great effort.

I think I came two or three times a week, either before an evening shift or after a day shift, for a few hours at a time. My duties were varied and I had to quickly learn their needs. It did take her a lot longer to get ready on her own, so I would help her with showers. I remember one time she asked me to hand her the shampoo bottle. She said, "It's the one with the rubber band on it." I said, "It's the one that says 'shampoo'." She laughed and said, "I forgot you can see." She did have ways of marking bottles and tubes and such to help her identify items.

Judy gave me lessons in Braille. She ordered a Braille writer for me and I used it to label many things for her. When I first got it, I wanted to show off my Braille writing skills to her and was going to write the sentence "I love you," but I reversed the dots in the "I" and it came out "E love you." I told her I meant to do that, because E was my first initial. I often said that sentiment to her over the years. Another way we developed to say that sentiment was when we were shopping for music CDs. She loved music and was worried that it would become inaccessible to her, so she bought many CDs. One time we bought Stevie Wonder's Greatest Hits and track 19 was the song "I Just Called to Say I Love You." She would often say "Number 19" and I knew what she was saying.

I used to think, if only she could see, everything would be all right, but I soon found out about Asperger's, a type of autism. Because of this she couldn't use a cane. When walking, she couldn't keep her hand on a railing. There were many times we went out to eat at a restaurant and many times that something would upset her and her behavior would make me want to crawl under the table and disappear. There was one time in particular we went to the Cheesecake Factory. I have a favorite appetizer I order for my meal and made sure that was ordered first and then I mentioned the salad. When the salads came, she angrily lashed out at the waiter. I couldn't understand why. I had expected my salad to arrive first and told her it was fine. I saw our waiter leave after that and our new waiter said it was a shift change. I secretly wrote a note to our waiter to say it's not you, it's her, and that I thought his service was fine. A lot of communication can be done using body language and eye contact, and I tried to hand the note to our waiter without Judy knowing what I was doing. The waiter did start to ask, but I put my finger to my lips and Judy started to ask what was going on, but I didn't need to tell her what had transpired. I was very angry at her response to the waiter and she couldn't tell me why she had responded that way. She talked it over with a friend, and they came to the realization that in her mind, I should have received the food in the order that I had ordered it, but that wasn't the way I wanted it. Oh well, lesson learned.

It turned out I had many more lessons to learn.

Patty:

A few years before Judy's death, Elizabeth moved in with her own parents in Elsah, Illinois to care for them. Eventually, Judy's physical problems overwhelmed her. After a couple of knee surgeries and partial recoveries, during which she became less mobile and less able to manage her diabetes, she became more dependent on Blair and hired caregivers. When Blair had a broken hip and then another, she had to be home alone while he was in rehab. This was very taxing on her, as he was such a support to her and a mediator between her and caregivers. Her latest neurologist, who understood autism, helped with many symptoms, but the combination of neurological, mental, social, and physical barriers intertwined to create insurmountable odds.

Over the last few months of her life, she began to tell her beloved husband Blair that she was getting ready to leave this world—not that she was suicidal, but that she was feeling ready when the time came. One night, at the age of 68, she called out to him in horrible pain. By the time the medics arrived, she was unresponsive. At the hospital, they offered to have her taken to another hospital where they could perform brain surgery, but the chances of returning to her previous level of functioning were unknown. Blair made the courageous and difficult decision not to pursue these measures, as he knew from many talks with Judy that she would not want them.

As I write about these difficult incidents and themes in Judy's life, I notice that the very things that made life so challenging for her—and sometimes made being with her challenging to others—are the things that were also her gold. Consider her compulsive insistence that things be literally as they said they would be: this mindset allowed no tolerance of hypocrisy or trying to wiggle out of anything one said, calling everyone around her to excellence and integrity. There was no one she held more strongly to these standards than herself, and this came through in her writing, her compositions, her intellectual arguments, and her commitment to seeking absolute truth and absolute love.

Judy's search for light in the darkness made her positive qualities—her love and wit and courage and determination—all the more remarkable, given the odds against her.

Blair R. Gleisberg, "Judy's Purpose":

This is not the chapter that I originally wanted to write. However, due to dear Judy's sudden passing, everything has changed. I fully agree with everything Judy has stated and I hope somehow this book will help others.

One of the big discussions Judy and I had over the years concerned the fact that handicapped people are placed in a mold, and if you don't fit the mold, forget you. This is probably the biggest reason why neither Judy nor I were popular with the blind community. We simply didn't want to fit into a mold.

Just because you may have a disability of some description, this doesn't necessarily mean you can't think. Let's talk about this for a minute. Judy was an excellent writer as you can see. However, she wasn't allowed to pursue this vocation because she just had to learn mobility. She went through about 18 mobility instructors, was so stressed out she landed in the mental hospital six times and still never mastered going places by herself. The problem is, she could never learn mobility—but so what? She could write, so let her do that. She could have made money to have someone guide her around. Deaf people can have interpreters, so why can't the blind have guides without being disrespected by the blind community?

What I am trying to do here is help bring this book to a conclusion and also make its purpose clear. When reading this book, you will see that Judy was unable to do things herself, but she could enlist others to help with things she could not do. These were some physical and logistical aspects of her life.

If you have a physical disability, you still deserve a loving home with a loving family. Some people seem to think that you don't. I remember very well when I was in a program in order to obtain employment, I was told I needed to leave my wife, go anywhere I was sent, and this for a nickel shooting job which wouldn't support my upkeep. Needless to say, I refused the offer and was labeled "uncooperative."

Yes, we do need organizations supporting different disabilities, but let's not do this on the backs of those who need the help. We do need volunteers, but let's not find these volunteers from the psychiatric community who are told, if you volunteer you will get better. This may be true, but let's not do this at the expense of the handicapped who need some help.

Judy: About My World

I can't say, as many blind people do, that blindness is merely an inconvenience, a minor nuisance that would become completely irrelevant if well-meaning sighted persons would just leave us alone to fend for ourselves. I can't say it because for me it isn't true. That darned Asperger's, or autism, or wherever I am on the spectrum that makes me peculiar and outcast and socially inept, and above all, unable to lie politely—a skill most neurotypicals take for granted—will not allow it. Everything I have achieved, everything I can do, is a result of hard work by my parents, my husband, a few dear friends and dedicated teachers, and myself.

As I've described, all my sensory experiences are intense and extreme; many sighted people have asked me if I ever had visual hallucinations or visual synesthetic experiences. I never have; I think that's because I have never seen. My eyes have never been stimulated by light. I probably wouldn't know a visual hallucination if it jumped up and bit me. When I bump my head I never see stars, or maybe I do see them and don't recognize it. I have never had one photon of input from my eyes. I have no idea what my visual cortex does in its spare time. My neurologist says it processes experiences more acutely than normal, and that accounts for my amazing memory.

My neurologist tends toward far-out hypotheses, so I have no idea whether any of this is true. I do know from listening and observing that most people's senses are half asleep compared to mine and that they don't experience the world nearly as intensely as I do. Most people cannot extrapolate to any experience beyond their own and I suppose I am no better than average in that respect.

People say, in an awestruck, eager voice (that I can only describe synesthetically as "gooey"), "Tell me about your world." I never can. Not in the way they expect. They want me to tell them that I have a magic way of distinguishing colors, that my guide dog gives me instructions for steering the car, that if I tap the bumper of a car, it will sound a perfect E flat, telling me instantly that it's a 1997 Ford. I can't tell them what they want to hear, that the magic always trumps the mysterious, or that all questions have easy answers. I can't tell them it is simple to pick up environmental cues from the sun on my skin and the wind in my hair. This book is my way of answering some of the questions about my world.

Editor: The following article was written by Judy in the early 1980s, while she was living with her parents and working on her doctoral degree:

"I Vote for the Trash"

I used to be afraid of the mailman. I used to be afraid of a lot of things—traffic noise that whooshed over me like ocean waves coming from all directions at once; uncooperative piles of sheets and towels that would fight to the death rather than be folded into neat stacks; fortresses of meat and vegetables, impervious to the feeble efforts of knife and fork; but most of all, I was afraid of the mail.

The braille and audio books it brought were never enough to offset the avalanches of print, all of which, with sighted help, had to be sorted into categories: handle now, read later, and pitch immediately. The trouble was that the sighted help was my dad.

I was living at home attending graduate school, working on my doctoral dissertation while teaching English composition. I was under constant pressure to get more and more done; and that was back in the days when technology was a manual typewriter and a braille watch. Digital reading and writing for the blind was still a gleam in a computer nerd's eye. My dad, then retired from his newspaper editing job, always said he wanted to be my eyes. He described everything, read me everything, tried his best to make sure I knew everything I would need to know to thrive in the big bad world. He insisted on reading me all the mail every single day. I remember once when I was trying to grade final exams and he spent over an hour reading me a long, pre approved application for a Mobil Oil credit card. I burst into tears. "Dad, I don't have time to read this. Besides, I'll never need a gasoline credit card."

"You don't know that," said Dad. "You never know what medical science will be able to do someday. Then you might need to know, and I won't be there to help you."

The reason Dad was so concerned was that I was an anomaly. No one could figure me out, not parents, not teachers, and most of all not myself. My IQ tests were always off the charts; my blindness skills were off the charts in the other direction. They still are. Which brings me to my point. Not all people with disabilities can ski the Matterhorn, climb Mt. Everest, or mountain bike through Europe. Sighted people pin much hope on the use of guide dogs for the blind, but contrary to these romantic notions, dogs have never been particularly useful to me for mobility. I've been through four guide dogs, but never have done my Christmas shopping alone at the mall.

I live every day with both blindness and autism. Sometimes I get lost in my own living room. Disability has not been an easy ride for me. All this relentless drive toward positive thinking, as if life with a major disability is one endless rah-rah college cheer, is both destructive and toxic. It's a standard I can't meet, and I doubt that I am alone.

So Dad read me all the mail. Dad's favorite mail to read me was the almost daily fund-raising appeal. We got letters from every blindness charity known to man. We didn't get autism letters because I wasn't diagnosed until years later; my only disability people knew about was blindness. So there was a huge discrepancy between my mental and physical abilities. The worst letters came from taping groups and guide dog schools. Each letter contained at least one breathless profile of a superhuman blind person: One girl was learning to be a molecular biologist; another was studying archaeology in Russia; the world seemed to be full of blind people who traveled the globe with their guide dogs. After reading each of these fund-raising pitches aloud, Dad would ask plaintively, "How come all these other blind people are doing it and you're not?"

He never clarified what "it" meant, but I knew. The things I wasn't doing were mobility, cooking, cleaning, sewing—all the skills included in what educators of the blind like to call the "expanded core curriculum."

A few years earlier I had won the Scholastic Achievement Award from what was then called Journal for the Blind. I had to submit a short autobiographical essay as part of my application. After the hype died down we received another fund-raising letter. It raved about yet another brilliant, accomplished blind person. One of the highlights of the profile was a long description of how that person traveled with her guide dog, Jerry, through the ruins in Mitla, Mexico. I felt a skewed, twisted sense of deja vu. All the pieces fit together. I had never said that I had traveled to Mexico with my guide dog. The travel in Mexico had been with my parents, ten years before I ever had a guide dog. There were other exaggerations as well.

When Dad finished reading, he exclaimed, "Isn't that an amazing person? Why can't you be like her?"

"But, Dad, I can't be like her. I am her. That story is about me."

Dad was stunned. He was probably more than a little embarrassed that he had missed it. He went back and read it again to himself.

"I'll be darned," he mused. "Of course it is. How could I have missed that? Even the dog's name is the same."

Although I had never seen one, I knew a light bulb had gone on over Dad's head, the way it does when a comic book character gets an idea. I had never seen that happen, but Dad had described it to me often enough, and now it was happening to him.

"I wonder how many of their other letters are exaggerations like that?" Dad's voice took on a note of thoughtful wonder that I rarely heard in our mail-reading sessions. "It's all about money, isn't it?"

I carefully refrained from saying that I had been trying to tell him that for years.

"Should we send them ten dollars as usual, or throw this letter in the trash?" His voice was smiling.

It didn't take me long to come up with the answer. "I vote for the trash." For the first time in a long, long, while, I was smiling, too.

About the Author

Judith Anne Dent received her PhD from the English Department of Washington University. She was born completely blind and finally diagnosed as autistic in her 60's. She grew up in an era that stigmatized blindness and didn't recognize autism.

Judith married and lived independently despite great odds. Her husband was also legally blind from birth.

Her home was in Kirkwood, Missouri. She is survived by her husband, Blair Gleisberg.

Acknowledgements

At the request of the author's husband Blair, and with his essential contributions, Judy's draft of this book was compiled and edited by Patricia Stout and Elaine Wiltse DeSmith.

For inquiries, Patricia can be reached at admin@womenscenterforhealing.org or (985) 264-8089

Printed in the United States
By Bookmasters